WHEN MEN
ARE WOMEN

WHEN MEN
ARE WOMEN

Manhood among Gabra
Nomads of East Africa

John Colman Wood

The University of Wisconsin Press

The University of Wisconsin Press
2537 Daniels Street
Madison, Wisconsin 53718

3 Henrietta Street
London WC2E 8LU, England

1   3   5   4   2

Printed in the United States of America

Library of Congress Cataloging-in-Publication Data
Wood, John Colman.
    When men are women: manhood among Gabra nomads of East Africa / John Colman Wood.
    256 pp.   cm.
    Includes bibliographical references and index.
    ISBN 0-299-16590-6 (cloth: alk. paper)
    ISBN 0-299-16594-9 (pbk.: alk. paper)
    1. Gabra (African people)—Social life and customs.   2. Gabra (African people)—Rites and
ceremonies.   3. Polarity.   4. Symbolism.   I. Title.
    DT433.545.G32 W66 1999
    305.89676—dc21   99-6427

For Carol

Listen to the story told by the reed,
     of being separated.
Since I was cut from the reedbed,
     I have made this crying sound.
Anyone separated from the one he loves
     understands what I say.
Anyone pulled from a source longs to go back.

—Jalal al-Din Rumi

CONTENTS

ILLUSTRATIONS

PREFACE

RESEARCH FOR THIS PROJECT was made possible by a grant from the Wenner-Gren Foundation, for which I am thankful. I also thank the Institute of African Studies at the University of Nairobi, with which I am affiliated, and the President's Office, Republic of Kenya, for giving me permission to study in northern Kenya. I also want to thank Emory University, which supported me with fellowship, travel, and write-up funding.

The book reflects field work done in summer 1991 and from September 1993 through March 1995. During those twenty-two months I came to like and admire my Gabra hosts. I thank them for tolerating, often encouraging, my presence, questions, and intruding witness. I especially thank Yara Gollo Kalacha, my assistant, traveling companion, and friend, who taught me more than he knows, was patient when I was impatient, and endured our long marches and cold nights. Several others were especially generous: Abudo Halake, Charfi Umuro, Tumal Orto, Katelo Bitacha, Jillo Ramata, Isakho Wario, Guyo Sake, Galgalo Duga, Galgalo Shonka, Ibrae Guyo, Molu Halake, Sarite Alkano, Waticha Boranticha, Gabriel Gindole, Guyo Saro, and Gumato Dabasso.

Many others helped. Toru Soga, an anthropologist from Japan, gave me my first lift to the Chalbi Desert in 1991 and introduced me to Gabra. His enthusiasm proved contagious. Henry Domman, a builder in Marsabit, became my friend; it was often on his lorry that my wife, Carol Young Wood, and I traveled between the desert and Marsabit. He and his family gave much and asked nothing. So did Herbert Anderson and his family of the African Inland Church at Kalacha. The priests and nuns at Marsabit, North Horr, Sololo, and Moyale were always kind and generous, as were Bishop Ambrose Ravasi and his staff. Curt Reynolds, then a development worker at Marsabit, was helpful during my 1991 trip. Claudia and Joel Leonard, volunteers at Laisamis Hospital south of Marsabit, became friends. They offered Carol and me a home away from home. Victor and Regula Wyss and their daughter, Nicole, lay volunteers from Switzerland, also befriended us. Deb and Gary Sharping kindly allowed us to stay at the AIC guesthouse in Marsabit. B. J. Lindquist and David Adolph, then of Intermediate Technology Development Group at Marsabit, hired me to make two visits to Olla Yaa Galbo, with which ITG had a veterinary medicine partnership, to help describe its organization and history. They also became generous friends.

Elsewhere, Paul Baxter of Manchester University, a mentor to all who study in the Oromo-speaking world, helped in numerous ways—not the least of which was his advice and considerable encouragement. Elliot Fratkin, Mohammed Hassen, John Hinnant, Naomi Quinn, Paul Robinson, Neal Sobania, and William Torry were generous with their time and advice on the phone and in person before I left for the field and after my return.

My teachers and colleagues at Emory were always supportive. They helped to get me unstuck when I was stuck, focused when I was unfocused. As a former journalist, I was more comfortable writing description than interpretation. Any theoretical merit in this discussion is due in large measure to their prodding. They are especially Donald Donham, Fredrik Barth, Corinne Kratz, Charles Nuckolls, and Robert Paul. Others at Emory were willing readers and advisers: George Armelagos, Peggy Barlett, Peter Brown, Carla Freeman, Marcia Inhorn, Ivan Karp, Sidney Kasfir, Bruce Knauft, Mel Konner, Michelle Lampl, Dan Sellen, Bradd Shore, Neal Smith, Debra Spitulnik, Pat Whitten, and Carol Worthman. George Armelagos, Steve Morreale, and Neal Smith also helped with the graphics. Peter Brown provided generous institutional support. Victor Balaban, John Bing, Margaret Buck, Jessica Gregg, Cameron Hay-Rollins, Alexander Hinton, Donald Jones, Daniel Lende, Wynne Maggi, Matsheliso Molapo, Theodore Schurr, and Mari Yerger read and listened and created a lively intellectual community. I would also like to acknowledge Rosalie Robertson, senior editor at the University of Wisconsin Press, for her faith and interest in the project; the helpful comments of Herbert S. Lewis, John C. McCall, James C. McCann, and Susan J. Rasmussen; and the careful editing of Jane McGary.

My thanks to all. No doubt there are others, whose names have temporarily slipped my mind. Forgive me. The strengths of this study owe much to many; its weaknesses are my own.

My family gave me the gifts of life, love, and support; they have always read, listened, commented, and encouraged. My parents, Kenneth and

Sandra Wood; sister, Melinda Wood; brothers, Peter Wood and, in spirit, Scot Wood; cousin, Timothy Colman; uncles David Colman and David Clark; and many others—to all I am grateful.

My association with Father Paulo Tablino was propitious. A scholar of Gabra himself, he allowed Carol and me to use an empty building at the Maikona Catholic Mission as a base. Father Tablino was well known to Gabra, particularly by the old men who were or had been d'abella. He encouraged me to study the d'abella, the "priests" of Gabra society. It was partly his insight, based on decades of life with them, that turned my attention to the role of symbolic dualities in their cosmology.

Carol, a social worker, generously took time away from her career to join me, for which I shall always be grateful. One could not pray for a better friend, companion, and partner. Her friendships with Gabra women provided insights to women's lives that I would never have had otherwise. Our conversations about our experiences together and apart proved invaluable. Much of what follows emphasizes the role played by the separation/attachment problem in shaping nomadic Gabra culture; this insight owes much to the frequent separations that fieldwork imposed on Carol and me. Carol, a former editor, read over the manuscript in several of its incarnations and made many suggestions. I could not have done this without her.

A Note on Language and Orthography

Gabra speak what they call *afan Borana*, a language they share with their Borana neighbors. It is an Eastern Cushitic language, a dialect of Oromo. In most cases I follow the simplified spelling of Ton Leus (1995) and avoid diacritic marks. The vowels are *i, e, a, o, u,* and a palatal *y.* When vowels are doubled, they are lengthened, but their other articulatory features do not change. I generally avoid double vowels in favor of the older and simpler, if slightly less accurate, spelling used by Leus.

Consonants are pronounced much as in KiSwahili, with several exceptions: *q* is a velar-palatal ejective, with a sharp sound in the throat; *g* is a velar plosive and is always voiced, as in "go"; *d'* with an apostrophe, as in "d'abella," is an alveolar implosive, which makes it softer than an ordinary *d*—it is produced using the tip of the tongue on the roof of the mouth just behind the teeth, and inhaling.

Nouns and adjectives are inflected for case. In most instances I give the accusative case, in which Gabra tend to suppress the final vowel, so that a non-native has difficulty hearing it: thus, *gala* "camel" sounds to an American ear like *gal*, and in some texts it might be written that way (see Legesse 1973:316).

More detailed orthographic notes are provided by Legesse (1973), Andrzejewski (1957), and Cerulli (1922). In this book, Gabra words are italicized on first use; subsequent occurrences are in roman, except for infrequently cited words.

The botanical equivalents for Gabra plant names are taken from Heine and Kassam (1985).

WHEN MEN
ARE WOMEN

Prologue
Red Is White,
Men Are Women

And yet relation appears,
a small relation expanding like the shade
of a cloud on sand, a shape on the side of a hill.
   —WALLACE STEVENS, "Connoisseur of Chaos"

THE NOMADIC CAMEL-HERDING GABRA of East Africa make elaborate use of binary oppositions. They routinely divide the world into right and left, inside and outside, red and white, senior and junior, masculine and feminine, and so on. Such divisions are common in structuralist descriptions of African societies. Gabra, however, would seem to make good *post*structuralists. They invert, reverse, combine, and recombine opposites in ways that evoke nuances of the ever-contingent spaces between symbolic poles.

Denge Doko, a Gabra and former seminarian, first tipped me off to the importance of oppositions.[1] I met Denge early in my fieldwork through an Italian priest. Denge thought of himself as a liaison between Gabra and the "outside," including church and state and the odd ethnographer. He straddled two worlds. In the nomadic world, he belonged to an important family that shifted with the *olla yaa*, a sort of mobile capital city. In the settled world, he was a catechist of the Roman Catholic church. (Some people in Bubissa, where he lived, addressed him as "father," as though he were a priest.) The day we met he wore a cardigan sweater that a seminary teacher had given him, a T-shirt, brown trousers, and sandals made of old tires. His fingernails and hair were stylishly long. His body was thick and soft, unlike most Gabra, as a result of his relatively sedentary life.

Denge's English was good, though sometimes difficult to follow. When he advised me about approaching nomadic camps, he spoke of showing

3

elders respect and greeting them in a special way. Then he tossed in this for good measure: "What is important is that you show respect, satisfaction, and rumination. Do you get me?" You had to be intuitive to "get" him. He overflowed with verbal enthusiasms. Ideas sometimes lay just beyond the reach of his English. It was an interesting if inadvertent choice of words to tell me to show elders "rumination." Gabra life centers on camels, and camels are cud-chewers—ruminants. Gabra do not worship camels, but the camel does serve as a model: it can walk long and far without having to drink water, an ideal Gabra set for themselves. That I should act like a camel was probably good advice.

As he talked, Denge propped himself on a wooden bench, crossed right leg over left, and leaned forward, one hand resting on his lap and the other cradling his chin. It was not a particularly Gabra posture; I imagined that he had learned it from European teachers. The pauses in his speech were homiletic. He was given to the pulpit, for which he had been trained but whose vows he forsook because he wanted a wife and children.

"Gabra," he said, "are complicated. Sometimes things look white but are really red . . . or they look red but are really white . . . ."

I scratched in my notebook: "Red & White?"

He was, for the moment, not describing himself. He had joined me on the bench and adopted my perspective. He told me that women in African societies are thought to have low status. He had read books about this. But, he said, a Gabra man must have a woman, a wife, to celebrate *Almado*, an important series of feasts in the Gabra calendar, while a woman does not need a husband to celebrate. This, he said, shows that women have higher status than men.

He was playing with idioms. He had collapsed the Gabra opposition between the colors red and white and the English notion that ideas are black and white—spelled out, like a contract. Denge, however, was pointing out that for Gabra, when things are red and white they are anything but as clear as contracts.

When Men Are Women

This book aims to make sense of a related puzzle. Gabra men are about as masculine and virile and patriarchal as they come. They carry knives and spears and, nowadays, even machine guns to protect their herds. They prize vigor and toughness, the capacity to walk long distances without food or water. A man who has killed an enemy and returned with his severed genitals is honored above others. Men (*d'ira*) say that women (*nad'eni*) are *nus*, or "half"; they say women are children. They exclude women from political and ritual activities. They denigrate women and feminine things.

Yet they regard their most prestigious men—the *d'abella*, who are ritual experts—as women.

Gabra ideas about gender, like their ideas about color, are complex and confusing. How can men be women? How can red be white? The reversals are puzzling in the way of all reversals, flipping a certain order on its head. But they also reinscribe the very binary oppositions they reverse. And this generates a theoretical puzzle. I went to the field after reading books that said structures, particularly binary and dualistic structures, failed to say much that was interesting, useful, or true about people's lives. They said that overarching ethnographic structures, such as binary oppositions, were Western inventions that had been imposed on others. Related books and articles in gender theory told me that gender was a cultural construction that had little if anything necessarily to do with human biology, and that the biological distinction most related to gender—sex—was itself a construction. Hence my consternation when Gabra spoke as though binary structures were important to their world view and their organization of gender, and that people's bodies—some having penises and others not, some bearing children and others not—were key to understanding their meanings. How was I to reconcile theory with what I saw, heard, and experienced?

This book is not just about gender reversal. It attempts to build a bridge across a theoretical gulf between one school of thought which makes structural generalizations about other people's lives, and another which sees this enterprise as an imposition and looks instead for the local, particular, and novel. My hope is to find the general in the particular—to follow a Gabra lead and reverse even this opposition. Gabra take seriously binary oppositions like male and female, masculine and feminine, or red and white: these are central concepts that they use at important rites and in everyday life to represent and think about their world.[2] I cannot in good faith ignore the oppositions or insist that they are not what Gabra really mean, because that would be as ethnocentric and neocolonial as if I were to impose those structures on the Gabra. However, their concepts of opposition are anything but monolithic. They are open, complex, contingent, and ambiguous in ways that Denge's comment about red looking like white only begins to suggest. It became clear to me that Gabra oppositions such as man and woman, red and white, inside and outside, us and them, or senior and junior, were not as diametrically opposed as they seemed; the poles were sometimes reversed, becoming their opposite, and the warp of this reversal was essential to their meaning.

When Women Were as Men

Gabra told me that men become women. They did not say women become men. They did, however, tell a story about an analogous role reversal. According to this story, there was a time when women, not men, dominated political affairs. The story illustrates how Gabra have used symbolic turnabouts to capture emergent complex meanings. After all, a world where either sex may dominate is a different sort of place from one where only one sex has ever held power.

> Banoye was mother of all people. She presided over meetings. She was clever and wise. Her word was law. But she began to make unreasonable demands. First, Banoye told people that they must move camp. When they began to load their camels, she came running and cut the ropes, making the loads fall to the ground. "I thought I told you not to move camp!" she said. Then, after the loads fell to the ground, she commanded people to gather them up and load their camels and prepare to move.
>
> The people were confused and unhappy.
>
> Banoye told everyone to take their camels out to graze for the day. But when they began to drive the animals to pasture, she told them to bring the camels back. When they returned, she told them to go, and so on.
>
> They shook their heads and complained to one another.
>
> One day Banoye ordered them to make her a special pair of leather sandals, ones with hair on both sides of the skin. People had no idea where to find such skin, because skin normally has hair on one side only. Banoye also demanded a bag full of fleas, which are so small that she might as well have asked them for all the stars in the sky.
>
> Now everyone was confused. These were impossibilities.
>
> They gathered to talk about what to do. They reached no solution. They asked prophets (*raga*), and still they could not think of an answer. As the elders returned from the shade tree, they met a boy, an orphan, who was returning with animals to the corrals. The boy greeted them and said, "*Akaku* (grandfather), what are you talking about?"
>
> Most of the elders ignored the boy, but two turned back and spoke with him. They told the others: "We want to hear what the boy has to say."
>
> They told the boy their problems. The boy said that getting a bag of fleas was simple. Take the dung of a donkey, he said, and tie it in a bag and tie the bag above the hearth in the tent. By morning it will be full of

fleas. As for the sandals, he said, that is also easy. Cut off a donkey's ears, both sides of which have hair, and make sandals from those.

The elders returned and told the others what the boy had said, and they agreed to do those things.

But Banoye's demands did not stop, and the elders approached the boy for his advice on what to do with their vexing mother.

The boy told them to go to the shade tree, where people met, and dig a deep hole. Over the hole, he told them to place a stiff cow skin, and put grass over the skin to hide it. Then, he said, take Banoye's stool and put it on the skin and call her to a meeting.

This they did, and when Banoye sat, she fell into the deep hole. The hole remains to this day at Liban, in Ethiopia, and is called Qile Ako Banoye (the deep hole of grandmother Banoye). As she fell, Banoye shouted to the women: "When your husband calls you, do not respond the first time, but tell him you did not hear; and when you go to pee, do it next to the house, do not go far away from the house."

"Banoye" is part of a series of stories that Gabra tell about how men came to dominate women.[3] The stories involve symbolic reversals. Once-powerful women are made powerless and low. Formerly helpless men, whose incompetence is underscored here by their appeal to an orphaned boy, become social authorities. What these stories do, among other things, is to place women at the center of the problem of social aggregation and dispersion, of making and moving camps, of coming and going with animals. Banoye tells people to pack up and stay, to go and come, at the same time. Women, in this way, come to embody the collective ambivalence for nomadic life—a life that we shall see requires intense solidarity and nearly constant fragmentation. Men speak of women as helpless and powerless; yet in stories and songs and private conversations, they describe women as formidable figures who are responsible for the basic dilemmas of their existence.

Gabra are structuralists: they talk about the world in terms binary and dualistic, making explicit links between patterns at different levels of their own analysis. But they are structuralists in poststructural ways. For Gabra, red is sometimes white; women are (or once were) more powerful than men; and men, as a matter of course, become women.

A Note on Methods

I set out to identify cultural models of manhood. Drawing on Naomi Quinn (1987, 1991), Quinn and Dorothy Holland (1987), George Lakoff and Mark Johnson (1980), Lakoff (1987), D'Andrade and Strauss (1992), and others, my plan was to infer overarching "cultural models" from metaphors and other tropes used by Gabra in ordinary speech. In the field, I found myself noticing parallels between different domains, not all of them linguistic. These tended to confirm expectations of models theory that people extend logics metaphorically across domains. To my ear, however, the word "model" evoked images of solidity, invariance, and control which, in writing about my work, I have sought to avoid. Instead, I use "pattern" and "structure," which strike me as less monolithic, even though I know that they carry similar connotations.

I looked for patterns in different places: I made camp censuses and kinship charts, conducted interviews, performed surveys, and compiled daily activity records. I constructed maps of nomadic movements, charts of rains and droughts, and diagrams of alternations between upland grazing grounds and lowland wells. I asked men and women to tell me stories about their lives. I recorded songs and proverbs. I attended rituals and feasts. I drew endless buckets of water for camels. Mainly, I was a participant-observer. I placed myself in and joined circumstances as many and varied as my legs would allow, and all the while I tried to keep my eyes and ears open. I traveled as Gabra travel, on foot with loaded camels. At first, I borrowed camels to carry supplies and water; later, I bought a camel, paying eight goats for it (worth about $100). Gabra did not at first believe that I could walk long distances. They said they had never seen a white person walk long distances. But they seemed to like me better because I walked, as they did, and because I traveled with camels. Six months into my stay, they gave me the name "Idema," which means "Walker." In all, I was nearly two years in the field—briefly in 1991, and then 1993 to 1995.

When I noticed salient patterns, I tested them, not simply by asking informants, but by looking to see if there were similar or different patterns in other contexts. For example, I was initially curious to discover differences in gender behavior between nomadic and settled Gabra. What I found out was that many settled Gabra were still engaged in pastoral life, a fact that confounded the apparent boundaries between these groups and made it difficult to identify clear differences or know what they meant. Throughout my stay, I paid particular attention to dualities and oppositions, interests that grew from my concern with gender opposition. I wondered whether Gabra manipulated other symbolic oppositions as they did the opposition between masculinity and femininity. I made notes on gender, space, seniority, and ethnicity, and I used these different categories to test and enrich my ideas about what Gabra thought about gender specifically, and about oppositions generally.

I have sought to write a thick description of these interlaced patterns of opposition. As I argue, it is in the juxtaposition, aggregation, and complex interrelation of opposites that an overarching understanding of a Gabra-typical logic of opposition emerges. In the chapters that follow, I write in both the past and "ethnographic present" tenses. The past tense indicates specific statements or events that happened during or before my research. The present tense, while it describes historically bound materials, suggests general forms and practices true at the time of writing. It seems absurd to say that Gabra "herded" camels, goats, and sheep, when in 1999 most still do. Similarly, it would be strange to describe a ritual such as a wedding (chapter 4) as a discrete event in the past when what I describe is in fact a composite of many different weddings. Here the point is not to describe a wedding but to say something general about weddings and how they were orchestrated at the time of my research. There is nothing fixed or essential or eternally present about anything Gabra do; however, there are general patterns that, at least at this moment, Gabra generally agree about. The ethnographic present marks these sorts of generalities.[4] Gabra oppositions also shine a bright light back on current debates about structure and contingency, form and variation, dualism and difference. Opposites such as these do not merely attract—they bleed into one another.

Plan of Discussion

Chapter 1 turns to structuralism's poststructural crisis. I show that structuralism was making poststructural moves all along, and that poststructuralism looks a lot like structuralism despite itself: my aim here is to collapse the false opposition between them. I take up gender theory, much of which in recent years has positioned itself against structuralism. My argument is that structural accounts of other people need not be static, monolithic, agentless, or ahistorical. Structure and opposition, when seen openly and contextually, are not the fixed forms that they have been made out to be. They can be lively and complex.

Chapters 2, 3, and 4 approach Gabra oppositions from different angles. Oppositions such as inside and outside, junior and senior, or masculine and feminine have different meanings for different actors at different moments and different periods in their lives. At no time are the meanings discrete; rather, they mingle like currents in a river. In these chapters,

I describe what Gabra do with oppositions at different times and places. By understanding oppositions generally, we may begin to understand the specific declaration that men are women. I look at how Gabra oppositions play out in social contexts, how they appear in individuals' lives, and how they are rehearsed in ritual performances. These are not exhaustive arenas, but they are diverse, and they indicate the range, depth, and importance of opposition in Gabra lives.

Chapter 2 is an ethnographic overview of sociality, space, hierarchy, and ethnicity. It takes up material circumstances and social exigencies, showing how Gabra manage the nomadic problem of aggregation and dispersion. The problem is not simply economic and environmental, although it does have an ecological frame. Gabra ideas of *olla* and *ala*, which I gloss as "inside" and "outside,"[5] resonate with issues of separation and attachment and the related concerns of ethnicity, seniority, and social organization. Oppositional poles relate also to each other: inside is sometimes outside, red is white, men are women. Gabra draw on ordinary experiences to connect different oppositions to one another. Symbolic oppositions become meaningful—indeed, motivating—by analogy: those that are cognitively associated come to be emotionally associated, so that white clay, for example, can evoke family love by way of its association with milk, main camps, and mothers. In the same way, images of separation evoke feelings of separation.

Chapter 3 continues these themes, but less generally and more concretely, with detailed accounts of two men whose lives illustrate the immediate and ordinary concerns of gender, seniority, and attachment. The poles of these oppositions—masculine and feminine, junior and senior, inside and outside—are experienced in life and stories, and it is ultimately experience that enables Gabra to imagine the unity of opposites and how they may be related.

Chapter 4 shows how Gabra ritual addresses these same issues. The polysemy of symbolic forms reflects their complexity and subtlety. The chapter takes a detailed look at the ritual cycle leading up to and including marriage. For Gabra, marriage ceremonies serve as arenas for dramatizing concerns and ideals about gender, identity, sociality, and seniority. I show how wedding ceremonies tease out the formal relations between masculinity and femininity, inside and outside, sociality and autonomy.

Finally, chapter 5 turns to the d'abella, the ritual experts, the men who are women. Drawing on a wide range of evidence and analysis, it shows how d'abella embody Gabra ambivalence toward attachment, seniority, and identity. My hypothesis is that gender categories, such as that represented by the d'abella, serve as metaphors for thinking about personal, spatial, and social dilemmas. Indeed, much as Robert Hertz (1973 [1909]) said of the right and left hands, feminine and masculine genders are good to think with. The d'abella's anatomy does not explain his being a woman; what does, or at least begins to, is that in becoming a woman the d'abella turns his attention away from the material and individual concerns of "outside" pastures to the ritual and collective concerns of "inside" camps and holy spaces. Gabra concepts of masculinity and femininity index the spatial distinction between outside and inside, but, as I show, in complex ways. The ambiguity of gendered symbols enables them to express precise ideas about social situations and personal experiences without smothering the complexities. My analysis is poststructural. The way to understand men becoming women is not by asking whether d'abella are really women; rather, it is by recognizing that they are in some ways *both* men *and* women, and at the same time *neither* fully men *nor* quite women. In the end, we must ponder the implications of these ambiguities.

1

"Post" Structure, Not No Structure

Let us ask: "What is it in the territory that gets onto the map?" We know the territory does not get onto the map. That is the central point about which we here are all agreed. Now, if the territory were uniform, nothing would get onto the map except its boundaries, which are the points at which it ceases to be uniform against some larger matrix. What gets onto the map, in fact, is difference, be it a difference in altitude, a difference in vegetation, a difference in population structure, difference in surface, or whatever. Differences are the things that get onto a map.

—GREGORY BATESON, *Steps to an Ecology of Mind*

I WRITE THIS ACCOUNT of East African camel herders at a time when the idea of "structure" is a problem. Current conversations in cultural anthropology are enamored instead of diversity, change, contingency, contestation, hybridity, fragmentation, instability, indirection, marginality, and deconstruction. As Bruce Knauft has observed of contemporary ethnography, "Coherent accounts . . . have become problematic" (1996:237). Ours is a *post*structural age.

But what does "post" structural mean: "after" structure, "beyond" structure, "goodbye" structure? Does poststructuralism leave behind structure, in the sense of integration and coherence? According to Micaela di Leonardo, poststructuralism "is antiscience, antitheory. It denies the existence of social order or real human selves, declaring the death of the subject . . . . It cannot affirm any truth or claim any political stance. It can only deconstruct" (1991:24).

How can one write about anything—diversity, contingency, and difference included—without appealing, at some level, to pattern, regularity, and coherence? I take "structure" to mean any pattern or configuration that affects, shapes, conditions, or generates other patterns. By this definition, structures are everywhere. Even chaos is now believed to have rhythm and regularity (Gleick 1987). Although it has become *de rigueur* in some camps to challenge and interrogate structuralist explanations, one cannot say goodbye to structure—not in its broad sense. And rhetoric notwithstanding, poststructuralists do not really reject structure, either; rather, they problematize structural relations. If anything, poststructuralists are more structural than self-styled structuralists, since poststructuralists continue to probe and worry and wonder about structures at a time when structuralists have come, seen, declared, and moved on. Poststructuralism, according to Josue Harari, "does not seek a clear or unified answer, but only tentative answers that may perhaps be reduced, in the end, to nothing more than a panorama only slightly different from that offered by structuralism" (1979:27). This is not the impression left by much recent poststructuralist writing. A zealous critique of structuralism has created, at least in American circles, a false opposition between structuralism and poststructuralism, which appears to force a choice between them that should not have to be made.[1]

Take the conundrum that Gabra men denigrate women yet regard prestigious men as women. On the one hand, men becoming women is a highly structured institution. Almost all men become d'abella, and therefore women, if they live long enough. Something organizes the shift from manhood to womanhood. This is done for reasons. It has meaning . . . *meanings*. To write about Gabra gender constructions, one must address structure. On the other hand, men becoming women is a fluid institution, born, as I show in the chapters to follow, out of conflict and contradiction; its meanings are open, contingent, multiple, and contradictory. The relation between gender and sex appears to be unstable, or as Harari put it, "tentative." One can say simultaneously that sex organizes gender and that sex does not organize gender. Both statements are true, and neither is quite sufficiently true.

The question, then, is not whether there is structure, but how to characterize, or represent, structure. It is about finding a voice, a position of sorts, between coherence (otherwise, nothing would be written, nothing at all, for it would not matter what one wrote) and ambiguity, or complex polysemy (otherwise, what was written would fail to express the complexity of ethnographic experiences). Identifying elementary structures need not oversimplify or reduce others in our view. As Robert Paul, a cultural anthropologist and psychoanalyst, has written:

> To say that the world is entirely composed of combinations of one hundred or so elements does not in any way deny the infinite multiplicity of all the

things in the world, nor does it produce a set of bloodless generalizations. This is because the manifest, diverse phenomena of the world have been reduced to a lowest common denominator, which then becomes the basis for a set of lawful and regular rules of transformation that indeed are capable of generating everything in the world, and of actually producing new things. (1982:5)

Gender, Structure, Ambivalence

The problem of men-becoming-women articulates with the anthropology of gender, because, like the Gabra, this literature has clouded the connection between gender and sex. The problem leads to structuralism and poststructuralism, because men becoming women raises questions about what structures gender assignments, if sex does not. Finally, it draws us to theories of conflict and ambivalence. I argue that men-becoming-women is a cultural formation born of paradoxical conflicts experienced by people in ordinary life. The following chapters show how ideas about gender and sociality grow out of material and historical dilemmas. These dilemmas have no stable centers, singular meanings, or final solutions. The fact Gabra gender assignments are uncertain and multivalent is basic to their meaning; it is their job, so to speak, to be ambiguous.

The Appeal of Binary

The structure most often challenged by contemporary gender theorists is binary opposition. Binary structure has come to be synonymous with the French structuralism associated with Claude Lévi-Strauss and his heirs (Dosse 1997, Ortner 1984; see Lévi-Strauss 1963, Dumont 1970, Ortner 1974, Bourdieu 1977), as well as with the British and American variations associated with Rodney Needham (1973), Thomas Beidelman (1986), and David Maybury-Lewis (1989). Of course, "structure" comes in myriad forms which are not always binary. But what critics have had to say about binarity suggests what they think of structure generally, since the complaint against binarity is that it is constraining, simplifying, and static.

My focus on binary structure also forms an analytic bridge to the Gabra, who think, and say they think, in binary terms. All good things in their world come in twos or dualities—even numbers, right and left, or male and female. They are disturbed, for example, by the hyena, an embodiment of wild and dangerous disorder, not just because hyenas move about at night and kill livestock, but also because female hyenas have what looks like a penis and testicles; hyenas do not as a species conform to the normal duality of the universe (see Kruuk 1972; also Douglas 1957 on the anomalous pangolin). The Gabra symbolic field abounds with binary oppositions. They say binaries make unities: *Lami toko*, "Two are one."[2] Theirs is a processual notion of opposition; the poles complement each other. It takes two to tango.

I find in the concept of binarity the very stuff its critics otherwise advocate: difference. Human experience generates and elaborates concepts of difference and distinction, between fragments of the self, between self and other, us and them, this and not this. Are making distinctions, finding differences, and thinking in binary terms so different from one another? Does it make people the same to say they are different, or that they negotiate differences?

The Roots of Structuralism

French structuralism in cultural anthropology, and the idea of binary oppositions with which it is associated, emerged from a perceived homology between the "deep" structures of language, identified by Ferdinand de Saussure around the turn of the twentieth century and later developed by Roman Jakobson and Nicolai Trubetzkoy, and the "deep" structures of culture proposed by Lévi-Strauss. One of Saussure's contributions to linguistic theory was the insight that "in the analysis of language, *relations of contrast and equivalence* . . . are methodologically prior to the units which the linguist postulates as the terminals of these relations in his descriptive model of the language system" (Lyons 1977:234, emphasis added). In other words, language can be broken down to elementary parts, and it is relations between the parts at that level, not the parts themselves, that carry meaning. These relations are binary: a "phoneme"—combinations of which form words—is either the same as another phoneme or different, according to binary "distinctive features" (Jakobson 1971, Trubetzkoy 1969). According to Saussure, the content of language (its semantic "weight") arises not from the value of its material constituents but from strings, or clusters, of phonemic *differences*, which have no content, or weight, but are only relations. "To mean," observed Barbara Johnson, "is automatically not to be" (1981:ix).

Just as Saussure noted a deep, or basic, structure (*langue*) behind the apparent structures of language use (*parole*), Lévi-Strauss (1963) posited a similar sort of structure behind the apparent, or surface, patterns of culture. Lévi-Strauss imported several key ideas from structural linguistics (see esp. 1963:33–36, 91, 209): the distinction between abstract principles, *langue*, and ordinary practices, *parole*; the shift in analytic focus from patterns of conscious to unconscious thought; the idea that signs are a priori arbitrary, and that there is no intrinsic relation between sign and signified (though the relation comes with use to be motivated); the idea that *relations* between elementary units are "methodologically prior" to concrete aggregates; and last, the idea that binary oppositions structure these relations—that the mind works by making meaningful distinctions. Like structural semantics, cultural meanings are supposed to be constructed from clusters of relations of difference—binary difference—among symbols. "The true constituent units of a myth," Lévi-Strauss wrote, "are not the isolated relations but bundles of such relations, and it is only as bundles that these relations can be put to use and combined so as to produce meaning" (1963:211).

There are strong family resemblances between the binary structuralism of Lévi-Strauss, on the one hand, and on the other, "dual symbolic classification" as promoted by Needham (1973, 1987) and others, and "dualistic thinking" as refined by Maybury-Lewis and Uri Almagor (1989). I am aware, as Clifford Geertz has observed, that "complete stability in the structuralist program from 1949 to 1979 is, to put it mildly, difficult to establish" (1988:31–32). There are more forms of structuralism than space in which to describe them (see Dosse 1997). There are also differences between "binary" and "dual." The key to binarity is difference—this or not-this—while the key to duality seems to be disjunction or alternation: this or that.[3] Levels of analysis differ between binary structures and dualistic classifications. Although dualistic theories draw heavily on French structuralism and presume a pan-human logic of binary opposition, dualistic structures often concern complex aggregates: the white clan and the red clan, this world and the nether world. Still, binary and dualistic theories seek to turn up structural principles behind aggregates. The broad aims of binary and dualistic thinking are the same. Binary structures are not necessarily static or unitary. Lévi-Strauss and Maybury-Lewis both argue that binarity is implicated in dynamic contradictions (see Lévi-Strauss 1963:229, Maybury-Lewis 1989:13–14). Such patterns offer the potential for multiple resolutions, or compromise formations, each dependent on context, historical moment, and the problems at hand.

Do Dual Organizations Exist?

For example, in 1956, Lévi-Strauss published an important paper on dualistic and binary thinking that asked in the title "Do dual organizations exist?" He is widely interpreted as having answered definitively, "No." As he concludes: "We should be well advised to reject the theory (of dual organization) and to treat the apparent manifestations of dualism as superficial distortions of structures whose real nature is quite different and vastly more complex" (1963:161).

This seminal work of Lévi-Strauss contains a bridge to his post-structural critics. The thesis of the article, aside from its ethnographic claims (and obfuscations; cf. Maybury-Lewis 1960, Fox 1989), is that cultural formations must ultimately be understood as interstitial; that is, their meanings occur in the relational margins *between* structures rather than in distinct and unitary structures themselves. As such, social organizations are conceived as involving "complementary distortions" between different and overlapping structures, as Lévi-Strauss explains in a 1960 defense of his essay. This means that social structures relate to one another in dynamic and nonessential ways. Because the relations are dynamic, they generate emergent, multiple, and unpredictable patterns, which are not reducible to their constituent structures. They are, as Lévi-Strauss acknowledges elsewhere, "gestalts" (1963:324). The dynamic space between different, mutually distorting structures is precisely what Jacques Derrida was calling attention to when he wrote, "We will designate as *différance* the movement according to which language, or any code, any system of referral in general, is constituted 'historically' as a weave of differences" (1982:12).[4] Structures cannot be understood discretely, but rather as multiplicities generated by relations between structures.

Lévi-Strauss was concerned with dual social organizations, such as the division of clans into intermarrying exogamous moieties or "halves." He wondered whether dual organizations establish the more or less reciprocal, symmetrical, and stable relations that many—including himself (1969 [1949])—thought at the time existed. In his search for an answer, he compared dual systems in various parts of the world. He called attention to variations in the ways different members of the same societies described social relations on the ground. From these accounts he posed a distinction between *diametric* dualisms, with different halves balanced against each other like equal weights on a scale, and *concentric* dualisms, with the different halves asymmetrically related such that one is more central, senior, and important than the other. The latter notion led him to a structure that was not dualistic at all but triadic, including a center, a margin, and whatever lay beyond.

Lévi-Strauss's critics (see Maybury-Lewis 1960, 1989; Fox 1989), who have done their own fieldwork in the areas he described, identify ethnographic errors and simplifications in his accounts of dualistic systems. They argue that he makes too much of the diametric/concentric distinction. My interest in Lévi-Strauss's article is not the facts per se, but in how they are used—his theory. This is not to say that the facts do not matter; however, quibbles over detail have distracted attention from the work's important insight.

Much of Lévi-Strauss's analysis recounts the various sorts of dualistic forms that crosshatch the societies he describes. Some of these divisions, he points out, separate people, while others unite them. As Lévi-Strauss describes the Bororo model, for instance, there is a concentric split in the village between male-public-sacred and female-domestic-profane, with the former located at the center and the latter at the circular margins. There is another dualism, superimposed on the first, between north and south moieties, and a third dualism splitting people into upper and lower divisions, or east and west. Each clan is further divided into upper, middle, and lower classes. The effect of these divisions is to unite people who are otherwise divided and to divide those otherwise united, creating multiple, overlapping, and contrasting groups within groups.[5]

Lévi-Strauss argues that dualities have external, or "ternary," factors impinging on them, creating patterns that are not simply dualistic. "The opposition between cleared ground (central circle) and waste land (peripheral circle) demands a third element, brush or forest—that is, virgin land—which circumscribes the binary whole while at the same time extending it, since cleared land is to waste land as waste land is to virgin land" (1963:152). There is thus a tendency in social systems to form hierarchies, with one side of a dualism inevitably closer to or farther from a desirable object or quality. Dualistic organizations, he says, express one sort of dualism in terms of another; for example, they may cast concentric, center-margin affairs as though they were diametrically symmetrical. This is part of what he means by "a complexity inherent in dual organizations" (1963:147). "In the first place," Lévi-Strauss says, "there is the juxtaposition of diametric structure with a concentric structure, including even an attempt to express one type in terms of the other. Actually, the East is *at the same time* east and center and the West is *at the same time* west and periphery" (1963:149; emphasis added).

Simultaneity is the key idea. The groups created by various social structures have more than one meaning at a time. What makes the divisions work as unifying structures is the fact that it is possible for the category West to be also North, or South also East, and for East to embrace both center and margin. Lévi-Strauss, in the end, does not argue that dualisms do not exist, but that "dualism" alone is too simple a way to describe complex social entanglements. His hypothesis is instead: "It follows that triadism and dualism are inseparable, since dualism is never conceived of as such, but only as a 'borderline' form of the triadic type" (1963:151). This echoes what he says earlier: "What we generally call 'dual organization' is in many instances (and perhaps in all) actually an inextricable mixture of the three types"—diametric, concentric, and triadic "dualisms" (1963:150).

Lévi-Strauss proposes that social organizations, as expressed by marriage practices, be understood as permutations of various basic oppositions.[6] Particular societies, or groupings within societies, are divided or united by these "distinctive features." The combinations vary with person and relation. The possibility of marriage between families of different units, for instance, alters the character of the division separating them; the division means one thing if they can marry, and something else if they cannot. Neighbors united by residence may be divided by clan; clan mates may be close in kinship but distant in space. The proximity of combined structures, like that of phonemes in a word, conditions them and alters their meaning.

What Lévi-Strauss's critics seem to miss is this idea that structures are superimposed on one another, that different structures occur together, simultaneously, and that they condition, alter, or distort one another. These distortions, and the endlessly different meanings they entail, are the very differences that fuel the poststructural project.

Gender's Divorce from Sex

The idea of two genders, masculine and feminine, made a certain intuitive sense when gender was thought to be structured by two naturally pregiven sexes, male and female. However, the essential connection between gender and sex and the binary structure of gender lost their foundation at two critical moments in the development of gender theory.

The first came with Simone de Beauvoir's declaration that "one is not born, but rather becomes, a woman" (1952:301). The point was clear: biology is not destiny. Much of feminist theory since has sought to show that there is nothing essential, universal, or inherent in females that necessitates their oppression or limits the range of possible gender expressions. If gender is not anchored by sex, then gender is not anchored by sexual dimorphism either. Not only might there be male women and female men, as Judith Butler suggests (1990:6); there might also be any number of genders. If gender is a cultural construction, then biology does not dictate the number or nature of genders.

The second rupture came when sex itself lost the material basis for its binarity. Anthropologists in the 1980s began to question whether sex was everywhere divided by humans based on the same facts of anatomy, reproduction, and chromosomes. Ethnographic accounts showed that sex was understood differently in some societies; people in Nepal, for example, distinguished female as flesh and male as bone, meaning that all people contained both sexes (Diemberger 1993).[7] Sylvia Yanagisako and Jane Collier summarized what all this implied: "We question whether the particular biological difference in reproductive function that our culture defines as the basis of difference between males and females, and so treats as the basis of their relationship, is used by other societies to constitute the cultural categories of male and female" (1987:48). If people in different societies might attend to other differences, these differences might not always be dual. Butler's *Gender Trouble* argued that the gender/sex distinction was itself artificial: "Gender ought not be conceived merely as the cultural inscription of meaning on a pregiven sex (a juridical conception); gender must also designate the very apparatus of production whereby the sexes themselves are established" (1990:7–8). The question then is not whether genders are "natural" pairs, but what cultural processes create and re-create dual or binary gender formations.

The Flirtation with and Flight from Structure

If feminists of the 1970s and early 1980s rebelled against the reduction of "cultural" gender to "biological" sex and anatomy, they did not abandon structure. Rather, they sought to discover structural reasons for what they perceived was a universal denigration of women. Sherry Ortner (1974, 1996) suggested that women's second-class status was rooted in the Lévi-Straussian opposition between nature and culture. She wondered whether "the universal devaluation of women could be explained by postulating that women are seen as closer to nature than men, men being seen as more unequivocally occupying the high ground of culture" (1974:83–84). What structured sex difference and sexism, Ortner suggested, was universal aversion to the lower, dangerous, and problematic functions of nature.

At the same time, Michelle Rosaldo (1974) argued that women's normative role as primary caregivers to children linked them with domestic as opposed to public concerns. What was thought to underlie women's low status in this view was not their sex per se but the relatively lower status accorded to domesticity than to politics. The domestic arena was linked to childcare, and thence to women, by virtue of their uterine and mammary investments in children. All this led back to women's "nature" and "biology." In a somewhat similar vein, Nancy Chodorow (1978) proposed that men's psychodynamic resentment of caregiving mothers organized the male animus against women generally. Marilyn Strathern (1981a) noticed the associations people made between women and family, or "selfish," interests, and between men and community, or "social," interests. This explained why, in the society Strathern studied, men occupied the moral high ground: women were too concerned with the particular interests of their children to be trusted with wider interests of community. These models were all binary. They sought to integrate gender with other institutions and to see gender as a set of beliefs and values that saturated social lives. All took for granted, with nods here and there to exceptions,[8] that sex organized gender assignments, if it did not always control what the assignments meant. They made efforts to distinguish gender from sex, not to reduce gender to sex. But concern for discovering universal structures of gender ushered sex in through the back door. According to these theories, it was women's biology, the anatomical fact of their bearing and nursing children, that set them apart from men and, within each society, helped to define their lower status.

Arguments against binary gender models emerged in the 1980s and took several forms. Critics faulted the assumptions that nature/culture, domestic/public, selfish/social, and male/female were universally and un-problematically recognized oppositions which occurred everywhere, and everywhere in the same way (see Ortner and Whitehead 1981, Strathern 1981b, Moore 1988). Butler (1990:12) has pointed out that even though these theories sailed beneath a feminist flag, they nevertheless assumed that gender reflected basic sex differences; that assumption, she said, failed to interrogate hegemonic constraints on women, gender, and sexuality. As she wrote in a later work, "If there is a point, and a fine point, to what I perhaps better understand as poststructuralism, it is that power pervades the very conceptual apparatus that seeks to negotiate its terms, including the subject-position of the critic" (1994:157). Feminist critics, in other words, unwittingly recapitulated the very structures they sought to challenge.

The supposed reality of dual sexes, male and female, was the "stable center" of gender that poststructural "deconstruction" destabilized. If sex differences were themselves constructed, then one lost the independent basis for their duality. Why were gender categories in so many societies dualistic? Duality's *raison d'être*, no longer reducible to two naturally pre-given sexes, was reduced instead to the interests duality served. According to Butler and others, a two-sex, two-gender model turned women into men's "natural" other and normalized heterosexuality. A feminist theory keen to challenge sexist and heterosexist norms would instead imagine multiple genders and sexes. The *binary* was thus wedded to ideas of male domination and what Adrienne Rich called "compulsory heterosexuality" (1980).

The Problem of the Binary

Thus the word "binary" became a term of opprobrium. The subtlety with which binary structure was approached by some became in time a caricature. The word now seems to be code for "modernist positivism" and "patriarchal hegemony." It represents limitation and constraint. In Judith Butler's analysis, for instance, gender is implicated, as are all cultural forms, in "fields" of hegemonic power (see also Foucault 1978). That is, the dominant interests of part of society come to be legitimated—regarded as normal, even natural—by the whole.[9] How this happens with gender, she argues, is that *binary* genders and *binary* sexualities are "lined up" behind a belief in naturally given *binary* sexes, male and female. For Butler, the problem with lining up sex, gender, and desire is not simply the serial linkage between the three domains, but the imposition of a particular order—the binary order—on any of them. "The binary regulation of sexuality suppresses the subversive multiplicity of a sexuality that disrupts heterosexual, reproductive, and medicojuridical hegemonies" (Butler 1990:19). The poststructural challenge to this structure is to ask if it might be otherwise, and if not, why not? If there is no prediscursive reason for binary sexes, there is none for binary genders. As Butler frames it, the concept of binarity itself is directly implicated in the socially constructed manacles of gender oppression. The task of feminist theory, she says later, "is not to prefer the feminine side of the binary to the masculine, but to displace the binary" (1990:126).

The binary has been tied by gender theorists to sex, biology, and bodies; to mention one is to evoke the others (see, for instance, Moore 1994:20). But the wholesale rejection of these concepts by self-described poststructuralists contradicts the inclusive ethos of poststructuralism. They re-create the very binary structure they seek to dispel. Is the concept of binarity really any different from the concept "difference" that is so celebrated in this same literature? One of the writers I am referring to, Henrietta Moore, even titled one of her books *A Passion for Difference* (1994). How did the term "binary," which in structural linguistics is identified with "difference" and "distinction," come to mean something restrictive and alienating: a simple dualistic disjunction between "this or that"—like "black or white," "love it or leave it," "be hip or be square"—rather than the more complex and truly binary "this or not this (but theoretically everything else)"?

"Post" Structure, Not No Structure

Much of gender theory's critique of structure has drawn on poststructuralism. The motives of both poststructuralism and feminism are partly political: to leverage change. An aim of feminism is to *liberate* women, not to lay on more structure. The strategy is to challenge assumed meanings, to turn up alternative or suppressed meanings—to find, in other words, chinks in the symbolic armor of the status quo (Butler 1994:168). Poststructuralists attend to *texts* and *discourses*, which are conceived broadly as systems, or fields, of meaning and understanding (Dosse 1997, Derrida 1974, Foucault 1978, Harari 1979). Discourses work to safeguard certain assumptions from alternative assumptions (Scott 1994:283–284). There are always multiple discourses, of course, so discourses compete, and certain ones come to dominate. The tools of poststructuralism are the ideas of *difference* and *deconstruction*. "Difference" harkens back to Saussurean linguistics and the idea that meanings arise from bundles of differences, or distinctions; therefore, meanings are not unitary but always contain within themselves alternative meanings. "Deconstruction" refers not to destruction, but to the process of disassembling, or analyzing, concepts toward an understanding of how they might be put together differently (Scott 1994:285–286; Johnson 1981:xiv; Johnson 1987:12; Derrida 1974:158).[10]

"Now, my understanding of what is most radical in deconstruction," said Barbara Johnson, a literary critic and translator of Derrida, "is precisely that it questions this basic logic of binary opposition, but not in a simple binary, antagonistic way" (1987:12). It is important to note that Johnson was not rejecting binary thinking here so much as adding to it. Thus, "Instead of simple 'either/or' structure, deconstruction attempts to elaborate a discourse that says neither 'either/or', nor 'both/and' nor even 'neither/nor', while at the same time *not totally abandoning these logics either*" (Johnson 1987:13, emphasis added). What deconstruction seeks to avoid is multiple-choice alternatives: A or B, yes or no, for or against. Instead, it entertains multiple or even contradictory meanings, but inclusively, not exclusively.

Poststructuralism is thus characterized as a never-ending search for new ways of understanding old materials. Harari, a literary critic, has summarized "Derridian deconstruction" as "the tracing of a path among textual strata in order to stir up and expose forgotten and dormant sediments of meaning which have accumulated and settled into the text's fabric" (1979:37). Similarly, Scott, a gender historian, has said that "an insistence on differences undercuts the tendency to absolutist, and in the case of sexual differences, essentialist categories. It does not deny the existence of gender difference, but it does suggest that its meanings are always relative to particular constructions in specified contexts. In contrast, absolutist categorizations of difference end up always enforcing normative rules" (1994:297). Bruce Knauft, a social anthropologist, has recounted the effects of the poststructural movement on gendered ethnography: "Personal experience or standpoint is accorded value even as its theoretical edifice may get dizzyingly abstract. Emphasis is placed on the re-creation of meaning, resistance, and identity by women, lesbians, and gays via the fragments and pastiche that have long been at the margins of masculine modernity" (1996:241).

But the search for alternative and multiple meanings, even the focus of attention on the particular over the general, does not eliminate structure. The question, as I said before, is not *whether* there are structures (which are plainly multiple, even infinite), but *which* structures and *why*, and *what* relations they have with other structures. "Fixed oppositions," according to Scott, "conceal the extent to which things presented as oppositional are, in fact, interdependent—that is, they derive their meaning from a particularly established contrast rather than from some inherent or pure antithesis" (1994:286). In this there is a sense that structures are ad hoc, unique to situations, and that their significance arises from historically contingent relations between oppositions rather than from anything intrinsic to their poles.

This is where poststructuralism, at least in some of its incarnations, puts persons, places, and times back into the study of culture and society. If structural relations are contingent, then their use and meanings depend on the motives and sensibilities of the people using them, and these in turn depend on local and historical circumstances. Where Lévi-Strauss has been accused of seeking a Platonic realm of eternal, universal, binary codes, some of his heirs have sought out the messy *practices* in all their particularity, the shadowy spaces between structural opposites (see Bourdieu 1977; Ortner 1984, 1989). This book aims not only to salvage the binary as a useful analytic tool, but also to reinsert persons and histories into the analysis of binary logics. Indeed, just as the philosopher Ludwig Wittgenstein argued that the meaning of language is tied to its use in language "games," the meanings of symbolic oppositions are tied to their use by persons in particular social "games." The chapters to follow show how binary gender symbolism is rooted in nomadic experience and history. These symbols were generally available to Gabra at the time of my research, but they were used to represent and make sense of life in different ways, depending on individual and circumstance. Thus, symbolic oppositions arise from local and historical contexts.

Scott, a historian, has suggested that gender systems are always binary, opposing masculine to feminine in hierarchical order (Conway, Bourque, and Scott 1989:xxix). But she has wondered whether this structure of binary difference is always or ever about sexual difference. In fact, she argues—much as I will—that gender serves in ordinary language use as a sort of trope to indicate inequalities of power. Gender, in other words, is good to think. "These interpretations," she writes, "are based on the idea that conceptual languages employ differentiation to establish meaning and that sexual difference is a primary way of signifying differentiation" (1988:45; see also Kratz 1994:49 and Ortner 1996:132). The symbolism is in the difference.

This is a *structural* exegesis that is *poststructural* in spirit. I am interested in exposing structural relations between concepts that are ambiguous and multivalent. Gabra symbols not only possess multiple meanings; they also imply the differences between what they signify and what they do not, between what they mean in a particular use and what their users purport to mean, and between their various uses alongside other symbols. That is, symbols contain their own semantic slippage. This was Lévi-Strauss's point in his essay on dual organization (see also V. Turner 1967:50–52, Barth 1987). The juxtaposition of representations creates emergent meanings and complexity. Meanings can be multiple and hybrid, though structures are more or less certain.

Critics of poststructuralism, such as di Leonardo, quoted at the beginning of this chapter, and Perry Anderson (1984), a Marxist thinker, warn that poststructuralism breeds intellectual nihilism. I argue that poststructural thinking need not be as anarchic and nihilistic as they suppose. Poststructuralism at its best asks us to reckon with complex, ambiguous, and multiple meanings. Derrida (1974:158) asserts that there is nothing outside the text. I take this in the way that Johnson does: "It is to say that nothing can be said to be not a text, subject to the différance, the nonimmediacy, of presence or meaning" (1987:14). If I understand them both correctly, they mean that there is nothing that is not a representation—an idea that is at least as old as Immanuel Kant's distinction between *noumena* and *phenomena* (1965). Human minds have no access to the "real" world, but only to meanings, texts, representations that they make. One can nevertheless be precise about the phenomenal world, about texts, or about representations. We can and do say useful things to each other.

Gabra gender symbolism represents a world view that is inherently contingent and uncertain. It would be mistaken to fix *the* meaning in Gabra society of, say, "man" or "woman," "masculine" or "feminine," "red" or "white," or to assign particular contents to those meanings. Such an effort would betray the facts. The concepts are ambiguous and polythetic precisely because they describe the complex, historically contingent experiences of individuals. Their meaning lies, in both structural and poststructural senses, in the space between their different meanings.

Precision and Ambiguity in Billy Budd

Barbara Johnson's exegesis (1980) of Herman Melville's last novel, *Billy Budd*, is a poststructural deconstruction that takes the middle way I seek. She manages to be precise about inherently ambiguous materials. I use Johnson's essay to show that a poststructural account need not be nihilistic about the world it describes—in this case a classic literary text, but conceivably any system of symbols and meanings. Johnson demonstrates the deeper understanding that can be achieved by retaining rather than eliminating ambiguity, and by attending to the interplay of multiple meanings. My ultimate analysis of Gabra d'abella, the men who are women, is similar to the type of analysis outlined here.

Melville's novel is a story about a sweet, naïve sailor, Billy Budd, who is falsely accused of treachery by the devious master-at-arms, John Claggert. Billy, enraged by Claggert's accusation but incapable of defending himself verbally, strikes Claggert and kills him. Captain Edward Fairfax Vere, who means well, must choose between compassion for Billy and military duty. He sentences Billy to hang.

This is a thumbnail sketch of a complex tale: to name but a few of its difficulties, one may read Billy as either naïve or treacherous, Claggert as evil or innocent, and Vere as just or unjust. Critics, Johnson writes, have tended to want to decide between these antinomies. They have seen the novel as a problem of ambiguity in need of solution. Was Billy really innocent? Was Claggert evil? Was Vere just? These are the sorts of questions critics have asked. Johnson says they are the wrong questions, because they presume that deep below its surface the novel contains certain answers.

Instead, Johnson argues, the world of *Billy Budd* is essentially ambiguous and undecidable. That undecidability—the multiple ways its characters may be read by readers, and the multiple ways the characters read each other within the novel—is the story. It is what the novel is about. Ambiguity, the "space between" possible interpretations, is its reality, its truth. An interpretation that decided these questions in just one way would misread the text.

Johnson makes a problem of the obvious contrast between Billy Budd, the naïve and innocent sailor, and Claggert, the evil cynic, by calling attention to the contrast between their presumed inner characters and what they do: Budd kills Claggert, thereby turning himself into a murderer and Claggert into an innocent victim; their characters change places. "If *Billy Budd* is indeed an allegory," Johnson writes, "it is an allegory of the questioning of the traditional conditions of allegorical stability. The requirement of Melville's plot that the good act out the evil designs of the bad while the bad suffer the unwarranted fate of the good indicates that the real opposition with which Melville is preoccupied here is less the static opposition between evil and good than the dynamic opposition between a man's 'nature' and his acts, or . . . the relation between human 'being' and human 'doing' " (1980:83). There is thus a secondary opposition between each man's "character" and "performance."

Johnson's method is always to probe deeper, finding ambiguity behind ambiguity and opposition within opposition. Melville, it turns out, tells the reader very little about Billy Budd or John Claggert. Their characters are inferred from an absence of information about them. Thus, another opposition emerges, as undecidable as the others, between what is known about the characters and what is unknown. In Claggert's case, lack of knowledge leads the reader (and other characters in the book) to believe that Claggert has something to hide and that he is evil or even Satanic. In Budd's case, it indicates goodness, innocence, or even divine origin (1980:95). The absence of facts leads others to make up stories about them, propagating a confusion of "readings" and "misreadings." "What Melville's tale tells," Johnson says, "is the snowballing of tale-telling. It is possible, indeed, to retell the story from a point of view that fully justifies Claggert's suspicions (of Billy), merely by putting together a series of indications already available in the narrative," which Johnson then proceeds to do (1980:95ff).

Under Johnson's attention, the text's uncertainties ramify like cracks in the wall, each leading to another, so that the text itself becomes unstable and the reader is not sure what to think. This seems to be the point. The novel draws our attention to these uncertainties: the fragmented, contradictory, nonunified character of selves and situations. Johnson believes that to draw a line between oppositions and between uncertainties, and to declare an interpretation that stands on one side or the other of the line, are to obliterate the "space between" the oppositions in which the life of the story occurs (1980:106).

Ambivalence: Motivation in Structure

There is a middle way through the antinomy between form and variation, between structure and contingency, and this way has a lineage at least as old as Kant. It runs through Hegel, Marx, Simmel, Weber, and Freud, and it continues in anthropology in Gregory Bateson (1958), Max Gluckman (1955), Victor Turner (1957), Lévi-Strauss (1963), Peter Berger and Thomas Luckmann (1966), Robert Paul (1982), Fredrik Barth (1987), Gananath Obeyesekere (1990), Margaret Trawick (1990), and Charles Nuckolls (1996). They and others have studied the essential role played by enduring conflicts, contradictions, and paradoxes in generating social patterns, personalities, and systems of knowledge.

A recent attempt to come to terms with the generativity of paradox, in a work by Nuckolls (1996), is useful to framing the present problem. Nuckolls seeks to synthesize cognitive and psychoanalytic theories toward an understanding of culture—to marry, as it were, the heirs of Weber and Freud. What makes his synthesis possible is that both these traditions share the notion of conflict as their organizing principle, and that of dialectic, a process of adjustment, as the perpetual response to conflict. The theories are structurally the same, even if they emphasize different aspects of experience (1996:269–270). The synthesis suggests a way to understand the intimate relation between psychological ambivalence and the open-endedness of cultural forms—precisely the concern before us.

Nuckolls shows how coherent cultural systems are organized around what amounts to incoherent conflicts and demonstrates that coherence and incoherence are intimately, inextricably related. Cultures and personalities, in this view, are built on paradoxes. Since paradoxes by their nature can never be solved, people are forced to make imperfect compromises, which are always in need of refinement. The ever-tentative compromise formations oscillate dialectically between the different sides of the contradictions. The tension born of conflicting desires moves people to refine their choices. "The variations of resolution are multiple, involving compromises and displacement, and continuous in one form or another, since the oppositional conflicts that call them into being cannot be resolved in most cases, at least not in any ultimate sense" (Nuckolls 1996:33).

Psychodynamic conflict is thought to originate in an infant's relations with its caregiving mother, whom the infant desires, from whom it never gets enough, with whom it identifies, yet from whom it must ultimately separate (Freud 1959:62–65; Klein 1986:70ff; Mahler 1968). The conflict of identification and differentiation is not unique to the infant-mother relation but persists in one form or other throughout an individual's life (Freud 1958:168; Bergmann 1971). Subsequent relations between an individual and others are thought, as a central understanding of psychoanalytic theory, to be conditioned by patterns established in prior relations, running back to an individual's first relations (Paul 1989:178). Developmental change is basically additive. New experiences augment and complicate rather than displace; older patterns continue to inform newer ones (see Oyama 1985:32). Learning, in other words, is always a matter of filtering new materials through what is already known (see, for instance, Lakoff and Johnson 1980). The problem of separation is, in some sense, the first paradox of experience, because separating from and attaching to objects in the world is a problem that cannot be solved: one cannot fully attach or entirely separate. "The result," Paul observes, "is an ambivalence which seeks simultaneously to assert independence, fearing dependence, and to long for complete dependence—to view union with the mother as both a balm and a nightmarish engulfment" (1982:148).

The ontogenetically original conflict is played out among child, mother, and father (Freud 1949:73ff; 1959:63). Psychoanalytic theory has evolved since Freud, and its practitioners have differing ideas about the important players, objects, and their relations. The key object, for instance, may vary in emphasis from breast to phallus, and the problematic other from mother to father, or some third party or dynamic (Lacan 1977). The make-up and internal dynamics of the conflict vary. For present purposes, what is important is the basic structure: *conflict*, arising from separation, and *compromise*, a truce between the contradictory demands of separation and attachment.

A central emotion in this process is, as Paul says, ambivalence, because the infant both desires and rejects its object. The child must strike a balance between contradictory wishes. A theory of ambivalence, provided by psychoanalytic work, has been missing from discussions of structure and variation; however, a growing literature on ambivalence in anthropology and sociology has begun to fill the gap (Merton 1976, Paul 1982, Lindholm 1982, Levine 1985, Trawick 1990, Obeyesekere 1990, Kratz 1995, Peletz 1996, Nuckolls 1996). The new concern with ambivalence is related, I think, to contemporary concerns with contingency and ambiguity. Ambivalence is a psychological state, one in which "the same object arouses positive and negative feelings . . . (or) conflicting wishes make it difficult or impossible to decide how to act . . . (or a person holds) contradictory ideas" (Merton 1976:3, crediting Freud and Eugen Bleuler, who coined the term). Because people possess multiple and contradictory dispositions, their choices, decisions, and actions address some problems but create others. People have ambivalent feelings about choices and outcomes: we cannot have our cigars and smoke them too. Ambivalence compels individuals to refine choices, to search for outcomes that finally resolve the tension of ambivalence, which is not always possible.

Robert Merton (1976) extended the study of ambivalence from individual to social processes. He focused on the "ways in which ambivalence comes to be built into the structure of social statuses and roles" (1976:5).

A doctor, for instance, is supposed to be both "clinical" and "compassion-ate" (1976:68); the objective remove demanded by the former character conflicts with the warmth and concern demanded by the latter. It is easy to recognize many such contradictions in American society: "honesty is the best policy" but "play your cards close to your chest"; individuals must "stand on their own two feet" but "it takes a village"; and so on. Ambivalence thus involves conflicting feelings, or dispositions, that arise from contradictions embedded not only in individuals but also in the shared values of groups. Conflicts between opposing desires generate anxieties, and anxieties make ambivalence motivating. Not all contradictions are simply mistakes; not all can be fixed. Some appear to be necessary aspects of life and sociality. Individuals, for instance, are likely to be ambivalent about society, upon which they depend and from which they derive needed support, but to which they inevitably owe obligations that conflict with personal desires (see Simmel 1968:58; Murphy 1971:129ff).

There are famous paradoxes in philosophy and logic, such as the ancient Liar Paradox—"I am lying"—or Bertrand Russell's set-theory question, "Is the set of all sets-not-members-of-themselves a member of itself?" Nuckolls argues that some paradoxes are important and central enough to shape the master principles of a culture. Culture, in this view, is perpetually setting goals that can never be reached (Nuckolls 1996:31). An example from American culture is the premium placed on individualism and the antithetical value placed on community and interdependence. Drawing on fieldwork in a Jalari fishing village in South India, Nuckolls (1991, 1996) shows how sibling relations are based on principles of unity and interdependence. Yet brothers, fulfilling their duties as brothers, set in motion processes of separation from their beloved sisters. "Although brothers and sisters want to remain tightly linked," he writes, "they are prevented from doing so by the very nature of the bond that relates them" (1996:46).[11]

Conclusion

Gabra nomads confront paradoxical imperatives, too. The exigencies of a camel economy in East Africa's Chalbi Desert require them to live apart from one another much of the time, yet all the while to form close, enduring attachments. The next chapter begins to illustrate how sepa-ration/attachment, or aggregation/dispersion, is a central and organizing contradiction in Gabra society. Gabra cannot once and for all aggregate or disperse. Every step toward one troubles the disposition to the other. An individual must always, and at many levels, manage an uneasy truce between them. One must do both. Such imperatives are hardly unique. At some level, the tension, or paradox, of separation and attachment is universal; however, nomadic Gabra experience the tension with special intensity and reconcile it in particular ways.

Poststructuralism's pursuit of the ambiguous "space between" makes it especially well suited for analyzing the circumstances of ambivalence. One of my arguments is that ambivalence generated by the separation/attachment problem, in both its psychodynamic and its social-symbolic senses, is related to Gabra men's ambivalence about gender. Ambivalence, of course, cuts several ways: women are ambivalent about leaving families at marriage, separating from children, and the myriad other attachments and separations that occur in their lives. This book is about Gabra manhood. Explaining men's ambivalence about women requires an understanding of gender, in particular of the "fans" of significance (V. Turner 1967:50) that link gender concepts with an array of others related to space and society, as well as of the fundamental conflicts or paradoxes of Gabra life. It is thus to Gabra circumstances that we now turn.

2

Nomads of the Chalbi
An Interplay of Opposites

And then: the first pure draughts of desert air, and the nakedness of space,
pure as a theorem, stretching away into the sky drenched in all its own
silence and majesty, untenanted except by such figures as the imagination
of man has invented to people landscapes which are inimical to his
passions and whose purity flags the mind.

—LAWRENCE DURRELL, *Balthazar*

And like the heat of the desert you silence the uproar of foreigners.

—ISAIAH 25:5

GABRA DWELL IN AN ARID AND SEMIARID LAND of rolling stone-strewn
plains, volcanic craters, and far-flung oases that spans the border between
Ethiopia and Kenya. They number around thirty-five thousand[1] and live
in many small, highly mobile communities, or camps, called *olla*, each
comprising from ten to one hundred persons. The camps are nomadic,
shifting often and opportunistically with news of rain or pasture. They
speak a dialect of Oromo, an Eastern Cushitic language common in
Ethiopia and part of Kenya (see esp. Baxter, Hultin, and Triulzi 1996).

Gabra are composed of five phratries, or mega-clans: Alganna, Sharbanna, Gara, Galbo, and Odola. The phratries are made up of numerous
patrilineal and exogamous clans, and the clans within each phratry cluster
into loosely exogamous moieties. Each clan contains sections, which are
amalgams of lineages (see also Torry 1973, Schlee 1989).

Gabra tend camels, goats, sheep, and some cattle; they have traditionally practiced no agriculture.[2] They share elements of a material culture
with the neighboring Rendille and Somali, and language and aspects of
symbolic and social culture with the neighboring Borana (Baxter 1954,
Torry 1973, Sobania 1980, Schlee 1989).

The land Gabra inhabit is among the harshest and least populated
areas of Africa (Torry 1973, Herlocker 1979). Afternoon temperatures

33

often exceed 40° Celsius. Average annual rainfall is between 150 and
200 millimeters, and this meager amount is unevenly and unreliably
distributed: one place might receive an entire year's worth of rain in
one extraordinary week while others get none in several years. It rains
generally in two seasons—October through November and March through
May—organized by monsoons from the Indian Ocean. But seasons may
come and go with little or no rain at all.[3] The Chalbi Desert region suffered
devastating and prolonged droughts in the early 1970s, 1980s, and 1990s
(see Torry 1973, Robinson 1985, Legesse 1989, Shongolo 1994b).

The Mega Escarpment in Ethiopia defines the region's northern boundary (see map, Figure 1). Camels fare poorly at higher, better-watered
elevations (Dahl and Hjort 1976, Field 1970), so camel-herding Gabra
are confined to the arid plains below the escarpment. The plains drain
gradually to the south and west, mainly into the Chalbi Desert basin in
Kenya. The desert, a vast, salt-encrusted dry lake, defines rather fuzzily the
southern boundary. Gabra do cross the Chalbi to exploit pastures beyond,
but at their peril, since Rendille, who are sometimes their enemies, live on
the other side. The desert is thus both an ecological and an ethnic border.
Lake Turkana's alkaline waters, fed by the Omo River in Ethiopia, define
the western boundary; a line running south-by-southwest from Sololo to
Marsabit describes, again fuzzily, its eastern limits. I know some Gabra
who have grazed livestock as far east as Wajir, but the farther they go east,
the greater is the perceived risk of Somali raids, so few venture there.

The landscape varies from skillet-flat, mainly in the south and east, to
undulant, like the open sea. Much of it lies between 500 and 600 meters
in elevation. The land is scored by wadi, or seasonal watercourses, which
Gabra call *laga*. Here and there a solitary crater rises above the plains.
A network of hills, ancient volcanic structures, rises to more than 1,000
meters in the middle north of the region. These hills are Badda Hurri, or
"Misty Forest" (though few trees remain); they appear on maps as "Hurri
Hills" (see Figure 2). Their high slopes attract moisture and fog, but little
rain, and they are more often green with lush tall grasses than are the
deserts below. Marsabit Mountain and Mount Kulal rise even higher in
the southeastern and southwestern corners, respectively; they are covered
with dense cloud forests.

The colors of the lowland plains change with place and time: the
brilliant white of Chalbi salt; the pale dunes north of North Horr; the quick
and ephemeral green following rains; otherwise, hues of leather, malt,
coriander, sandalwood, turmeric, rust; lavender and rose at dawn, scarlet

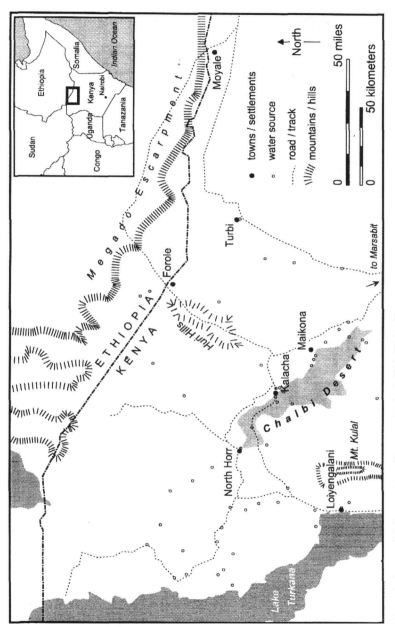

Figure 1. A map of Gabra territory. (Cartography by Jeff McMichael.)

Figure 2. A view of the Gabra plains looking north from Maikona toward Badda Hurri, the distant mountains.

before dusk. The soil is usually visible, exposed like a balding scalp below thin or nonexistent ground cover. The ubiquitous basalt boulders are black as clotted blood. Pebbles on the southern grass plains (*ramata*) are pinkish purple. The alluvial mud at the Chalbi shoreline is baked yellow as adobe. My memories of visual distances quiver from the heat. In the afternoon, great whirlwinds of dust and debris rise a hundred meters into the air and swirl across the land. They can demolish a Gabra tent in their path.

I have walked across the plains for several days and not met but two or three travelers. Indeed, this region encompassing more than forty thousand square kilometers has less than one person per square kilometer. The wind is incessant as surf and sails almost always from the east. For all its aridity, the open air smells oddly fresh, especially in the morning, of cucumber and melon and strong tea.

A quirk of geology has separated water from pasture. Where there is grass and brush for animals to eat, there is no permanent drinking water, and where there is dependable water at wells and springs, there is little for animals to graze. When rain falls, it drains quickly in the sandy soil or flows along seasonal riverbeds, much of it filling a vast aquifer below the Chalbi Desert (Bake 1991:54–55). Here where nothing grows owing to the salt on the surface, there is reliable, if often alkaline, water beneath. For Gabra, grazing tends to be better in the north, while wells and springs tend to lie in the south.[4] Small settlements have sprung up beside dependable watering holes at Maikona, Kalacha, North Horr, Bubissa, and Dukana. Here merchants sell goods to herders when they bring animals to water. Here is also where missionaries have set up shop, where relief agencies distribute food, and where the government has posted soldiers. It is also at these centers that impoverished (or, in fewer cases, exceptionally wealthy) Gabra have settled.

The division of two essentials, water and pasture, means that during the dry seasons—which comprise most of the year—herders and stock must separate into small, highly mobile camps and shuttle back and forth between pastures and wells. The enterprise of watering stock involves crushing labor: it is not unusual for herders to march forty or fifty kilometers with camels to water, and after they have drunk their fill, to march the forty or fifty kilometers back to pasture, just to repeat the trek a week later. The exigencies of the camel economy in this environment divide social groups and keep them moving. The need to shift between grass and water shapes social organization and informs ideas about space.[5]

So sparse and variable are pastures usually that communities also spend much of the year divided between main and satellite camps. Gabra explain this partly as a function of distributing risks, partly as a matter of what any one pasture will bear, and partly as a recognition that different livestock eat different types of forage and benefit from different pastures (Dahl and Hjort 1976). Main camps (*olla*) include tents, women, children, older men, and most of the milking stock. They move every month or so, loading tents and containers for water and milk on the backs of castrated male camels. The tents, the defining features of main camps, are domes made of an armature of wooden poles covered with woven mats, skins, and cloth. Tents are owned by and associated with women; main camps are thus feminine spaces. Gabra have a saying: *Wara jecum nad'eni*, "Home means woman."

The smaller satellite camps (*fora*) include younger men and older boys, who tend the remaining herds in the relatively more dangerous distances, generally farther away from permanent water than the main camps.[6] Satellite camps shift weekly, if not daily. In contrast with olla, they are seen as masculine spaces. There are no tents in fora. At each camp, men build new corrals out of thornbush and stones; they sleep under the stars on the bare ground beside their animals.

The Sacred, the Social, and Rain

Rain is one of the prime concerns of ritual and prayer. The Gabra divinity, Waaqa, is associated with the sky. Sky and divinity are not the same: sky is understood as the location of divinity, not its essence (see also Evans-Pritchard 1956, Lienhardt 1961). Nonetheless, *waaqa* also means sky. During and immediately after rains, main and satellite camps may reunite. Then there is sufficient water and grass in one place to suspend the long treks to wells. For several weeks—even a month or two, depending on the rainfall—there is plenty of forage for animals to eat, milk for people to drink, leisure, and conviviality.

These times of social aggregation, in contrast with the more usual circumstances of dispersion, are associated with sacred moments. The association is complex. Sacred gatherings do not always occur in the relatively lush days after rains. Rather, rituals, which typically involve sacrifices of animals or milk and feasting, are performed according to a calendar that cycles more or less independently of the seasons: a seven-day week, with days set aside for particular activities and prayers; twelve lunar months, with ceremonies occurring at new moons and Sorio Nagaya sacrifices on certain days within three special "camel" months (*jia galla*); a 365-day year, with extended Almado ceremonies at its beginning and end; and seven-year "week" cycles, corresponding to the seven days of the week which are the namesakes of sequential years, and in some of which Gabra make pilgrimages to sacred grounds to initiate new officers and d'abella (see Tablino 1989, Robinson 1985). Only when people gather at main camps, in the presence of tents, may they perform rituals. If a living father, mother, or eldest son is absent, the family may not sacrifice animals, acknowledge the new moon, or perform a marriage (see Wario's story, next chapter). Above all, these and other rites must occur at main camp, often literally in the shadow of the tents. Gabra are enjoined, whatever the season, to return with their herds to main camps to participate in certain rituals.

Ceremonial gatherings are linked in people's minds with the less formal gatherings following the rains. Both of these sorts of gathering, the formal and the informal, are times of sociality and feasting. They are linked by rain: gatherings occur when Gabra ask for or receive rainfall. Ritual gatherings are culturally organized moments, held in the interests of inviting rain and peace, which imitate and reproduce the gatherings organized as if by nature during rainy seasons. The crucial point is that ritual moments are moments of social gathering. The sacred and social occur together.

Pairs of Oppositions

This book is a symbolic analysis of Gabra culture. Gabra divide the circumstances that I have been describing into binary oppositions, and these derive their meaning, their motivational force, from experience. If we are to understand the oppositions, we must also understand the experience: the laborious contrast between taking animals to water in the south and driving them to pasture in the north; the division of families between main and satellite camps; the punctuation of the year by dry and wet seasons; the contrast between lush highlands and arid lowlands; and the alternation between moments of dispersion and aggregation. The oppositions are gendered by Gabra as feminine or masculine, in that women are identified with places and moments of aggregation and men with outlying pastures and dispersed satellite camps. There is a sense, among Gabra, that much as men and women require each other to procreate, these other oppositions require each other as well—that unity is achieved through duality; hence the saying *Lami toko*, "Two is one."

I once asked a wizened elder, Waticha Boranticha, why Gabra always repeated prayers an even number of times. Waticha was past ninety years old and thought to know more than most about such things. In fact, he was fixated on *ada*, law or tradition, and often harangued younger men about the need to follow tradition. "Waaqa made everything in twos," he declared. "We have two eyes, two ears, two legs, two arms. We have day and night, sun and moon. We have black men and white men. We have male and female. It shows respect to Waaqa to pray in twos."

Gender and Space

Let me draw several observations from what I have described so far. The first is that the geographic and moral fields are coterminous and related; they overlie each other. The social center, the main camp, is also the moral center, the location of ritual action and efficacy, where Gabra identity and tradition are rejuvenated. Images of one evoke the other. The second observation follows from the first: women characterize and define the social center and thereby also the moral center. The proximity of women to ritual, and the link Gabra make between ritual and the procreative capacity of women, gives ritual concerns and practices feminine associations. This is so despite the fact virtually all ritual activity is performed by men, albeit supervised by d'abella, the men who are women. The third point is that the association is reciprocal: as women feminize the social and moral center, the center "socializes" women, linking them inextricably with the idea of Gabra tradition and ethnicity.

Variations in Gabra dress illustrate the link between space and gender. Men wear baggy, hand-stitched, heavy muslin shorts and wrap themselves over the shoulders in a large muslin sheet with angel-hair fringes tied at both ends; this sheet serves as sun protection in the daytime and bedroll at night. The type of white cloth is precolonial, common throughout the Horn of Africa. They wear thick-soled sandals made of old tires and carry long wooden staffs or spears. A married man may tie a white cloth around his head as a turban. Some also sport a bracelet, earring, or finger ring made of metal or ivory. These often have special meanings: a particular bracelet called *arbora*, for instance, signifies that the wearer has killed an enemy. Still, in contrast with some of their more bangled neighbors, Gabra men are like the American Amish: plain dressers. The overall impression is white.

Women are more colorful. Before the colonial era, and as late as the 1950s (Baxter, personal communication), they wore animal skins. Now they wear multicolored cotton cloths called *wilki*, with a bias to the colors red, dark orange, and blue. The contrast between the women's reddish-brown skins and men's white cloth is preserved by contemporary women's colorful dress. A woman wraps several layers of cloth around her torso, like a toga, tying the cloth over her left shoulder and gathering it around her waist with a string or belt. She may also drape her head with a similar cloth. Women are not veiled or—except briefly after childbirth—secluded. But a woman does use her head cloth as a sort of veil, especially when flirting with men, by drawing the cloth across her mouth.[7]

Gabra women adorn themselves with distinctive jewelry. They prefer necklaces of square aluminum beads, called *kalim*, which are made by Konso blacksmiths from discarded cooking pots and polished as bright as silver. They wear bracelets made of aluminum or iron, signifying marriage and the birth of sons. They wear long strands of red and yellow beads, which incorporate, as segments, beads worn by their children as protective charms after birth. The beaded necklaces are graced with medallions, formerly silver dollars, called *nira*. Women of certain phratries also wear a triangular crown, called *malmala*, made of a thong wrapped with spirals of flat burnished aluminum. Women wear sandals like those of men; they rarely carry staffs and never carry spears.

Those are basic outfits. When Gabra go to town, to visit or stay, the outfits change, but more for men than for women. Towns are, in some measure, outside the Gabra moral universe. Since men identify with the outside anyway, when they go to town there are few moral impediments to their adopting the dress and performances of "modernity." In the towns of Marsabit, North Horr, Maikona, and others, one can see men in Muslim skullcaps and Somali sarongs, T-shirts and trousers, sport coats and shoes. There are men in American baseball caps and African safari hats. There are sunglasses, flip-flops, wristwatches, sneakers, nylon training jackets, and camel-skin Bata desert boots. These urban adornments have been introduced by lorry drivers, occasional adventure tourists, and young Gabra who have left and returned from jobs and schools. Men see these items as urban and modern, representing the "way the world is going" as opposed to how it was or how it is still in the "reserves" (see Tablino 1996). This is the quintessence of "modernity": an imagined future rather than a remembered past serving as model for the present. Men in nomadic camps also wear modernity in bits and pieces—a skullcap, a broken wristwatch, an army hat, a shirt—bought, borrowed, or scrounged from friends in town. Urban fashions are distinctly male. Women in towns, by and large, look like women in camps. True, when nomadic women visit town they wear their best cloth. They show off, but they show off as Gabra women.

The men who are most conservative in their dress are d'abella, the men who are women. The centerpiece of their outfit is a turban made of heavy cloth scrolled into a cylinder, stitched fast with thorns, and plastered a brilliant white. Instead of shorts, d'abella wear a sheet tied at their waists and fixed on the left side, like a woman's dress. Likewise, when they anoint themselves with blood or ceremonial paint, they do this on the left shoulder. They wear distinctive blue beads and a plain iron bracelet. Like women, they may not carry a knife or spear, but only a stout shepherd's staff. They wear special sandals, which are in fact the sort of leather sandals worn by Gabra before tires became accessible. Other men may embroider their cloth with colored yarn, but d'abella should wear only plain white cloth, which they regard as traditional, representative of the Gabra past. In other words, in dress d'abella are extra-traditional Gabra.

Space, I have said, is implicated in the organization of Gabra culture, particularly the distribution of people, the location of rituals, and the construction of gender. Men tend to locate their interests and identities outside main camps, at the margins, beyond the bounds of feminine aspects of their society: they draw on images and practices of outside spaces to construct masculine identities. These include spears and guns and staffs, walking long distances, and tending animals. Women tend to locate themselves inside main camps, the centers of Gabra sociality, tradition, and feminine gender: they draw on the images and practices, the colors and textures, of inside spaces to gender themselves. These include the dome tents, globular water and milk containers, round cooking pots, and the circular hearth fire.[8] Boys become men as they leave the relative security inside the main camps for the dangerous and distant satellite camps. Later in life, when men shift their attention from "outside" to "inside," when they become d'abella, their dress becomes ethnically and morally more conservative than other men's dress, and their gender undergoes a semantic slip from masculinity to femininity.

Women

Gabra say that d'abella are women (*nad'eni*), but d'abella are not the same as female women. They are male women, and there is a difference.[9]

Female women's status in Gabra society is complex. On the one hand, they own their own tents and have considerable control over what goes on within them. Their labor involves matters of great import to men, but it is performed largely outside men's control and supervision: men may not weave the exquisite milk and water containers, or even know much about them, just as women may not carve wood. Men care for camels and other livestock; women load animals, move camp, and journey for water. Both stay busy, working long hours, especially during the lengthy dry seasons. It is as if men and women occupy separate but parallel worlds that intersect at discrete moments but otherwise remain apart. Men own most of the livestock, but their wives generally own the fruits of that livestock: the milk, meat, fat, and oil. Women decide who eats and drinks, when, and how much. A husband would be rude to look inside the family's milk and oil containers. Women may not meet in large groups, but women do spend their days almost exclusively in the company of other women: collecting firewood, traveling for water, weaving, caring for children, talking, and singing. They have considerable freedom of movement. As far as I could tell, women and men alike came and went as they pleased, within the constraints of fulfilling household responsibilities.

Women and men share extramarital sexual freedoms. Indeed, both wives and husbands are expected to have lovers (*jala*, masc., *jalto*, fem., literally "friend," but across genders, "lover") outside of marriage,[10] though they are discreet, even secretive, about them. Husbands and wives do not especially like their spouse's having a lover, but there is nothing socially acceptable that they can do about it. Women's lovers give them gifts and clothing; they are the subjects of women's songs and stories. A woman's lover may be the biological father of her children. While the father (*abba*) is always the mother's husband, the man who paid the bridewealth, a special relationship (*abbera*) exists between progenitor and child.[11] The abbera may give the child gifts, including livestock. The lover may give the woman livestock, which may form the basis of her own herd, a sort of insurance against widowhood.

On the other hand, women have little reliable access to wealth outside their own tents. Gabra inheritance favors sons, particularly the firstborn son, who receives all of the father's stock that his father has not already given to others before his death (Soga 1997). Since women are usually much younger than their husbands, they are likely one day to be widows, at which point most women become dependent on sons. Women are excluded from most political meetings and are not permitted to hold meetings themselves under a shade tree. Nevertheless, I often saw men consult women about decisions, and many men confessed that women were as wise or wiser than men.

Women are all but excluded from ritual activity: they do not pray or share in sacrifices, though they may and do bless others. A woman's presence is usually required for her husband and sons to sacrifice an animal, but the extent of her actual involvement in the event is to cook the meat. Women, however, do play key roles at Almado, or New Year, ceremonies. It is noteworthy that this one series of ritual events that includes women has milk, as opposed to blood, as its central symbol. Women told me that their favorite ritual time was not Almado but *sorio* sacrifices, when all are enjoined to return to main camp. Sons do not always return for Almado.

Although it is collectively discouraged, women may be beaten with impunity by their husbands. Gabra say the right eye of the wife belongs to her husband, and he may poke it out if he pleases. Men believe women are contaminating: sexual contact with them weakens men through loss of sperm; neither a woman nor a man who has had recent sexual contact with a woman may milk a freshened camel, for fear that the woman's body fluids will get on the camel's udder and endanger the calf. On the other hand, most men and women that I asked told me that women are superior to men as camel trainers, and experience confirmed this: women had much more success than men in managing my obstreperous camel.

In countless ways, men tend to disparage women and regard them as beneath men, as children (*intala*), as "half" persons. Galgalo Shonka, who appears in the next chapter, was not the only old man I heard refer to his wife—an older woman herself—as a child. And yet this denigration of women, which I seldom heard from women themselves, hides men's apparent admiration of women and attention to their attitudes and beliefs. A woman's teasing can move a young man to take absurd risks to prove himself (see, e.g., Kassam 1986b). Women can be leaders of parties drawing water from wells. They take their husband's place at Almado if he is absent. They are the sources of human life.

There is no formal equivalent to the d'abella institution among women, by which they "become men." Women, however, are seen by men and women alike to have a hard, masculine side, which emerges when they herd animals, draw water at wells, or taunt and criticize men in songs. Unless a woman bears too many children or fails to get enough to eat, she is said to grow every bit as physically strong as a man. Women are celebrated in songs and stories for their superior endurance at drawing water for livestock. When women journey long distances for water, materials for tents and containers, and favors from family and friends, they enjoy masculine freedoms if not masculine identities. Widows in particular may become independent if they are lucky enough to have their own sheep and goats. There is a large literature on the changing roles of women as well as men, and their changing status over the life course, a process I take up in more detail in chapter 5 (Rasmussen 1997, Katz and Monk 1993, Blacking 1990, Boddy 1989, Gutmann 1987, Brown and Kerns 1985, Poole 1981, Keith 1980, Goody 1958). I knew several women who had been widowed or abandoned by husbands and who lived almost always in *arjalla* satellite camps with their own flocks. They had lovers they visited, from whom they could ask favors. These women did not call themselves men (*d'ira*), but they chuckled when I asked and acknowledged that they lived like men.

Main Camp

I remember waking up in main camps in the gray desert dawn. Even though there were sleeping people all around me, it was one of the rare moments when I felt alone. My assistant, Yara, and I slept outside on the cow skins we used as loading blankets for our camels. Gabra, especially men and boys, often sleep outside, where the air is cooler and fresher and space less cramped than inside the tent. I would wrap myself in my heavy muslin sheet against the chill morning wind and stand and gaze at the awakening camp.

Yara and I were usually guests of the *abba olla*, "father of the camp," after whom the community is named. Thus, Olla Ali Duba was the camp of Ali Duba, who was its abba olla. Ali Duba was the man whose name had come to be associated with this community. He was not necessarily the oldest or the richest, or from the most senior clan, though he might have been. Nor was he formally elected. Gabra say somewhat tongue in cheek that the abba olla is determined by children. A passing stranger asks children what camp they come from, and they say "the camp of so-and-so," and thereafter so-and-so is abba olla. The abba olla is the one to organize meetings, distribute resources, and mediate minor disputes. It is partly his leadership that holds people together despite conflicts, disagreements, and other pressures that might otherwise divide them. However, he has little if any authority, beyond his influence.

Gabra tents—shown in Figure 3—look like half-buried coconuts. They are made of bent saplings lashed together into a sturdy dome armature and overlain with fibrous sisal mats,[12] skins, and cloth (see Prussin 1995 for an analysis of nomadic architecture, including Gabra tents; also Rasmussen 1996 on Tuareg tents). The typical camp has between five and ten tents, or households (Torry 1973:182–184; O'Leary 1985:167). I knew several with more than thirty tents, and depending on the year, the phratry capitals, called *olla yaa*, may have fifty or more. The tents are pitched in a line running north and south, with all doors facing west, away from prevailing winds (Figure 4). *Mirga*, "right," also means "north," and *bita*, "left," means "south"—the default point of view being within the tent, looking out. Right/north is senior and more important, though, as we shall see, concepts of seniority and value are complex. The order of tents in the north-south line reflects phratry, clan, and family seniority.

In front of the tents, on the western side of camp, are goat and sheep corrals called *mona ree*, which are made in circles with branches cut from thorny trees and bushes.[13] These are designed as much to keep predators out as stock in. The corrals have gates facing the tents and a thorny bough for a door, pulled into place for security at night. Between the corrals and tents are small enclosures made of stones piled atop one another like hollow cairns; these are pens for the kids and lambs, to protect them from

Figure 3. A Gabra tent or *mina dasse*. The pieces of wood scattered on top help to secure
the mats against the desert winds and may later be used as firewood.

predation and prevent them from suckling their mothers. (I remember my
surprise the first time I heard a pile of rocks bleat.) Sometimes, to frighten
away hyenas, Gabra also pile rocks to look like human watchmen in profile
against the night sky. They also keep small but scrappy dogs for the same
purpose.

On the privileged, upwind, eastern side of the tents are the camel
corrals, called *mona galla*, also usually made of thorny branches. Each
corral is five to ten meters across, depending on the size of herd; the
fence may be taller than a man. There is usually one corral for the camels
belonging to each extended family. Within the corral are separate pens for
calves, so they are close to their mothers but cannot suckle at will. Each
corral has at least two entrances: one facing the tents, called the "door for
milking"; and another opposite, facing away from camp, called the "door
for grazing." In all the camps I visited, these arrangements seldom varied.[14]

Tent: Inner Sanctum

The order within each tent, or *mina dasse*, is as fixed as the order within
camp. The floor plan is circular; Figure 5 shows a typical arrangement.

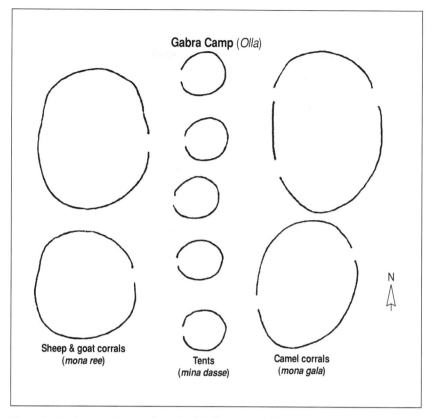

Gabra Camp (*Olla*)

Sheep & goat corrals
(*mona ree*)

Tents
(*mina dasse*)

Camel corrals
(*mona gala*)

N

Figure 4. A schematic layout of a typical Gabra camp (*olla*).

The dome is between three and four meters in diameter and about two meters tall. The size of a tent varies over a woman's life: it has this more or less "standard" size at her wedding (see chapter 4), grows as she bears children and acquires additional materials for it, and then shrinks as she gives parts away to marrying daughters and other relatives. An old widow is left with little more than a thimble for shelter.

The doorway consists of a gap in the armature and is covered with cloth curtains for privacy and protection from the afternoon sun. Inside, the tent is divided into halves: a public area in front, called *bad'a*, where the woman kindles her fire, and a private sleeping area in the rear, called *dinqa*. I use the words "public" and "private" for lack of better terms. Guests, even strangers, are usually invited to enter the private half,

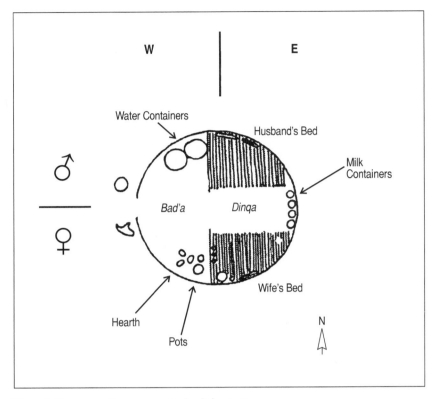

Figure 5. The internal arrangement of a Gabra tent.

where they sit on the beds—two raised pallets made of long sticks lashed together, built into the structure of the tent. But the two rooms within the tent are separated by a lattice, called *korbo*, and curtains. When the family wants privacy they draw the curtain so anyone looking in the front cannot see into the rear. Within the tent there are thus an inside and an outside.[15]

The tent also has a north-south division. The northern side is masculine, the senior position in the Gabra domestic compass. This is where the husband sleeps, when he sleeps inside, and the wall where he hangs the bags and baskets that contain his possessions. The space just outside to the right, or north, of the door is reserved for the husband, the *abba wara* or father of the house; here he sits on his stool in the evening or early in the morning. The southern half of the tent is feminine. This is where the wife sleeps with her children, when she does not lie with her husband. On the southern wall beside her bed she hangs her bags and baskets. In the front half, she builds her cook fire on the left, or southern, side, amid three hearthstones. The space just outside the door to the left is hers; here she, the *had'a wara* or mother of the household, sits in the evening.

The divisions of the tent are not clearly uniform or symmetrical. A man leaves his "masculine" spear and relatively "feminine" staff outside, leaning against the tent; the spear (*worana*) leans at the south or feminine side of the doorway, while the staff (*ororo*), a symbol of husbandry but not of violence, leans at the masculine north side of the doorway. Similarly, it is inside on the masculine north side of the tent that women store water containers (*butte*), which are tightly woven watertight baskets, holding twenty to twenty-five liters of water each (or, increasingly, like-size plastic jerricans). The water, usually drawn from southern wells, is a feminine substance, the province of women, who are responsible for its collection, storage, and distribution. On the feminine south side of the tent, however, women tend their fire, a masculine resource, which though tended by women may only be lit by men; men own the *uchuma*, or fire sticks, a wooden drill and platform for making fire by friction. In this way, Gabra suggest each gender's dependence on the other.

Inside against the rear eastern wall of the tent the woman hangs her milk containers (*chicho*, see Figure 6), received as gifts from the couple's relatives at their wedding. These tightly woven baskets, like butte only smaller, each hold four or five liters. They are made with the tough bark of wild asparagus roots, and they are treated with resin and scorched with hot coals between uses to disinfect and flavor them. Here too on the back wall hang the family's ritual sticks, one each for the father, mother, and sons; these are used in ceremonies and are adorned with strips of skin from sacrificed animals. Here the father hangs the dried scrota of goats he killed when his sons were born. Between the beds and near the wall the woman keeps her *mano*, a small structure made of bent sticks and leather, a miniature of the tent's armature, which she and her husband use to fumigate themselves and their clothes. Incense like this has ritual as well as practical significance: making something smell good is a way of making it healthy, and this is related to its being in right relation with Waaqa. The rear wall forms a kind of shrine, though the term probably sanctifies it too much. It is not a place of worship. The wall symbolizes the household's procreative capacities. It is this wall that faces the stiff turbulent winds, that the woman braces with extra support when she builds

Figure 6. Gumato Dabasso (*second from right*) with her children. She holds a *chicho*, a tightly woven basket for storing sour-milk yogurt. (Photograph by Carol Young Wood.)

her tent, that serves as a metaphor of the family in women's songs. For nomadic Gabra, the wall carries associations Westerners give to keystones and foundations (see Prussin 1995).

A Day in the Life

The day in camp is marked by oscillations of activity and rest. Under certain conditions, people rise before light and take camels out for grazing in the relatively cool morning; they return midmorning for milking and a break during the heat of midday, and then leave again to pastures for late afternoon and early evening. I hardly ever saw this, however, though many said it was "traditional" practice. Ordinarily, people rose at daybreak, around six o'clock. Women, who must be more modest about such things, would take advantage of the darkness to walk away from camp to relieve themselves. Women rouse fires from coals banked for the night. They pour water and milk for tea. Wisps of smoke from the tents rise in the soft morning light. Husbands emerge, if they slept inside, or rise from their skins outside, to sit on stools by the front doors, drink their milky tea, and chew tobacco. By seven-thirty or eight, the men shift to the camel corrals to visit, watch the animals, and supervise milking. They might also pass by the sheep and goat pens to talk with those, mainly wives and daughters, who are busy milking there. Only sexually inactive (uncircumcised) boys, or in some cases celibate men, may milk freshened camels with new calves (*hirmana*), for fear that lingering odors and fluids from women will harm the calves.

This is a busy time: calves, lambs, and kids are bawling, youngsters are running to and fro with milking bowls, and men are discussing where the animals should be grazed that day, giving instructions to sons, and making plans.

Animals, especially camels, are sent to pasture at the same time as other camels of the several corrals within a camp. Camels are difficult to manage once they see others leaving for pasture without them. Gabra consider it rude for one impatient herd-owner to send his camels off early, before the others are ready. When it happens, it is grounds for heated arguments and sour feelings.

Between nine and ten o'clock the camels leave for pasture in mass, though they might graze in different areas up to ten kilometers from camp according to their owner's wishes. They are tended by boys and young men. Sheep and goats usually leave earlier than camels, to different pastures and rarely so far from camp. They are tended by girls and boys.[16] The father often stands by the entrance to the corral to say a prayer for his departing sons and camels, asking that they graze in peace and return unharmed.

Boys and young men tending livestock seemed to consider this their own time. They have to keep their eyes on the animals, of course, but aside from this, and the tasks of driving stock to pasture, rounding up strays, and driving them back at night, they are free much of the day to chat and explore and play. I sometimes saw boys with bows and arrows shooting birds, lizards, and snakes. Boys did not generally welcome my company or that of other adults. Their fathers would grin and wink. "Let them go," one man said. "They want to be alone."

Older men spend the day in camp repairing, embroidering, or tying fringes on their cloths, carving wooden camel bells, stools, and implements, visiting with others, playing the board game *sadeka*, or holding meetings in the shade of a nearby tree to make decisions or settle disputes. Men may join others in taking livestock to wells. They may visit friends at neighboring camps or undertake a long journey to visit and request favors (*imaltu*) from family or friends elsewhere, all depending on the season.

The rainy season is best for long-distance travel: walking is easier (one need not carry water), and since during rains there is usually plenty of milk, receiving guests is easier too.

Women, meanwhile, tend to infants and younger children, weave dasse mats or make other materials for tents, weave water or milk containers, repair clothing, collect firewood, keep the fire, and prepare food. The food is mainly fresh and sour milk, milky tea, and meat, usually from sheep or goats. Relief maize distributed during and after droughts is also available, but it requires considerable water and firewood to prepare; it is thus more common closer to wells and settlements. Women may trek with loading camels to distant wells for water, which will take them away for as long as thirty-six hours. They might make their own long-distance journey (for imaltu, or for materials for tents and milk containers), which could last several weeks. If they remain in camp, their day is spent, much like men, alternating between different tasks.

With the animals gone and children off with animals, the camp is as quiet as a library most of the day. As the day grows hot, people retreat to the dark within the tents or the shade beneath a tree to nap, visit with neighbors, and loll away the hours until late afternoon.

Figure 7. Two girls engage a visitor from the safe folds of their mother's tent while their father looks on.

Close of Day

Women prepare tea again late in the afternoon,[17] just before the older men set off near sunset to meet the younger men and boys returning with the stock from pasture. Their assistance is especially needed with the camels, which do not always return willingly for milking. Boys may also need help at this time with sheep and goats, which wander and lag behind and get lost in the growing dusk.

The time the stock return, called *galchuma*, seemed to be a favorite for men. They would prolong their walk to meet the boys, stopping to chew tobacco and gaze across the plains. It was one of the rare times that I saw them suggest an esthetic appreciation for anything besides animals and women. Some men would round up camel calves, which graze separately near camp. Others would meet returning boys and herds and accompany them to the corrals. If a father did not go to meet his herds, he would likely meet them at the gate of his corral. The standard greeting at this time is *Galchumi nagaya?* "Have you and the animals returned in peace?"

There follows an hour of visiting and talking about the day's events. The boys report what they have seen: they might have come upon lions eating an ostrich, for instance, or the location of a den of hyenas, or met passing strangers from whom they learned of goings-on in distant places. The exchange of news is important business and is taken seriously. Later in the evening, men might visit others in camp and repeat the stories told by their sons, just as the sons visit their friends and tell each other what they have heard about the day's events in camp.

Milking occurs, once the animals have cooled down from their journey, in the several hours after the stock return and may last up to ten or eleven o'clock. There is the same flurry of activity as in the morning, but now under cover of darkness. There are fires rekindled for tea and, if someone has killed a goat, meat. During and after evening milking is *ware*, a time of day for visiting, telling stories and jokes, drinking fresh milk, resting in the orange light of the fires within the tents, or sitting outside under the stars, talking and making plans.

Satellite Camps

After a reunion—during the rainy season, say, or for a sacrifice during a camel month[18]—the father sends dry animals and sufficient milking animals to sustain the herders back to fora, the satellite camp. There is a certain private ceremony to the departure of sons and camels to fora. The times I saw these partings, mother and father accompanied their son or sons to the outer gate of the corral, where mother and son would speak with each other as the camels lurched ahead. Then the father would accompany his son and animals for the first few hundred meters, or even a few kilometers, offering last-minute advice and instructions. Men prefer to have their camels close at hand, where they can see them, but they also want them to graze on better pastures; these partings are thus full of ambivalence. The same ritual would be repeated at each corral in camp, whose owners are likely to pool resources in a common satellite. A fora camp may even include camels from several different olla.

Fora stay on the move, sometimes shifting daily but more often every several days or week, always seeking superior pastures. Camels in the driest seasons must drink every twelve to fourteen days. If their forage is green, they may go three months or longer without drinking (Torry 1973:80; O'Leary 1985:213; Dahl and Hjort 1976). Men meet their liquid needs with milk and blood drained from the necks of living camels. This relative independence from water allows camel herds and their husbandmen to range across the distant and less-populated northern pastures of the region.

There are no tents in these camps, or many material signs of order. A camp consists of a single corral for all animals, with separate doorways for each family's stock. I have seen some camps dispense with a corral when the camels were tame and unlikely to wander and where there was little concern for predators. Men erect a windscreen of sorts with branches, called *gosse*, which offers no more shelter than a bush. They sleep on skins, if available, or on the bare ground, having cleared away stones and perhaps gathered together a bed of dry grass. There is a saying, *Dao fora d'amocha indoartu,* which means "The shelter of fora will not protect you from cold." Fora is *outside* the moral space of the camps. I knew one man who was *chabana*, literally "broken bones," an outcast, and as such no longer allowed to participate in ritual activities.[19] He complained to elders about another man, but they refused to hear his case. The old men said the outcast was now in fora—lost in the wilderness, so to speak. Complaints against others, they said, must be made at main camp, inside the olla (see Wario's story, chapter 3).

There may be one or several hearths in fora camp, depending on the number of households represented in it. Men and boys in camel fora live almost exclusively on milk and blood. Camels are seldom killed for meat. The men may also dress and cook game, if they are able to kill a giraffe, oryx, or gazelle.[20] In arjalla, the satellite camps for goats and sheep, they may slaughter stock for food. The normal age range in fora is between ten and thirty years old (O'Leary 1985:192). Young and old agree that life in the camps, sleeping on hard ground, drinking blood, staying up late at night, singing songs, and following camels for long distances, makes them strong and virile and dangerous. As one man told me with gleeful pride: "When you're in fora, you are just like an animal." By contrast, young men regard life in main camp as debilitating. They say they grow soft in camp, where food is thought to be more plentiful and work less arduous. Mainly, they say, they are weakened by women. They believe that ejaculating sperm drains their strength. Sperm comes from bone marrow, and to lose too much sperm ultimately hollows one's bones. It is better to remain in fora, for in fora men grow strong, *jaba*, and huge, *gudda*. When the rains come and extended travel is easy, the same men, toughened and bonded by their experiences in fora, may plan and execute raids on enemies.

Despite the privations, there is considerable order in fora. Every camp has a leader and assistant leaders, depending on the number of men and animals present. Leadership falls to the man most involved in constituting the camp. Together, men and older boys make younger boys endure special hardships, in a sort of hazing. They give them demanding, even impossible, tasks to perform. They might be told to go alone on a journey at night. They might be sent to look after animals with nothing to drink for the day. They might be ordered to collect firewood, tend fires, or cook tea. Youth, they say, are the women of camp. Young boys, like women, are subjected to the discipline of the men in the group. If anyone gets tobacco from home, he must not keep it for himself but give it to the leader, the abba fora, who distributes it to everyone. (The association between youth and femininity occurs in ritual arenas as well: certain sacrifices demand a female sheep, for instance, but if none is available, I have seen owners substitute a *young* male.) Men at fora organize meetings to resolve disputes. They say fora teaches them how to conduct themselves in public meetings, a task that will occupy much of their time as older men and fathers. Boys are beaten if they do not submit to their elders.

It is at fora that boys hear stories of raids against enemies such as Rendille, Dassanetch, or Somali. It is by making raids (or defending against them), killing enemies, stealing stock, and proving bravery that men establish distinct reputations—reputations that follow them the rest of their lives, as we shall see in the next chapter. The camels, sheep, goats, or cattle a man brings home from a raid are an enduring witness to his achievements: he may give a camel to his sweetheart, to his family, to his uncle. He will receive a female camel—a female marked in this case with the collar of a *bull* camel—from his maternal uncle, in honor of his having collected a trophy, the testicles and penis of a slain enemy.[21] It is during a man's years in fora, outside the main social center of camp, that he distinguishes himself, individuates, builds a reputation, enters his own and other men's memories as a distinct figure, and becomes a character in songs that are sung in main camps and fora even beyond his death to celebrate his heroic achievements.

Interestingly, given what it says about Gabra notions of their ethnicity (Wood 1997b), it was at fora that some Gabra say they originated. The story, told particularly by Galbo and Odola phratries, is that their ancestors were Somalis. Gabra do not generally consider themselves to be Muslims, but the special turban worn by d'abella is said to be a substitute for the holy Koran. It seems that men from a Somali fora stayed away so long they forgot over generations how to read, and when they returned for a new copy of the Koran, the Somalis back home refused to give them a copy, since they could no longer read. The Somalis gave them cloth for the d'abella's turbans, or *hitu*, instead. These turbans are wrapped in many layers and plastered a brilliant white with clay; d'abella store protective and sacred objects—a bit of lion's skin or claw, a porcupine quill, bits of salt, chunks of myrrh—within the folds. To this day Somalis supply the cloth for these turbans.[22]

Gabra in fora see themselves at once as central, for their husbandry of camels, and marginal, distant, and out of touch vis-à-vis the main camps. This tension extends to relations with neighbors, such as the more numerous and powerful Somali and Borana. The concern that men might be lost to fora—might leave main camp and never return—finds expression in the story Gabra tell about the origin of baboons: baboons, it seems, descend from men who failed to return from fora, who stayed outside in the wilderness too long.

Fountains of Life

The quintessential opposite of wilderness is, interestingly, not so much main camp (though that too), but wells (*ela*). Although wells are often great distances from main camps, they are supreme centers of social aggregation.

There are many wells and water points in the region (shown on the map, Figure 1), but the largest and most reliable are the wells and springs along the Chalbi rim (Bake 1991). These include Maikona, Gamura, Korawe,

Kalacha, North Horr, and Balessa. The wells at Maikona, which I know best, occur on the flat barren expanse of what must have been a bay on a now extinct, salt-encrusted lake. From a distance, you can see a couple of tall doum palms, which suggest the water below, and three shady acacias. You can also smell the wells downwind—a wet salty odor like that of the sea. There are thirty-two wells at Maikona, clustered into a sandy depression the size of two or three football fields. Each is a tiny crater, no bigger than a backyard swimming pool or hot tub. The water table is shallow, so water is at most two to three meters below the surface. Some wells are salty, and camels prefer these. Others are sweet, and these are reserved for people to draw their drinking water. Beside each well, running along the mound of dirt that was dug out to make the well, is a mud trough perhaps four or five meters long. At Maikona usually two persons—men or women, but mainly men—stand in the well, one below in the water and one above on a ledge, and pass stiff giraffe-hide buckets full of water between them to fill the troughs, like a vertical bucket brigade. They sing while they work. Some wells elsewhere are so deep that they require scaffolding and a chain of six or eight persons to lift the water from the bottom; I have heard about wells in Ethiopia that require ten or twelve. A visitor may come upon wells on the Chalbi and see animals, and smell the sea-salt air, and hear the rich, rhythmic, hypnotic songs, but not see people—only buckets of water rising and splashing into the troughs.

The wells are carefully organized by a committee of elders, called *nama herega*, who are appointed by men of the many camps using the wells. These elders assign every camp a well, a day, and even a time of day for its animals to drink. In the dry season, goats and sheep must drink every five days; camels, every twelve to fifteen days.

Early each morning, small groups of men wrapped in the customary white sheets, spears tilting across shoulders, the "advance" teams, march down from the stony plains above Maikona to the wells. The day before, these men and others would have trekked from pastures with their goats and sheep and camped an hour or so away for the night. Several of them set out for the wells at dawn, before the animals, to prepare the mud troughs. About an hour or so after the advance teams, others follow with the goats and sheep. One herd may number a thousand head, too many to drink at once. The shepherds hold the flocks back, about half a kilometer away, and release small groups, or *murnya*, of ten to twenty on signals from others standing beside the wells. As each group finishes drinking, a man lifts his staff, signaling his partner to allow the next group to spring forward.

Now to imagine the scene at the wells, keep in mind that at any given time there may be two dozen herds, each with hundreds of bone-thirsty sheep and goats, waiting on the periphery. As they wait, each herd sends forward small groups of stock, all wildly dashing for the water that they have been able to smell but not taste for the last couple of hours. So this is the scene: there are animals waiting to drink, animals running to drink, animals drinking, and animals resting after drinking. Thousands of them. There are people, of course, inside the wells, furiously drawing water; others standing nearby, directing traffic; others dashing and shouting here and there through the confusion, sticks raised, looking for strays. There are men whose flocks are waiting their turn who are pressing the previous men to hurry and finish. Others, mainly women, now begin to arrive with caravans of loading camels (*oro dane*) to fetch drinking water for their camps. The camel trains march in single file through the rushing sheep and goats, seemingly oblivious to the apparent confusion around them.

Then, usually late in the morning, come the great herds of camels, appearing on the horizon before the sheep and goats have left. They too must be held back, with their masters sending groups of ten or twelve forward at a time. Soon there are more than a thousand camels on the plain.

The scene is not finished. Nomads are hard to find, but they must bring animals to water, and so anyone wanting to meet anyone eventually comes to the wells. They come to buy animals or to sell. They come to settle a disagreement or collect a debt. They come to visit, pass messages, arrange marriages, hear news. The wells are focal centers of olla dotted across a vast region called *mada*—a water point and the area it supplies. There are many encampments whose only regular contact with one another is at the wells. People from the nearby settlement of Maikona wander over, sometimes for no other reason than they have nothing else to do. Men from town buy sheep and goats for resale at Marsabit or Nairobi markets. Others have cloth or tobacco or flashlights to sell. Some meet friends or family to help draw water in exchange for milk. All this activity kicks up dust, and with the winds adding to it, the air above the wells is soon shrouded by a gritty yellowish fog.

And yet by end of day, by some miracle of divine agency or human intelligence, every person and every beast has drunk and gone, the dust has settled, and there is nothing to see from a distance but the two palm trees and three acacias.

Insides and Outsides

So far I have sought to distinguish between inside and outside in an effort to draw attention to their distinct as well as overlapping characteristics. My brief to this point has been structural, and to point out structural relations, I have simplified differences. Thus: inside places are feminine, wet (or contain containers of milk and water), round, soft, social, sacred; outside places are masculine, dry, straight as thorns and spears, rugged, asocial, profane, nonceremonial.

In fact, Gabra notions of inside and outside are complex and open. The following discussion grows out of an old interest of anthropology in the structural contrasts between culture and nature, sacred and profane, domestic and wild, or village and bush (see Needham 1973; Beidelman 1973, 1986; Ortner 1974; Riesman 1977; Bourdieu 1977; Kassam and Megerssa 1994; Rasmussen 1996). My analysis contributes to the conversation by introducing and elaborating the Gabra contrast between inside and outside, *olla* and *ala*. "Inside" and "outside" are deictic relational terms, having no enduring attributes or fixed places. Thus, as I have indicated, space within the tent can be divided between inside and outside, as can space in the distant fora camps. By contrast, ideas like "culture" and "nature" tend to exclude each other. Even if such terms as "village" and "bush" are used metaphorically, they have specific referents, which anchor meanings to particular places and associations. It is more of a stretch to say of a place that it is at once both village and bush, than it is to say that it is both inside and outside.

Prototypically, "inside" means within the tent. Owned by women, tents house not only people but also water and milk containers: the tent is a sanctum sanctorum, a container of containers. Here is where women kindle cooking fires, consummate marriages, conceive and deliver children. The thick mats covering the tents are ethnic markers, for Gabra are *wara dasse*, "people of matted tents," in contrast to their neighbors, the Borana, who are *wara buyo*, "people of grass houses." The tent is more than an enclosure, a material inside. Virtually all rites, prayers, and blessings are held in the main camps, within the tent or within its shadow: no tent, no ceremony. It is that clear-cut. Tents are physical, social, *and* moral centers.

Gabra extend the inside/outside distinction metaphorically from tents to the larger encampment. Indeed, the term "olla," translated here as "inside," is the term for main camp, the nomadic community.[23] The ecology is so spare that households normally divide their stock between main and satellite camps. If main camp is inside, satellite camp or fora is quintessentially outside. There are few comforts in fora—no women, no tents, and no ritual performances. Once, on a long trek to a distant camel camp, a friend and I sought rest and shelter from the afternoon sun in the shade of a tree. My friend, Abudo Halake, was glad to be returning to his animals. He looked at me and with a smile said, *Ali al*, "Out is out." It was, I think, the same as saying "It doesn't get any better than this." To be outside, away from social pressures, free and alive, and above all among men, was a pleasure for him. It was a common sentiment.

The inside/outside, center/margin distinction also encompasses relations between wells and camps. As we have seen, wells are large-scale centers, visited regularly by people and herds from hundreds of outlying camps. Like tents, wells are dark, relatively cool containers. Wells are sometimes called *wara*, a word more commonly used for family, or the site of one's tent. The wells are social centers, "inside" places, in contrast to the dispersed character of the rolling plains "outside."

As the diagram in Figure 8a suggests, there is a series of nested inside/outside, center/margin relations along a south-north axis: southern wells are focal centers for northern encampments; and main camps are centers for a scattering of more distant satellites, often farther north. Inside/outside relations radiate northward: Gabra gather, or at least touch base, at southern camps and wells, and they disperse to superior pastures to the north.

Space on Its Head

There is an inverse dimension to the inside/outside pattern. It begins at sacred ritual grounds in the far north and radiates southward. Gabra ceremonial grounds lie near the Mega escarpment in Ethiopia (Tablino 1989:91; Schlee 1990; O'Leary 1985). The most sacred of these grounds are mountaintops. Sites at the base of the mountains are revisited by pilgrimages every fourteen or twenty-one years. These infrequent events, which are known as *jila galana*, "feasts of the return home," last several months and are years in preparation. Here new generations of d'abella, the men who are women, perform transition rites and assume office. The rites evoke themes of returning to places of origin, reestablishing social unity, and rekindling knowledge and enthusiasm for "tradition" or ada. Having been scattered during the intervening years, they now return to the center of Gabra space. During these ceremonies, d'abella are said to "give

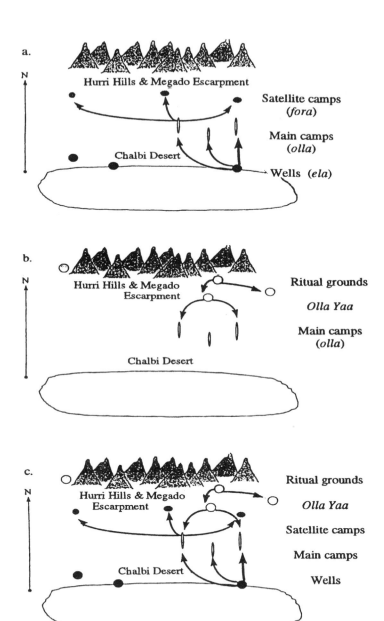

a.

N

Hurri Hills & Megado Escarpment

Satellite camps
(*fora*)

Main camps
(*olla*)

Chalbi Desert

Wells (*ela*)

b.

N

Hurri Hills & Megado
Escarpment

Ritual grounds

Olla Yaa

Main camps
(*olla*)

Chalbi Desert

c.

N

Hurri Hills & Megado
Escarpment

Ritual grounds

Olla Yaa

Satellite camps

Main camps

Chalbi Desert

Wells

Figure 8a–c. Schemata of Gabra territory showing dynamic relations between locations.

birth" to tradition; they enter seclusion (*ulman*), explicitly analogous to the seclusion of mothers and newborn infants in that other sanctum, the tent.

In addition to ceremonial grounds, each of the five Gabra phratries has a nomadic capital, a camp called *olla yaa*, where elected and hereditary leaders dwell.[24] All Gabra are expected to follow tradition, to make periodic sacrifices and perform certain rituals, but none is so important as those performed in yaa. Prayers, rites, and blessings here are ultimately what keep Gabra straight with the divinity Waaqa. Yaa elders are the courts of last resort, the final arbiters of disputes. Yaa camps are the centers from which all others are thought to have separated. As one story goes, Gabra once consisted of only five camps. Over time, each grew large and people left to establish separate camps elsewhere, but the original five remained foremost, senior, and original. These five are the five yaa. The belief that the yaa are the original communities is underscored by the fact all Gabra camps, except yaa, are called *cheko*, which means to be cut off or lonely. Unlike cheko, which are free to shift wherever and whenever their residents want, the yaa are tradition-bound to remain in the northern reaches of the region, within striking distance of the ceremonial grounds.

An inverse set of nested center/margin, inside/outside relations has emerged (see Figure 8b): holy grounds in the far north are periodic focal centers for yaa and other camps to the south, and yaa camps are centers for a scattering of others, generally farther south. The ceremonial grounds in the north are analogous to the southern wells; they are the hubs to which Gabra return periodically to quench their thirst for tradition, their collectivity. Likewise, the yaa are analogous to ordinary camps, except that instead of always remaining within striking distance of wells, yaa remain close to the ceremonial grounds. Finally, cheko camps, the ordinary Gabra communities, stand in relation to the yaa camps as fora, or satellite camps, stand in relation to main camps. Thus there are two series of nested, center/margin, inside/outside relations (Figure 8c). Each center is a hub for radial movements: people come and go from tents, camps, wells, and ceremonial grounds. The southern wells and northern ceremonial grounds are as far away from and peripheral to each other as they can be in this region. Each center is the other's margin; each margin, a center. Inside is outside, outside is inside.

Inside, Outside, Us, and Them

The keys of a piano extend left to right, from low notes to high notes, but they repeat the same scale over and over. Notes change and remain the same. Relations at high octaves are structurally identical to relations at low octaves. Structure on the Gabra keyboard is not about musical notes, but about relations between inside and outside, near and far, central and marginal, senior and junior, strong and weak, male and female. Gabra extend inside/outside relations beyond themselves to encompass their neighbors as ethnic others. In a region where, recent literature suggests, people have historically crossed and recrossed the divides between ethnic groups (see Sobania 1980, 1988, 1991, 1993; Waller 1985; Spear 1981; Spear and Waller 1993; Waller and Sobania 1994), concepts such as inside and outside or central and marginal—concepts that admit the possibility of inversion—are particularly useful.[25]

Take, for example, the Borana, Somali, and Rendille, Gabra's neighbors to the north, east, and south, respectively. Not long ago, Gabra were thought to be a lowland camel-herding branch of the upland, cattle-herding Borana. Their language and dress are much the same. Gabra sometimes call themselves Borana. They tell a story about a Borana father with three sons. The old man fell and his cloth dropped and exposed his naked body. One son rushed forward to cover his father, another covered his eyes, and the third laughed. The father declared that the son who had covered him would be Borana; the son who laughed would become Waata, a hunter-gatherer (see Kassam 1986a); and the son who averted his eyes, who was quiet and respectful, would become Gabra.[26] Some Gabra lineages, particularly among Alganna and Sharbanna phratries, trace their origins to Borana. All Gabra follow a loose variation of the Borana generation-set system called *gada* (see Legesse 1973; Torry 1973, 1978; Baxter and Almagor 1978). At transition rites, certain Gabra make offerings to the Borana *qallu*, a hereditary high priest or ritual king (Legesse 1973, 1989; Baxter 1954).

Just as Gabra exchange livestock for Borana blessings at transition ceremonies, they exchange camels with Somali for the special cloth used to make the d'abella's turbans, an exchange thought by Gabra to suggest their Somali origins. Gabra lump themselves with Rendille and Somali as *wara dasse*, "people of matted tents," in contradistinction to Borana, who are *wara buyo*, "people of grass houses." Gabra more closely resemble Rendille and Somali: they share a common material culture, centered around camels, as opposed to Borana, who keep cattle.

Günter Schlee (1989) argues that Gabra emerged from what he calls a "proto-Rendille-Somali" (PRS) society which, centuries ago, populated the arid lowlands of what is now southern Ethiopia and northern Kenya. According to Schlee, part of PRS society fell under Borana hegemony some time after its sixteenth-century expansion; this group adopted the

Borana language and some of its political institutions but retained many camel-centered symbolic and ritual forms.[27] Schlee compares family and clan names across a number of regional ethnic groups, including Gabra, and concludes that Gabra origins lie among the ancestors of present-day Rendille and Somali. He brings to this thesis a number of supporting myths and ritual forms, shared by these groups, that suggest a common set of interests and values, if not also a common origin; some of these stories are recounted in the next chapter.

Neither theory—that Gabra are a branch of Borana, or that they are a Borana-dominated splinter of proto-Rendille-Somali culture—captures the ethnic flux and identity-switching that has characterized the region's history (Haberland 1963, Lewis 1966, Sobania 1980, Hultin 1982, Donham and James 1986, Spear and Waller 1993, Fratkin 1992b, Waller and Sobania 1994). Many of my Gabra friends could name their fathers back fifteen generations. Often, after so many generations, the names became recognizably Rendille, or Somali, or even Nilotic Maa-speaking Samburu, but often too they were Borana-Gabra all the way back. No doubt there were polyethnic ancestries among these other ethnic groups (Spencer 1973, Sobania 1980). Moreover, people in Africa, as elsewhere, are well known to invent lineage relations (Evans-Pritchard 1940, Kopytoff 1987). I am not trying to suggest that there are no overarching patterns, or biases, in the flux of interethnic relations: Borana did wage a campaign of expansion that lasted several centuries. They very well might have come to dominate some PRS people in the Chalbi region. But for present purposes, the actual history is less important than the current fact that Gabra understand themselves to be at once distinct from their neighbors and yet also related to them. Their identity is expressly interstitial, derivative, and amalgamated, unlike the Borana or Somali, who regard themselves as original. Gabra thus have the cultural means at hand to play up different or common origins as the need arises.

The Borana-centered Oromo movement in Ethiopia has sought to recruit Gabra under the banner of a common Oromo identity, but at the time of my research without much success. The Gabra I knew were unconvinced that a Borana-Oromo identity was in their best interests. On the other hand, Borana and Gabra have joined forces to raid Rendille livestock to the south, and Gabra have succored Borana fleeing north to Ethiopia from those raids (Legesse 1989, Shongolo 1994b). Gabra have explained these alliances by saying that "Borana are our brothers. We are one." Legesse (1989), Schlee (1989), and Shongolo (1994b) describe long-standing partnerships between Gabra and Borana, in which Gabra have aided Borana and Borana have aided Gabra when they lost stock to disease, droughts, and raids. Still, immediately before and during the time of my fieldwork, Gabra and Borana disputed access to ritual grounds in Ethiopia. Borana and Gabra also clashed, with several fatalities, over possession of a son born of a failed Borana-Gabra marriage, and Gabra refused to join Borana in clashes with Burji at Marsabit Mountain (Wood 1997b). Their loyalties are split and contested.

Relations between Gabra and Rendille oscillate between friendship and enmity as well. My Gabra assistant's great-grandfather, Turo, was a Rendille who became Gabra. I met countless Gabra with similar histories. Several Gabra clans identify themselves as Rendille clans. The d'abella institution, universal among Gabra, is shared by one Rendille clan, and this clan shares its name, Odola, with one of the five Gabra phratries. Odola of both Gabra and Rendille recognize mutual kinship. Nevertheless, in recent years Gabra and Rendille have fought and killed one another, sometimes with automatic weapons, over livestock (Fratkin 1992a). I knew Gabra camps that shifted near the settlements of Maikona and Kalacha because they feared Rendille attacks. Word was that Rendille did the same at Kargi for fear of Gabra.

Overlying these interethnic complexities are the international complexities of dwelling across a border. Gabra occupy space that is marginal, both literally and economically, from the standpoints of Ethiopia's and Kenya's centers. As Schlee (1989) has observed, this land between nations has been important to either state only insofar as it served as a buffer against the other. Gabra complain that neither Ethiopia nor Kenya has much interest in them. They have ambivalent feelings about both: on the one hand, governments offer police protection (somewhat unevenly) in times of conflict, which is valued; on the other, they periodically demand livestock payments (to generate cash for a new district officer's house and office at Maikona, for instance) or make restrictions on movements, which are resented. Abdullahi Shongolo, a Moyale researcher, has reported trans-border "forum shopping" by Borana and Gabra, who look for sympathetic institutions (1994a and personal communication). The women and men whom I asked all agreed that government could do a better job keeping peace and providing markets—that is, higher prices—for sheep and goats.

Symbolic Reversals

Structural homologies cut through the differences between Gabra and Rendille. As groups, they are like opposed hands of the same body, different and yet the same. Even their respective geographic landscapes mirror each other. Picture a huge basin nearly five hundred kilometers across, with highlands rising far to the north (the Mega Escarpment) and far to the south (the Nyiro and Ntoto mountains). In the middle lies a true desert, the Chalbi, where nothing grows, but where there is reliable water. Nowadays at least, Gabra dwell mostly north of the Chalbi and Rendille mostly south. Both herd camels, as well as goats and sheep, and cattle if they can manage. Gabra have relations with Borana cattle-herders to their north; Rendille have relations with Samburu cattle-herders to their south. They have complex relations with each other.

Gabra regard north as right and masculine, and south, toward the wells, as left and feminine. Rendille, by contrast, regard south as masculine and north, toward the wells, as feminine. In a Gabra tent, the woman's fire is on the left, or south, side, and the husband's bed on the right, or north, side. A Rendille tent is just the opposite: the woman's fire is on the north side, and her husband's bed is on the south side (Spencer 1973:41, Beaman 1981, Fratkin 1987, Schlee 1989). There is thus the sense that Gabra, in close relation with Rendille, have fashioned themselves into an antithesis of Rendille, but a mirrored antithesis, one that looks enough like the other to make the other intelligible, a familiar "stranger" (Simmel 1950:402–408). The two groups ride an ethnic see-saw: opposed—when one side is up, the other is down. Yet, by virtue of being on the same board, pivoting on a common fulcrum, they are related, bound by their structurally similar differences.

Something like this apparent reversal between Gabra and Rendille could explain the variety of different ethnicities among the pastoralists in this part of East Africa, as well as the remarkable resemblances among them: it is as if they have all, at some time in the past, been each other, or preserve that fiction as a precautionary possibility. Gabra understandings of relations with neighbors can be seen as extensions of internal social relations between main camps and their satellites. The center/margin, inside/outside dynamics between main and satellite camps, wara and fora, olla and ala, serve as structural metaphors for the wider field of social relations. The familiar experience of aggregation and dispersion, social connection and separation, provides a basis or model on which Gabra can understand non-Gabra others. Gabra believe that they descend from the lost fora of Somali. Their stories of origin speak of a prodigal son leaving Borana fathers and brothers to tend wild camels in the bush, thereby becoming Gabra. Rendille include among their numbers "lost"

Gabra; and Gabra, "lost" Rendille. It is a particularly pastoral idiom, this ambiguous tension between "us" and "them," inside and outside. Among nomads, every "them" is potentially "us," everywhere "outside" is potentially "inside," and every "domestic" space, when abandoned, is "wild."

Junior Fathers, Senior Sons

Thus far I have sought to show that Gabra social, spatial, and ethnic oppositions are complex, and that the poles contain aspects of their opposites—a fact which, among other things, facilitates the symbolic resolution of oppositional tensions. If one is ambivalent about separating, he may nevertheless know that in doing so he also attaches. The same is true of being inside or outside, being Gabra or Rendille, because each is at once distinct and same.

This logic—the capacity of opposites to reverse and mirror, to merge into each other—also organizes Gabra notions of seniority. There is, we know from Louis Dumont (1970) and others, something essentially binary and contingent about the junior-senior relationship (but see Needham 1987). It should not be surprising that this relationship is complex. If we understand the basic template of senior-junior relations as between fathers and sons, then the possibility that senior and junior positions would fold into each other reflects a basic dilemma of father-son relations. Fredrik Barth (1981), writing on Middle Eastern notions of manhood, has called attention to a paradox in the relationship between a father and his son in societies that admire virility, independence, and aggressiveness in men. How are fathers to rear sons to be *both* aggressive and obedient? The concern is now widely noted (see Herdt 1981, Lindholm 1982, Herzfeld 1985, Meeker 1989, Gilmore 1990). In some societies, sons leave home when they become adults, so the problem is relatively short-lived. Gabra sons, however, customarily live with their fathers all their lives. Their households share common herds that may not be divided until the father's death. The tension between fathers and sons is potentially great, especially as sons become mature men with divergent interests and the fathers become old and less vigorous men.

One way Gabra resolve this tension is by distributing roles differently over the life course. It is not accidental that old men, ideally d'abella, are identified with home and hearth, rituals, and feminine things, in contrast with younger sons. Given the Gabra pattern in which men marry late, by the time fathers and sons are likely to compete with one another, when the sons are adults, the old men are too old to compete—at least physically. This would not be the case if men married at twenty. But Gabra men typically do not marry until they are thirty-five or forty, to women who are often fourteen or fifteen years old (see chapter 4; also Torry 1973:289–290; O'Leary 1985:162–163); this puts a father in his sixties or seventies when his sons come of age. A man of sixty is not as capable as a younger man or older boy of following camels for weeks, months, or even years on end with little food and no shelter. Nor is the old man likely to make as good a soldier. By the time his sons are mature, the father usually remains at main camp (or visits other fathers in other main camps), serving as the formal head of his family and stock, while his sons who venture forth with the animals are in many respects the de facto owners.[28]

The arrangement of tents in camp reflects the ambiguity of seniority between fathers and sons. Gabra pitch their tents by order of seniority, with more senior phratries or clans north in the north-south line and less senior ones south. These relations vary from context to context. There is one order for going to Jila Galana, or transition rites, another for saying prayers, another for distributing the spoils of raids, and another for arranging tents in camp. Moreover, one sometimes hears different orders cited by different people. What I most often heard was that among the five phratries, Sharbanna tents were most senior, pitched farthest north, followed by Gara, Galbo, Alganna, and Odola.[29] Each phratry has a number of clans, and each clan, a number of families, all with their own relative positions. In all cases, the logic is senior equals north, and junior south.

Gabra sons, as I said, usually remain with their fathers until their deaths. Upon marriage, each son becomes the head of a household, with a tent owned by his wife and given to her by her family at her wedding. Within these extended families, the tents of sons sit north of their father's tent. The tent of the first-born son (*angafa*) sits farthest north, followed in order of birth by those of other married sons, with the father's tent farthest south, in what amounts to the junior position. Thus fathers, the senior men in families, are also, at least with respect to the position of their tent, the junior men. The father is senior, because he is older, the prime mover of his family. He is also the owner of the animals as well as the owner of his family. The word for father, *abba*, means "owner."[30] One reason Gabra give for a father's taking the junior position "behind" his sons is that, like the owner of livestock, he drives them forward, as a shepherd follows his flock. The "junior" position for the "senior" man suggests something of the interdependence between "owner" and "owned." Sons are also owners, of course, since they inherit the stock and may make reasonable claims (ones that would convince community elders at a meeting) on the herds while their father is alive. By virtue of shouldering the greater burden of caring for the animals, sons also exercise much day-to-day control over the herds. Ownership, and seniority, are thus split between fathers and sons.

Complex Seniority

Gabra express the idea of seniority with the term *angafa*, or "firstborn." The word means to be first, prior, but it also connotes stronger, better, fitter, and superior. The firstborn son is angafa; those who follow are *mand'a*. In the Galbo phratry, the Jiblo moiety is senior to the Lossa moiety. Its seniority is expressed by its tents being pitched north of Lossa tents, by its officers (see the section on generation sets below) having the last word over Lossa officers, and by its precedence in prayer and ritual performance. At Olla Yaa Galbo, the phratry capital, there is a central prayer ground, a thorny enclosure called *nabo*, with two doors—one to the north for Jiblo, and another to the south for Lossa.

The seniormost Jiblo clans are said to descend from Waata, the region's supposedly autochthonous hunter-gatherers. A group of Waata are said to have overpowered a section of Gara (another Gabra phratry) with bows and arrows and seized their camels.[31] The Jiblo clans of Massa and Chako are senior because as former Waata they are autochthonous: they "own" the land (see Kopytoff 1987). On the other hand, the seniormost clan of Lossa, Barawa, is thought to have descended from a lone and anonymous figure atop Forole, a mountain said to be the place of Galbo origin; on this mountain Galbo induct new generations of d'abella (see chapter 5). Thus, in one sense, the junior moiety (Lossa) is senior to the senior moiety (Jiblo), because their man from Forole originated the Galbo phratry. But in another sense, the senior moiety (Jiblo) is senior to the junior moiety (Lossa), because it descends from the original owners of the land. Just as ritual seniority is "split" between the moieties, it is split within them as well, since not all Jiblo descend from Waata, but just the two senior clans; and not all Lossa descend from Barawa, but just that clan. The seniority of moieties and clans is largely ceremonial. But the notion of split, or complex, seniority pervades seniority even in its ordinary sense, in that there are opposing values, or measures, of seniority: one is age, as old men are undoubtedly senior to young men; the other is strength and vigor, and in this respect young men are "senior" to their elders.

Moreover, there is another, psychodynamically important dimension to the complex relations between fathers and sons. As I said, men do not generally marry until they are in their late thirties or early forties, while women ideally marry in their early to middle teens, so wives are typically at least fifteen and often twenty-five or more years younger than their husbands. Wives and husbands are expected to enjoy romantic relations outside marriage, often with age-mates. Sons, of course, do not compete with their own fathers for sexual access to their mothers; but sons belong to a generation of young men who do in fact "compete" with the older generation as potential lovers of the older generation's wives. The seniority of fathers is hardly monolithic, but rather is split, shared, and contested by sons. This complex view of seniority, which admits hierarchical inversions, seems rather basic to the Gabra worldview: what is senior is also junior, and what is junior is sometimes senior.

An old man once told me that the color red was senior to the color white. Both are symbols of blood and milk, and these in turn are symbols of death and life, violence and peace, masculinity and femininity. Later in our conversation, however, he said white was senior to red.[32] I asked him how this could be. He said red was senior to white because a drop of blood quickly alters the color of a bowl of milk, but a drop of milk has no visible effect on a bowl of blood. Red was more powerful than white, and thus senior. On the other hand, he said, most animals' coats are white (*adi*, white or light-colored), and blood is derivative—it comes after, or follows behind, the living animal. So, he said, white was senior to red. Red and blood are associated with violence, spears, and younger men. Young men, for instance, paint their faces at new moons and other ceremonial occasions with a paste made from red clay called *walmale*. White and milk are associated with peace, femininity, the round plastered turban of d'abella, older men, and d'abella themselves. Men of all ages in certain clans paint their faces with paste made from white clay, called *shila*, but d'abella must use the white shila only, never red walmale.

Generations

I have described how seniority among men is not monolithic and uniform but distributed. This split, or distributed, seniority is codified in the generation-set system. All men belong to a group of men, or set, which passes through a series of grades, each with a specific status and set of responsibilities. Gabra sometimes call the system *gada*, after the better-known and more elaborate system of the Borana (Baxter 1954, 1978; Legesse 1973; Torry 1978; Bassi 1994; see also Hinnant 1978, 1989, on the related Guji). Gabra more often call their version *luba*.[33] Luba systems differ among the five phratries: Gara have one, Alganna and Sharbanna another, and Galbo and Odola yet another, and there are variations within each. Torry has described the Alganna system (1973, 1978), and Tablino has taken up aspects of the Galbo system in various places (1989, 1991). I collected materials on all, but I know the Galbo system best and will use it to illustrate my larger point.

Luba sets are organized by generation rather than age. Each set consists of sons of men in a previous set, so the men of previous sets are generally older than those of subsequent sets, though this is not always the case, as I will explain. Galbo have six sets which cycle through three active grades, or offices (see Table 1). The sets are named in order Wakora, Gurjab, Afat, Mangub, Damballa, and Wagura. The men of Wakora are the fathers of men of Afat, who are fathers of Damballa, who are, in turn, fathers of Wakora. Gurjab are fathers of Mangub, who are fathers of Wagura, who are in turn fathers of Gurjab, and so on. There is thus one set between the sets occupied by fathers and their sons.[34] The generations Wakora-Afat-Damballa are distinct from Gurjab-Mangub-Wagura; they form what amounts to two generationally organized "moieties" that cross-cut the Jiblo and Lossa phratry moieties.

The sets pass collectively through a series of three active grades: qomicha, yuba, and d'abella. Since there is one set between sets occupied by fathers and their sons, sons enter the first active grade and become

Table 1. Galbo generation sets

Grades		Sets	Relations
		Wakur	Fathers of Afat, deceased
Retired	→	Gurjab	Fathers of Mangub, mostly deceased
D'abella	→	Afat	Fathers of Damballa; sons of Wakur
Yuba	→	Mangub	Fathers of Wagur; sons of Mangub
Qomicha	→	Damballa	Fathers of Wakur; sons of Afat
In waiting	→	Wagur	Sons of Mangur
		Wakur	Sons of Damballa

Note: When current d'abella retire, all the sets will move forward in the schema: Mangub will become d'abella, Damballa will become yuba, and Wagur will become qomicha.

qomicha when their fathers become d'abella. Sons become yuba when their fathers retire from d'abellahood and become *jarole matta bufatte*, old men who have retired their "heads," or leadership.[35] The timing of these entrances and exits is determined by a seven-year cycle; men who are not ready to enter a grade either wait, fall back into a subsequent set, or leave the system.

The system imposes distinct roles and responsibilities on fathers and sons. Qomicha, for instance, are political elders. They are for the most part active men in their prime who are concerned with the economic and political affairs of the larger group. They are called on to solve problems and settle conflicts. In contrast with d'abella, qomicha aspire to ideals of strength, physical discipline, political acuity, and aggressiveness. They exact justice. They are inclined to violence toward non-Gabra enemies and Gabra troublemakers.

Yuba constitute an explicitly transitional grade. They advise qomicha on the one hand and train to be d'abella on the other. Their greater experience gives them influence over qomicha. Some yuba told me that their job was to "look after" qomicha. At meetings, yuba men tended to hold the floor, and arguments were often pitched to them. But Gabra are clear that qomicha, not yuba, occupy the "seat" of authority: *Qomichi barchuma qaban*, "Qomicha have the stools." Ambiguity over which grade has power is a feature of the system, since authority is divided among the grades.

D'abella are ritual elders whose office is mostly concerned with leading prayers, saying blessings, and overseeing rituals. Their primary duty seems to be to promote peace. Like the Nuer leopard-skin chiefs, d'abella are sanctuaries: a man has only to touch a d'abella's cloth or grasp the center pole of his tent to gain an advocate for mediation with his enemies.[36] D'abella are regarded as women (nad'eni). They do not dress like women or act like women, though they regard their dress and aspects of their behavior as feminine. D'abella are not transvestites or transgendered. They *say* they are women. Others refer to them with feminine pronouns. There are special rules governing their behavior, and that of others toward them, which place d'abella in the same category as women. Offenses against d'abella, for instance, are adjudicated and punished the same as those against women. D'abella tie their cloth on the left side, like women. They walk behind men, like women. When a d'abella urinates, he squats and does not hold his penis, as if, like a woman, he did not have one. D'abella should not carry spears or knives; they should not, in fact, utter the words "spear" or "knife" (see also chapter 5).

D'abella and qomicha, fathers and sons, are in many ways antitheses of each other. Qomicha and younger men, or *qero* (an age-related status of warriorhood and pastoral vigor), conduct raids against other ethnic groups. They make and enforce judgments against other Gabra. They are associated with spears, blood, violence, and the color red. D'abella, by contrast, oversee tradition, say prayers, and preserve peace. It is d'abella in the olla yaa, the nomadic capitals, who offer morning and evening prayers. They are associated with the shepherd's staff, milk, peace, and the color white. In the yaa, d'abella are custodians of the sacred drum (*dibe*), a feminine symbol for its roundness, while qomicha are custodians of the sacred horn (*magalata*), an elephant's tusk, a masculine symbol for its phallic shape. The dibe is pounded to call the phratry to prayer; the magalata is sounded to call men to meetings and war.

In countless disputes, where d'abella typically sit as dispassionate judges rather than disputants, I heard d'abella stress the greater importance of a peaceful settlement than a true settlement. A man may have been wronged, but eventually he will be asked by elders to forgive, or even to make the larger concession, in the interests of peace. Of course, any man may exercise these skills, and not all d'abella share them. They are part of the role's character.[37]

Old fathers are not only situated in different places from their sons—in the main camps—but they also aspire to different ideals, methods, and goals. Being at the olla, fathers are more disposed than sons to a concern for the organization of social, interfamily affairs, ritual performances, and right relations with Waaqa. It is interesting, and probably not accidental, that as their ability to look after their own livestock diminishes, their horizons broaden toward the collective and cosmological (see Paul 1982, 1990, 1996a, for a comparative case of Tibetan Buddhists). And though not all old men are d'abella, d'abella are quintessentially old men: the institution is an aspect of the formal organization of old age, maturity, and generation.

I was told by men in different grades that qomicha and d'abella want to delay the next transition because they would prefer to remain in office; those in line to be qomicha and d'abella are said to be impatient for the transition.

Each set, when it is constituted at transition ceremonies held by each phratry, names two *hayu*, or supreme judges—one for Jiblo and one for

Lossa. Hayu are drawn only from certain clans: in Galbo, they come from Chako or Golole, which are Jiblo clans, and Odolale or Koshobe, which are Lossa. They are anointed by the rest of their set at periodic celebrations with blood from a sacrificed camel. They receive *qumbi* (myrrh) and incense from the high Galbo *qallu*, a ritual office occupied by the senior man in the senior lineage of the senior Massa clan. Hayu wield power that is extraordinary in nomadic societies where people can "vote with their feet." Gabra compare them to government chiefs. I heard one influential elder say of hayu: *Ini hayu. Wan ini tolchu jed intolchan*, "He is hayu. What he says to do we must do." Most people, of course, live well beyond the hayu's immediate reach and attention. Hayu function as chairmen or chief judges. People come to them with particularly serious disputes. Theoretically, all decisions are made by consensus, but certain individuals hold more sway than others, based on their wisdom, charisma, friends, and reputations, and hayu seem to have most sway of all. They have the final word in any decision, and unless they speak in concert with the group at the end of a meeting, the group has not yet made a decision. These decisions often involve fines, with one family ordered to pay livestock to another or to the yaa. The most serious sanction available is banishment, which amounts for men to a kind of ritual shunning. Hayu hold office for life and are active as long as their luba occupies one of the three active grades. At any one time then there are six active hayu within each of the five phratries—two for each of the three sets in office. It is not required that all hayu live at the phratry capitals, the yaa, though at least one should. During my visits to Yaa Galbo, there were two hayu living in the yaa encampment, and one living in another camp nearby, representing each of the three grades. Luba also elect any number of *jalaba*, who are clan leaders, or "judges," throughout the region. They represent the yaa and convene local meetings.

Since men may have sons over many years, the range of ages within sets is potentially wide, and it tends over time to grow wider (see Legesse 1973 and Torry 1978 for analyses of this apparent structural weakness in generational systems). It is thus possible for members of an "older" set to be younger than some members of a "younger" set. The discrepancy is partly corrected by requiring that men attain minimum levels of maturity before joining their cohort in certain grades. For instance, men must be circumcised, which formerly occurred in their early twenties but now more usually in the middle to late teens, before joining their luba and entering the first grade of the system. Likewise, men must be married, which normally occurs after they are thirty-five or forty years old, before they may enter the d'abella grade. In some phratries, such as Alganna, immature men are forced to leave the luba system, becoming *hafto*, "lost" or "left-over" (Torry 1978); in others, such as Galbo, they may wait and join their own cohort later, when they have gained suitable maturity, or they may fall back into a subsequent set. Despite these corrections for age, there is still quite a span of years represented in each luba. It happens that men die of old age before becoming d'abella, and I have known d'abella in their youthful forties.

At the time of this writing, the Afat luba were d'abella, Mangub were yuba, and Damballa, the sons of Afat, were qomicha. Gurjab were retired d'abella, or jarole. At the next transition, probably in 2000 or 2007, Afat will retire, Mangub will become d'abella, Damballa will become yuba, and the sons of Mangub will constitute themselves as the Wagura luba and become qomicha.[38]

The luba system imposes a formal order on the generations, such that d'abella are interested in peace, while their sons, the qomicha, are interested in political order, justice, and war. In this way, responsibilities are divided among men. The system also splits and cross-cuts intergenerational relationships. One is supposed to regard his own cohort, the members of his luba, as brothers. Fathers regard all men in their sons' set as sons. Men of Afat, for instance, may not sit on the stools belonging to any of their "sons" in the Damballa set. But within the system, one also regards members of the adjacent set above his own as titular fathers and those of that below as sons. These are the men who serve as advisers to the following set. They accord each other a somewhat more familiar, more avuncular respect. It is the adjacent set, not the set belonging to the actual fathers, that hands over the responsibilities and the sacred objects of a grade to the next set in the system. A man inherits stock from his father, but he inherits social, political, jural, and ritual offices from the set immediately before him in the system, not from his father's set.

The generational logic of the luba system is not monolithic but split. D'abella are senior to their sons, who are qomicha; they are, after all, for the most part older than the men in their sons' luba. D'abella have authority over ritual performances. In certain other arenas, however, the qomicha enjoy a certain seniority, or priority, over d'abella. It is up to qomicha to make political decisions for the rest. It is the younger men's *gadoma*, or time. Even this context-specific reversal is not uniform, however: ultimately, each set requires the consent of the other to act. Each is senior to the other—d'abella in the arena of prayers, qomicha in the arena of politics. Yet within the system, they are dependent on one another, each explicitly senior *and* junior to the other, going before and following after the other, much as fathers and sons arrange their tents in the camp line-up.

Conclusion

This chapter began by illustrating the problem of social separations and attachments, and then turned to the structural similarities between this and other problems, such as the spatial divide between inside and outside, the ethnic divide between "us" and "them," and the hierarchical divide between senior and junior. Gabra solutions to these problems of opposition involve splitting opposed moments and joining aspects of each with its opposite—making the poles trade places, so to speak—such that in times of aggregation there are aspects of dispersion, and in times of dispersion there are aspects of aggregation. The symbolic formation of splitting and combining opposites constitutes a cultural logic apparent in many aspects of life. Ultimately, I will argue later, Gabra do something similar with gender. The logic acknowledges that the very absence of a substance or quality has a presence, exerts an influence on its opposite, and that what is present, because ephemeral, arouses the anticipation of its absence. Rain is a concern whether it is raining or not. Seniority of a sort is possessed by juniors as well as seniors. Following this logic, femininity can be imagined to be a property of manhood. This is the conclusion to which I am leading.

In the next chapter, I return to the problems of separation and attachment, being inside and outside. Now, however, the level of description and analysis shifts from the general to the particular and distinctive: I tell the life stories of two very different individuals. The materials this chapter has explored are studied in a different dimension. Rather than *tell* the reader that inside is sometimes outside, I *show* how men live these oppositions, belonging to the inside and the outside simultaneously. The meta-analysis of chapter 3, much of it implicit, is that these men *live through* and thereby *encompass* the oppositions of separation and attachment in the ordinary course of their normal—as well as unique—Gabra lives.

3

Two Lives
The Ins and Outs of Two Men

> . . . every man is tabernacled in every other and he in exchange and so on
> in an endless complexity of being and witness to the uttermost edge of the
> world.
>
> —CORMAC McCARTHY

THE PROBLEM OF SEPARATION AND ATTACHMENT is normally thought
to concern an infant's growing independence from its mother. Many have
also recognized that the problem features in other dilemmas later in
life, and one of these is the nomadic tension between social aggregation
and dispersion. People experience these push-me-pull-you tensions as a
multitude of small matters, daily irritations, deviations, and noise, which
require adjustment and decision, particular courses of action, choices:
one or the other, this door or that. One goes with the flow or resists it; one
is included or excluded; or, more likely, one charts (or follows) a course
between. Individuals, after all, are *both* products and producers (Berger
and Luckmann 1966:61).

What follows are partial accounts of two men's lives. Their stories offer
insights about the textures and varieties of Gabra life. They show some of
the ways Gabra negotiate dilemmas of separation and attachment. Each
man struggles with his own marginality and seeks contact with the center.
Each makes an epic journey to the periphery that shapes his identity at
the social core. Each in his own way stands outside "tradition" yet also
squarely within its sweep. Indeed, the cases demonstrate that separation
and attachment, outside and inside, are not mutually exclusive moments:
one can separate and attach at the same time. It is the take-home lesson of
these cases that the space of separation and attachment is non-Euclidian;
near can be far, distance may establish connection, parallel lines may
converge.

The first case is that of Galgalo Shonka, a leader whose life course oscillated between center and margin. The second is that of Wario Elema (a pseudonym), whose marginality and outsider status as a drunkard, long ago rejected by his father, was balanced against his curious position as a Gabra insider.

Why describe these two especially? All writing is selective. I chose what I thought best represented the whole. In many ways, however, these two are atypical, non-representative. Few men had the stature of Galgalo Shonka. He was one of Gabra's highest officials. And though alcohol was encroaching on impoverished settlements, its use, let alone abuse, was rare: Wario was one of the few Gabra alcoholics. Galgalo and Wario are extremes—old and young, central and marginal, nomadic and sedentary, sacred and profane. Yet their atypicality illustrates the typical. They reveal how Gabra of all stations negotiate the dilemmas of separation and attachment, being inside and outside. Their lives are different, but they are also structurally similar, and it is this overarching pattern—their ambivalent relationship with the center—that they share with each other and with Gabra men generally. The pattern makes them typical and representative. In telling their stories, I chose parts that they emphasized. I am of course aware that the narratives were shaped by them and me, in the telling and retelling—that they are, in Vincent Crapanzano's words, "double edited" (1980:8). I was nevertheless a relatively passive interlocutor, a good listener. At the times of the conversations recounted here I was not consciously pursuing a theme of separation and attachment. That two such different men told such structurally similar stories suggests the strength and importance of the theme.

Galgalo Shonka

When I met him, Galgalo Shonka was eighty-two, a d'abella, and a patriarch. As *abba dibe*, or "father of the drum," of the Galbo phratry, he was among the most important figures in Gabra society. He dwelt at Yaa Galbo, the nomadic capital. He was a Massa, a member of the most senior clan of Jiblo, the senior Galbo moiety. We met early in my field work. For that visit, my assistant, Yara, and I arrived after dark under a three-quarter moon. We had walked all day across a plain of tall yellow grass and few trees from the Torbi reservoir with a caravan of the yaa's water camels. As we approached in the pale pewter light of the moon, I could make out silhouettes of domed tents within the thorn-branch walls surrounding the encampment. We had been hearing bleating goats and barking dogs and the tonkling of wooden camel bells. Now the air carried the soft wood smoke of cooking fires.

The camels, walking in single file ahead of us, disappeared into a gap in the branches. I watched their loaded humps glide away above the thorn-bush walls. Our escort from Torbi, Katelo Guyo, led us into camp by a different door. We were to be Galgalo Shonka's guests. He was expecting us. We had sent word from Torbi through Katelo's son that we wanted to visit and had learned that morning that the yaa had given us permission to come. But this was my first visit, and I was nervous. The stories I had heard suggested that the yaa was leery of foreign visitors. I worried that after coming this far we would be told to go away. The descriptions I had heard back in Maikona had given me the impression that the yaa was a sort of Oz, with leaders like wise but temperamental wizards.

After a stop for tea at Katelo's tent, we were taken to Galgalo. The abba dibe was sitting on a low stool in front of his tent, wrapped against the night chill in a white cloth. We exchanged the special greetings used for d'abella in the yaa, which I had learned and rehearsed at Torbi. The old man remained seated. He answered in a hoarse, almost whispering voice. He gestured for us to sit on wooden stools beside him. I noticed that our bags, which the camels had carried, were already piled nearby. I told him we had brought the customary gifts of tobacco and coffee berries.

Galgalo said that he was pleased that I had learned the proper greetings for an old d'abella such as himself. He said young people, who had been to mission and government schools, had forgotten or never learned these greetings. I told him, through Yara, that I wanted to write a book about Gabra, which pleased him. While we talked, Ele Galgalo, the old man's wife, emerged from the tent with cow skins for us to sleep on; before we slept, she brought us huge bowls of fresh camel's milk to drink for our supper.

I rose at first light and stood and stretched and looked around. A skinny mongrel at a neighbor's corral noticed me and yapped for awhile. The air was cold and gray. Here and there the smoke of early fires rose above the matted tents. The camp was arranged differently from others I had visited. The tents formed a great circle rather than the customary north-south line. I counted thirty-two. The *mona gala*, the camel corrals, lay in a ring outside the circle of tents. The corrals were nearly contiguous, so that they formed a thorny outer barrier. The *mona ree*, the corrals for goats and sheep, lay inside the circle of tents, protected against marauding hyenas. In the very

Figure 9. Galgalo Shonka, abba dibe of Olla Yaa Galbo and a d'abella, one of the men who are women, carves a wooden camel bell in front of his tent.

center of it all was the *nabo*, the closest thing Gabra have to a temple or mosque. Here men, especially d'abella, pray every morning, afternoon, and evening; here ceremonies are held and judgments are blessed. Formal meetings among elders generally occur outside camp, under a shade tree. When men reach consensus, they return to the nabo for blessings.

The nabo looked like a corral. It was made of thorny branches, like corrals, and had two entrances, one on the north side for the Jiblo moiety and one on the south for Lossa. Inside, along the western wall, was a fire which burned continuously. Gabra call this fire *bakalcha*, after the morning star, around which they imagine the universe revolves. When the yaa moves, the nabo fire is first to be kindled, and all the tents must light their hearth fires with embers from it. The nabo fire is explicitly reminiscent of the fires in satellite camps and is therefore an image of both center and distant margin.

The nabo disappointed Yara and me. Never having been to a yaa before, we had imagined something larger and more elaborate. People had told us the nabo was the most important place in the land, where messengers came and went at all hours and high officers held court. Our Maikona informants, who had obviously never seen the nabo, described it as a sort of theater with a stage and auditorium. I pictured guards at doors, flags and banners, uniforms. Instead, we found a circle of thorn branches defining a space the size of a volleyball court, a much-trampled dirt floor with a few stones for stools, and a fireplace deep with smoldering ashes.

Galgalo emerged from his tent soon after I stood to look around. He stooped to get through the doorway. He was tall and thick-wristed, and vigorous for someone who had been born in 1912. He must have been physically powerful in his youth: his shoulders were still broad and his back straight, and though he carried his six-foot frame with the stiff deliberateness of an old man, his legs remained long and muscular. He had an easy, reassuring smile, the more notable because so many other elders were dour and distant. Galgalo wore the customary accouterments of d'abella—white cloth, a brilliant white-plastered turban, and a necklace of sky-blue beads.

As father of the drum, Galgalo was custodian of the yaa's most sacred object. He kept it in a large leather sack at the back of his tent, removing it only for ceremonial occasions. The drum was big and round and squat as a hassock. Its walls were carved from a hollow log, and it was covered by the taut skin of a camel that had belonged to the Barawa clan, one of the founding families of the Galbo phratry. There were seeds inside that rattled when shaken. Galgalo brought the drum out and beat it and sang prayers at each new moon and on other auspicious days. The yaa held three such objects: the drum; the horn, made of an elephant's tusk; and the firesticks, made of *mad'era* wood and used to light the nabo fire. The drum was central. Each of the five phratries was supposed to have its drum; Gabra spoke of the five phratries as *dibe shani*, "five drums."

After a breakfast of milk tea, Galgalo led Yara and me to the nabo. It was time for regular morning prayers and our formal introduction. As Galgalo's guests, we entered with him through the north doorway. Several d'abella, including our escort Katelo Guyo, were already inside, having spent the night sleeping on skins near the fire. We greeted one another and Galgalo spoke with Katelo. Other d'abella arrived, wrapped in white sheets, wearing white turbans, and carrying wooden staffs. They talked among themselves and mostly ignored Yara and me.

Eventually one of the old men said it was time to pray. The men squatted on the stones and removed their sandals, and as they prayed they extended their open hands in front of them, as if to catch the divine Waaqa's blessings. They opened and closed their hands in rhythm with the chorus that accompanied each prayer: "La . . . la . . . la. . . ." The prayers of d'abella are filled with mysterious words, many of whose meanings Gabra themselves claim to have forgotten or never to have known. Much later, when my language improved, I noticed that parts of these prayers alternated sacred place names such as Melbana, Megado, and Forole with the words *nu d'ur ol*, a refrain asking for Waaqa's guidance (the text of a representative d'abella prayer appears in chapter 4). Each man prayed in turn, according to his office and clan seniority. The prayers had a hypnotic sing-song quality: the praying d'abella said a word, the rest answered "la" in chorus; he said another word or phrase, and they answered "la," and so on.

Prayers done, Galgalo introduced us. He told them that I was studying Gabra traditions, *ada Gabra*. I handed over the gifts. One d'abella, Abudo Mamo, who was a hayu, asked why I wanted to learn about Gabra. I told him it was part of my work toward a degree.

"What will you do with the degree?" he asked.

"Perhaps teach people in my country about Gabra," I said.

"Why would they want to know about Gabra?"

"Because it is good for people to learn about each other."

"Why? Are they going to come here?" he wondered.

Galgalo saved me. He told Abudo that I was going to write a book, and that Gabra in schools could read the book and find out about their own traditions. Abudo half smiled. I sensed that he remained skeptical. Nonetheless, the old men welcomed and blessed us.

It was nearly time for the camels to go for grazing, and so the d'abella drifted back to their tents and corrals to see their animals off for the day in the care of their sons and grandsons.

When the camels had gone, we joined Galgalo in the shade of a small acacia near his tent, and while he carved a wooden camel bell with an adze, I asked questions about his life.[1] This became our custom. It took a while to get used to talking with the old man. Questions, I discovered, could not be too direct. Pointed questions made for short answers. I wanted him to talk at length, to free-associate, to ramble. I wanted to let him determine the pace and direction of the conversation. He tended to speak more if my questions asked for an elaboration on something he had already said. His stories were often difficult to follow. Even Yara expressed bewilderment at the strange narrative turns. Not until I got tapes and transcripts back to the United States and began to study them did I realize that the turns he made were not at all the mindless meanderings I had imagined, but in fact had logical—and suggestive—shifts.

Figure 10. Galgalo Shonka and Ali Roba, both d'abella at Olla Yaa Galbo, relax by a camel corral. Ali Roba's granddaughter stands beside him.

For example, Galgalo would start telling us a story from his child-hood—say, about his family's migration from one place to another. The migration might have occurred as part of a larger movement of the wider community. Without warning, and apparently without transition, Galgalo would be telling us about this larger migration. There are structural analogies between the epic stories Gabra tell about their origins, the ordinary courses of their lives, and the daily travails of taking animals to water or pasture and returning. Events relevant to one are relevant to the other; only the scale seems to change. Galgalo's stories confused us because we did not always know that he had switched levels.

The apparent equivalence between levels supports my argument that family attachments inform understandings of attachments with the wider community, and vice versa. The family tent represents camp, which represents community, which represents tradition; to invoke one is to invoke the rest. The fact that Galgalo and others switched levels when they talked about themselves offers important insights about how Gabra understand the boundaries, trajectories, and cycles of their own life courses (see Kratz 1997).

No sooner had we settled into a new dimension than Galgalo would shift again. He might have associated the migrations that occurred in his lifetime with some historical or mythical migration from the very distant past. For men like Galgalo, events of long ago bore a structural resemblance, or even an identity, to present or near present events (Robinson 1985). Elders spoke of the present as a repetition of the past. Thus, Galgalo might begin telling us about his childhood and then talk of migrations that occurred before Gabra emerged as a distinct group of people.[2]

The story of Galgalo's childhood was typical of those I heard from dozens of others. It followed a script. As a boy he played with other boys, molding camels and cows out of clay made with dirt and spit. They made tiny corrals with pebbles and twigs. By the time he was five years old he was carrying a shepherd's stick, looking after kids and lambs from his father's flocks. With makeshift bow and arrows, he shot birds and lizards. By ten, he was tending larger stock, spending days with the grazing herds, returning at night to his parents' tent, though by now he was sleeping in the corral with the camels. As a teenager, he left the main camp for extended periods of months, even years, to live with older boys and younger men in the fora camps. These satellites roamed great distances over the lava-strewn plains with camels not needed at the main camp.

Once, before Galgalo was born, his father and another man took their animals to fora.[3] The two men wandered north from the Ewaso N'giro River area, where their olla was camped. They eventually found themselves at a place called Lagga Loko (Logologo) in what is now Rendille country south of Marsabit. The grass was good. Galgalo's father thought there might be water beneath the ground, so he and his friend dug a well and found water. The well, known as Rete, still produces water. Between the grass and water, the place was an ideal fora camp, and the men remained there many weeks.

Meanwhile, back at Ewaso N'giro, Galgalo's mother worried. She had heard no news from her husband, and she was pregnant, close to delivery. She loaded her tent on camels and set out to find her husband. Guided by news collected from others met on the way, she found him at Lagga Loko. Soon she delivered a son, their first-born, Galgalo. Now she had *ulma*, a period of seclusion lasting nearly two months after childbirth, during which time the family could not shift back to their community. The olla sent scouts, however, and eventually the community moved to Lagga Loko.

Several years later, the Ethiopian government in the north reinvigorated an old policy of taking tribute (*gabar*) from Borana and Gabra, driving many south toward Marsabit and beyond to avoid debt slavery (Sobania 1980, 1993). At about the same time, the British colonial government in Nairobi bolstered its presence at Marsabit, partly to police the influx of people from Abyssinia and partly to watch the border. Galgalo, as a boy, heard the stories.

"Marsabit then was no town," he said.[4] "There was no town. Qalla Rasa [a Gabra leader who became liaison to the colonial government and then its appointed chief] was there. Samburu were there. One white man was there. One white man, at the top of Aite well. He had placed a tent there. The only person who would go to the white man was Qalla Rasa. The others feared him. At first it was the cattle, do you understand? The white man wanted a contract for milk when he came. He didn't have any soldiers; he had one, a game scout, a Somali. He asked Qalla Rasa to recruit soldiers.

"I was eight years old, eight years. The Hofteh, who are [Borana] people of Marsabit, ran away from Ethiopia and came in large numbers to Marsabit.[5] It was at this time that soldiers were recruited for the white man, many soldiers for himself. Most of them were Somalis. Other white men came. There was no post office, no road, even these white people came on horses and mules. People don't know about vehicles at this time. The white man got soldiers, and he got a place to stay, and he asked for girls. He said he would engage them, pay bridewealth, and girls were found. Four girls."

"What did he do with the girls?" I asked.

"He married them."

"The white man married the girls?"

"Yes. Four girls. One was a daughter of Qalla Rasa. One was the daughter of Guyo D'ole, a Gara [a Gabra phratry]; she was the sister to Wato Elema. One was the daughter of Godana Burale, the father of Tullu, the sister of Tullu, a girl called Arao. She is an old woman now, this Arao. And another girl."

"He married all four?"

"All these girls he married. He married. When he was transferred, he gave them all property, animals. He gave them property and left. The one who was daughter to Qalla Rasa, she was later married by Halkano, Halkano Gura. The daughter of Godana Burale, Arao, was married by Kalicha Musa. The daughter of Guyo D'ole was called Jirma. She was the sister to Wato Elema. She went home. Her children, their uncle is Wato Elema. The father they have is Wato Elema. She never married.[6] She just owned those animals. Those who are alive now, the animals that are theirs are from these."

I asked if he remembered the white man's name.

"I don't remember," he said. "It is something of long ago."

According to Galgalo, Qalla Rasa was procuring girls and recruiting soldiers for the white man. And he was apparently amassing power to himself by playing the white government off against Gabra and any others he could muster. The British, for example, wondered about the Hofteh. The Hofteh denied that they were Borana and they denied they were Gabra.

"This time," Galgalo said, "when the Hofteh said they were Hofteh, the white men said, 'We have heard of Borana and we have heard of Gabra but we have never heard of Hofteh.' Those Hofteh gathered and fled to Kalacha. Now, when Qalla Rasa was asked, he said: 'Yes, all these are my people.' He said: 'Even those who say they are Borana, they are mine.' So Qalla was told to shift those people at Kalacha, even those at Waso [Ewaso N'giro], to Marsabit. Qalla took soldiers and went to all areas, even Merti [near the Ewaso N'giro] and shifted them back to Marsabit."

"Who was he moving? Only Gabra, or others?"

"Only Gabra. Gabra, Gabra. Sharbanna, Alganna, Gara, Galbo, all these [Gabra phratries]."

"Were some Gabra in Ethiopia?"

"They were there. Yes. And these Hofteh [from Ethiopia], they were saying, 'Abba, don't tell them we are Ethiopians.' They were all on Qalla's side."

Gabra, he said, were grazing their livestock from beyond Badda Hurri in the north to Waso in the south, and Qalla Rassa made a sweep of those areas, rounding up the Gabra toward Marsabit.

"Bonsa was an elder like Qalla," Galgalo said. "They were one *milo* [the same clan]. Then Bonsa said, 'You have collected all your tribe, and I will not participate.' He complained. He complained about the people who were made soldiers. He complained about the girls who were collected for the white man. Bonsa complained about all of them. 'How can we *gibir* [give as tribute, but in this context also force or drive] human beings?' he said. 'We gibir animals, but we will not gibir human beings,' he said. Now the senior chief was Qalla, and so this time he and Bonsa disagreed with one another, and Bonsa went back to Waso with his people."

"So Gabra separated?"

"They were cut greatly. Those others remained at Waso and the others remained here."

Marsabit Mountain was now shared by Borana and Gabra, whose livestock grazed the north and east slopes, and Samburu and Rendille, on the south and west slopes. I asked Galgalo whether the people on and around the mountain raided one another, stole each other's animals and fought each other, or whether they lived together peacefully. He said the colonial government was serious about keeping peace: "The *kolon* gave warnings," he said. "Anybody who kills will be killed. Yes. The government was feared."

At this point Galgalo's story shifted back to a time he later said was "before our birth, when our fathers were born." The year, he said, was Talassa Loni Segel, the Tuesday year the cattle were raided at Segel, a plain west of Mount Marsabit.[7] Galgalo said the Samburu raided Gabra camps west of North Horr toward Lake Turkana near a place called Uranura.[8] Word soon spread to Gabra and Borana at Marsabit, and men went to help. On the way, despite a peace treaty between Samburu and Gabra-Borana on the mountain, the men raided a Samburu cattle camp at Segel, killed some men, and stole some cattle. The stolen cattle were sent to fora elsewhere on the mountain. The men continued their journey, routed the Samburu beyond North Horr, and returned to Marsabit Mountain.

There was a heifer among the stolen Samburu cattle that became pregnant by a Gabra bull in the Gabra fora. When it delivered its calf, it refused to leave the calf and go with the rest of the cows for grazing: "For two days it refused to go. Two days. Two days. Finally, the third day, it went by force. The third day, it accompanied the other cattle for grazing. When they got to the place for grazing, the herd boy was protecting it. The cow ran away. It ran and ran and ran. Some Samburu near there had taken their spears and gone out, and they were dancing with some girls there. They were dancing. The cow ran into the place where they were dancing. The cow ran among them. The cow was making noise. Woo, woo! The Samburu recognized the cow. They saw it was one that had been taken at Segel. Now they got excited. Woo, woo! They started killing there, and they took and took all the way to Ires Filla [near the crest of the mountain], all this side. They killed."

The cow, representing a double separation—first from its Samburu owners and then from its calf—caused a third separation when Samburu killed and drove their enemies from their homes.

The Gabra and Borana, chased by Samburu *morani* (warriors), fled north to Elle Bor, a hill on what is now the Ethiopian border, 140 kilometers north of Marsabit. Here, apparently, they joined forces with Borana from the north and drove the Samburu back. It was after this, according to Galgalo, that *tiriso*, literally a formal friendship and in fact a patron-client relationship, was established between Borana and Gabra. Borana were understood to be the more numerous, powerful, and aggressive patrons, owing to Gabra dependence on Borana protection.

Once again Galgalo's story shifted. It was as if tiriso reminded him of less peaceful times, or, more likely, reminded him of oscillations of war and peace, the one making sense of the other. If the conflict with Samburu occurred in his father's lifetime, the next event he recounted happened during or before his grandfather's time, in a quasi-mythical moment before the region's ethnic groups separated from one another. Indeed, the following episode, give or take a few details, was told to me by many elders. It is in a sense their Exodus story.

Galgalo and others said that the journey, Kedi Guura, occurred at a time called Iris (see Schlee 1989, Robinson 1985, and Sobania 1980 for variations). What is interesting is the connection Galgalo makes between the oscillations of separation and attachment experienced by him and his contemporaries and those experienced by his ancestors. The story he tells below is structurally the same as the story about his own family's journey to Lagga Loko: a departure, a transformation, and a return. The mythic story seems to help Galgalo make sense of his life. The story conforms to a Gabra conception of the life course: initial social unity, followed by outside adventures that threaten one's connections with others, that particularize and shape an individual's character, and then a return to the fold of social unity, at once the same as before but also transformed by the experience, now *both* separated and attached.

Gabra, he said, kept camels while Borana had cattle. A disease killed the Borana cattle but spared the Gabra camels. "The Borana didn't have any animals but the Gabra had some few animals. So the Borana organized *raba* [a section of young men devoted to conquest], and they started to raid the Gabra. . . . The Gabra missed *finna* [life, or a state of affairs conducive to life]. They had nowhere to raise their children. So they ran away. They crossed the Chalbi Desert, passed through the Dassanetch, and came to a ford in the river called Malka Oda. The Borana forced them to cross through Malka Oda."

As Galgalo understood it, Malka Oda lay at the very northern end of what is now Lake Turkana. Some versions of the story indicate that the lake was already there, but sufficiently shallow or dry for Gabra to cross. Others suggest that the journey antedated the lake. In any case, after Gabra reached the other side, the lake rose and they were cut off from the land whence they came. Eventually they decided they wanted to go back. Galgalo said the Borana wanted peace with the Gabra after all: "The Borana said, 'We are finished. We don't have finna.' So Borana sent someone to Gabra, and said, 'Gabra, come back.'" The problem was how. The water was too deep to cross.

The elders, Galgalo said, summoned a *raga*, a diviner, and asked him for advice. The diviner said it was possible to cross the lake, and he told them what to do. He asked if they had a camel somewhere in their herds that had no owner, a strange camel. He told them to find it and bring it to him, which they did. That camel had delivered a calf the same day. Then he told them to find a young woman of the Kibibe clan who had given birth that day to her first child, a son. When the woman was brought, the diviner said she should milk her breast into the water, and the water would part. This was done, and the water parted. The diviner said to load the newborn calf of the strange camel on a *rocho*, a loading camel, and send the rocho in front of the herds as the people crossed the lake. However, he said, the mother of the calf, the strange camel, should be held back and made to follow the herds at the rear. In no case, he said, should they allow the strange camel to walk forward among the other camels. These things were done, and they began to cross where the lake had parted.

They crossed in a long line between the walls of water which were held back on each side by divine force. Before they were all across, however, the strange camel, eager to find its calf, slipped away from its tenders and ran forward among the other camels. At this, the water rushed in and filled the divide. Some people were already across. Some were in the lake and were drowned. And others remained cut off on the far side, and their descendants remain there today, called *wara gaala gababo*, "people of the short camels." It was at this time, according to Galgalo, that the people who made it back across the lake separated into distinct groups, Borana and Gabra, and by other accounts, Turkana, Dassanetch, Rendille, Samburu, and Somali. In other words, they left relatively undifferentiated; they were cut off, separated from the rest; and then they found a way to return, but in doing so, they became more complex, divided into different groups. This is not unlike the experience of young men, who travel off to camel camps, are often cut off from the rest, and eventually return to the camps as older men to marry and start families themselves. The stories suggest the profound anxiety and fascination Gabra have about separations from family and camp.

That evening, Yara and I accompanied Galgalo for *galchuma*, the time when elders set out to meet the herds as they return from the day's grazing. The sun was setting on the desert, the fading light was softening the harsh landscape, and the heat was abating. Over our heads, sand grouse, in teams of three and four, darted this way and that homeward across the darkening sky. Galgalo began to talk. He said everything in the universe depends on everything else in the universe. He said Waaqa made the universe that way. Everything in the universe, he said, is one, *toka*. Women need men to reproduce. People need animals. Animals need grass. Grass needs rain. Rain needs prayers. Prayers need men. "People forget that they cannot do anything by themselves. That is why they fight and steal. They always want to prove that they are more powerful than Waaqa, and they always fail."

We walked for awhile in silence. Galgalo broke the quiet to tell us that Guyo Dido, the *abba uchuma* or "father of the firesticks," had moved his tent out of the yaa and was staying in another olla nearer his cattle. He said the *abba magalata*, "father of the horn," the third sacred object in the yaa, was also spending much of his time these days in another olla, with the family of his father's brother, whose son had died. That family, he said, should be in the yaa, not outside. Most of the *hayu*, leaders of the generation sets, who customarily dwell in the yaa, had also shifted away, to be closer to their animals. All of these officers, he said, were pursuing private interests at the expense of the collective interests of the yaa, and therefore, of all Gabra people. People, Galgalo implied, were speaking different languages, following separate interests. Galgalo worried the center, the yaa, the tradition of the yaa, would fall apart. Traditional values are tied up with social attachments at the yaa; its break-up, the separation of the leaders, would entail not only the demise of the camp, but also the ritual practices and the sacred meanings with which it is identified.

Next morning, we resumed our conversation with Galgalo, returning to his life's story. Once again he squatted with his back against the trunk of the shade tree, using an adz to nick form into the knot of wood in his hands.

"Our family was at Lagga Loko. The road from Isiolo was not yet completed. What we saw were these people of missionaries, you know, the ones called Kirigi (Christians, probably from the Bible Churchmen's Missionary Society, who established the first mission at Marsabit in 1931). These people came. Kirigi. They had a donkey that pulls a cart, a cart pulled by an animal. That was something people did not know. There was a white man with them. He had cattle. His herders were Meru. There was one white man with them and they came and settled at Rete, near my father's well. By this time I was somebody who could shift for cattle fora. I was as big as I am now.

"So these people, Kirigi, came on foot. They came to the well and asked who was the well for. They asked for water. People said the well belonged to my father, so the man came to my father. They shifted and reached the Rete area. This well. My father gave them permission to use it. Later, the white man called the old man and told him, now he is Kirigi, we shall stay together and have this as thanks, and he gave a roll of cloth to my father and some *posho* (maize meal). He also gave tea leaves, which we didn't know about, and sugar, which was referred to as *woni mioftu*, the 'sweet thing.' At that time honey was known but not sugar. These people and my father became friends and they trusted each other and stayed together. A day for his cattle (to drink at the well) was fixed and since then there is no day that a cloth was not brought, posho, sugar, and tea leaves. Eventually, those people shifted to Sokorte [a crater lake on the mountain]."

How did his father communicate with the white man?

"There was a translator, a Somali. He was called Mohammed Shaba. A Somali. He was translating for the D.C. [district commissioner]."

Was his family alone at Rete or camped with others?

"There were days we were alone, and there were days we were with others, just like this, concentrated. When people came to Rete, we stayed together in a big olla. But mostly we stayed alone. After Kirigi went to Sokorte, we shifted to that side, along the road to Sokorte and camped near there."

The colonial government was then encouraging Burji farmers and Somali traders to move to Marsabit to provide food and services to government workers, missionaries, and other settlers. Galgalo said the Burji, who came from Ethiopia, were first to send their children to school. "The others refused," he said. "The other people, the Borana, the Gabra, refused learning.

"It was at this time that the white man and my father became friends. Rendille watered their camels at Sokorte, and the white man bought a camel and said he was going to use it for safaris. He asked my father to take care of the camel for him. The white man never used that camel, so after that the camel was ours.

"The Burji increased. They came one by one. They became workers for the Kirigi people. They were taught about timber and building. They were taught about medicines. The first white man was transferred, and another white man came, and this one was called Bwana Haylett.[9] This white man was teaching the tradition of God. Later he always came to visit my father and told him, 'Give me your son, and I will employ him and educate him.' He kept asking, and finally I joined his work. What he said was he was not married, and he told me to teach him the [Borana] language like he was a child, just the language of Borana. There was another Gabra, a Gara, Dabasso Wabera, working for the white man, too.[10] Dabasso is the one who was killed [assassinated, years later, presumably by Somali rebels, having been appointed by the newly independent Kenya as district commissioner of Isiolo]. When his father died, his mother married a Burji, and Dabasso became Burji. The Burji had started learning and the others refused that learning. The Borana said that boys do not work as maids. They refused learning.

"I was washing clothes, like a turnboy, but cooking was done by somebody else. I was working in the house. Dabasso then was very young. He was among the children who went to nursery school. This time I was a big person. Bwana Haylett said I should go to school. He told me education was important. We stayed together one year, and the second year he said he wanted to marry and went home to marry. He said when he came back, I should return to work with him. So he married and brought his wife here.[11] "I didn't have any other work but teaching his wife the Borana language. I was young and she was young. The two of us stayed together.

"Bwana Haylett, you know, had a license to kill animals like rhinos, elephants, gazelles, all these. Later on, we went together to the mountain of Kijabe and we hunted colobus monkeys. Even these monkeys we hunted together. I was teaching his wife the language, and we stayed together. His wife and I stayed together, and Bwana Haylett hunted animals in the day. Sometimes he took me with him. I threw stones to make the monkeys jump from tree to tree. He shot them when they passed between trees. He taught me to use the rifle. The first time, I put the rifle on my shoulder and when I pulled the trigger it nearly knocked me on the ground."

After Kijabe, Galgalo's father asked Galgalo to come home. It must have seemed strange to the family for Galgalo to live away from home. Sons, especially firstborn sons, typically stay with their fathers until the fathers' deaths. Moreover, ceremonies may not be performed without the family's firstborn present. The trip to Kijabe may have alarmed Galgalo's father. But Haylett resisted letting him go. Somehow, perhaps with the promise of no more extended excursions, Galgalo's father agreed to let his son stay.

Soon after the hunting expedition, Haylett's wife gave birth to a child. Galgalo's duties shifted from teaching Borana and washing clothes to tending the infant. The family needed a trusted worker in the house. Haylett's wife had difficulty in childbirth and remained bedridden. She never recovered, and two months later she died.

As Haylett prepared to leave Marsabit with his infant son, three missionaries came to replace him: a man called E. J. Webster, who went on to translate the Bible into Borana, and a husband and wife team whose names Galgalo remembered only as "Hawkin" or "Awking."[12] The wife was a doctor, and the husband a pilot.

Three of Haylett's young servants accompanied him and the baby to Mombasa, where he boarded a ship for England: Galgalo, Dabasso, and a Burji boy named D'era, all of whom had been baptized by Haylett. Galgalo said the plan was to enroll them all in school in Nairobi.

"At Mombassa, Haylett went away from us. He wrote a letter and said we should give it to the government and then, he said, we could go to school at Karatina. We were taken by a car to Nairobi, and there a government official, the one of Nairobi, read the letter and told us we were to join the school at Thika or at Karatina, whichever we wanted. But my father refused. He got the D.C. in Marsabit to make a radio call to Nairobi. He told them to bring back his son. So the other two joined school, and I went back home. Dabasso was very young then. D'era was already a young man. He attended a school for adults and married a Kikuyu girl at Karatina. He became a priest. He came back and became a church leader. Dabasso was educated there and then when he finished classes he came back to Marsabit. I left them and came back. Since the old man refused to let me go to school, I went home and stayed."

Why didn't his father want him to go to school?

"He said, 'I can't put on *qumbi*[13] without him. I can't do sorio [sacrifices] without him.' The government man said, 'Let the boy continue with school.' The old man said no. After that I stayed with my father. I looked after animals—until the Italians defeated the Sid'am [Ethiopia]."

There is a tension between fathers and sons, writ peculiar in Galgalo's case: fathers want sons, especially the eldest, close at hand for rituals, which are essential for livestock and cannot be performed without the firstborn, but they also need sons to attend livestock and other chores, inevitably far away. Galgalo's experiences were unique in that few in his generation had (or wanted) the intimacy he enjoyed with European missionaries. Yet they were also typical: all young men had adventures outside the reach of their fathers and struggled at the limits of their fathers' tether. The tether was tested again during Britain's war with Italy in southern Ethiopia.

In the wake of Italy's occupation of Ethiopia, the British government in Kenya drafted men in the northern frontier zone who could read and write, making them clerks and eventually soldiers. Galgalo never went to school, but Haylett had taught him to speak and read KiSwahili. By this time, Dabasso had returned from school in Karatina. The two, among others, were pressed into service. Galgalo remembered fighting throughout Ethiopia, under the command of a man named Said Bare, a Somali. Galgalo said he was in charge of a battalion. His memories of this time were spotty. No one seems to have let him in on the big picture. He remembered that his battalion fought as far north as Addis Ababa. He remembered burying fallen soldiers where they lay. He remembered concealing weapons so they would not fall into enemy hands. He remembered skirmishes in different places. He remembered where planes were shot down: at Oboq, Addis Ababa, Daka Ngor, Magado, and Walmale. But he did not connect these memories to one another; they were as isolated from each other and everything else as lost land mines. His stories from this period lacked a trajectory until the end, when he began to take charge of his own destiny.

"The Italians ran away. Just like that, the *banda*, who were the African soldiers, and the Italians ran away into the forest and became *shifta*, bandits. Then the armies were brought together and selected. The war was over, but there were shifta still in the forest. The prisoners who were captured during the war were gathered together. Now the war was over. Now the bodies of those people, those people who were on our side, the British, the Africans, all those people, we were told to dig them out of their holes so that, together with the coffins, they could be carried home.

"We dug the holes and laid a cloth beside them and then identified the bodies. You know, this leg is this, and this scar is this. I was slightly hurt, wounded, though I had not known it, but I had a small wound. We went back and dug the holes and removed the bodies and just from this I fell sick. I was very sick.

"The old man was alive then, and he was engaging for me this girl, this mother here [Ele, his wife]. But someone told them I was dead. They were told I was probably dead. Every day the old man went to the office, to those government people, and they said they had not heard over the radio that I was dead. My father didn't know whether I was dead, so he could not slaughter *awala* [a burial sacrifice] for me. It was not possible.

"When my health improved I continued to dig up bodies, and then we were finished digging up bodies. Said Bare took us east. The Borana this time had been raided by Degodia, the Somali, and they had taken all the Borana animals. We went back to the east and reached D'adacha Worab. We were traveling on foot, and any bandit we met with a gun we were shooting. An airplane dropped food to us as we walked along. Villages with shifta were burnt. Two villages, animals and people together, were burnt. Where there were no shifta, we collected animals but we did not harm people. We brought these animals to Nagele, these Borana animals. I was in charge of distributing the animals. Those animals were captured from the Somali for the Borana. We went to Webi, where the Borana had gathered and were sitting under trees, and gave their animals back to them. Even at Soda the Borana came together, and we gave animals to them. We finished at Mega. All the animals were given back.

"When the Borana got their animals, we were told to return to our work. Said Bare told me to continue in the army. But the war was over. I didn't know whether my family was alive. I didn't know whether my father was alive. I didn't know whether my mother was alive. I told him I was not able to work. I was told I was talking useless words, nonsense. We became bad to each other. That day, it was said, shifta had come to a place, and Said Bare told me to go alone and fight. And so I went alone. It was at Mega. There was a station of airplanes. It was fenced with wires, like the houses of those people of prison. The big house of airplanes had four doors. He told me to go and fight the shiftas. He threatened me if I refused his orders. I told him, 'I will not refuse your orders. I will go and fight.' I went. I left on foot.

"The shifta had arrived at that station the night before. They had captured two Borana women and some cattle and they slaughtered cattle at the station and ate and left that night. I came closer and closer to the station and when I reached it, there was nothing there. When I reached there, a vehicle, which had been sent after me, arrived. We heard the shifta had gone to a house that the Italians had been forced to leave. I was told to get into the vehicle and together we went to that house and found the shifta. We found them eating meat. They killed one of us. We killed seven of them. The others ran away. We took our dead man and went back.

"The next day at assembly, Said Bare told me to take my battalion and go back to my job in the army. Said Bare told me. I told him again I was not able to go. I wanted to go home. Said Bare said, 'How many people want to go home? Hold up your hands.' In addition to me, seven others held up their hands. All of us were people of Marsabit, Gabra. Said Bare said to me, 'You have spoiled all these people. You have spoiled them, and that is why all these people want to leave. You influenced them,' he said. He said, 'You must work.' I told him I can't.

"I asked him what he wanted me to do with the army clothes. He told me to wash them and put them there on the ground. 'You won't carry anything from here,' he said. He asked the others whether they were the same, and they said that they would do what I did.

"Said Bare called on the radio to a big judge [a white colonial official] and he came and asked us and said, 'Are you all the same? Do you all want to go?' We said we wanted to go. He said, 'Because of your mistake, there will be no rewards or benefits according to the army. If you want to go home, get out.' Right then we started washing the clothes . . . They told us to go away from Mega, to go home. We told him, 'We were collected by force. It was not our wish. We assisted the government. The war is over. We don't have the weapons we had. We have returned our weapons. Unless you take us back, there is no way we can leave. We have no weapons.' The judge thought to himself, and he gave us a car, and it took us home to Marsabit.

"That day we went home to our people."

Galgalo, now in his early thirties, returned to Marsabit. He married within the year, and a year after that, his father died.

His life was spent tending animals, shifting camp and herds from as far west as Kubi Fora, at the shore of Lake Turkana, to as far east as Wajir. He offered no stories about his life after the war. When I pressed for accounts of this time, he said that he looked after animals; he did what every other man did. He buried his father. He raised a family.[14] He spent his youth distinguishing himself as an individual, necessarily apart from the society at large. On his marriage he entered a script of conformity, a period when social attachments and obligations were more important than individual distinctions, and the sorts of stories he told about himself changed. In this way his stories can be seen to be mediated by culturally specific expectations of the life cycle (Kratz 1997:40).

Until Galgalo became a d'abella in 1986 and was named abba dibe, father of the drum, he had never dwelt in the yaa. I asked him what qualified a man to be abba dibe. He said the abba dibe was always chosen from the Massa clan. "But there are many Massa," I said. "How is one chosen?"

He said the abba dibe should be someone who has been careful to observe Gabra traditions. He should be someone who is strong, fair, honest, and generous. Gifts to the yaa, for instance, are given to the abba dibe and distributed by him to the rest. If he was not fair, the others would mistrust him and they would squabble with him and each other. The abba dibe, he said, must not show favors. "If you are abba dibe," he said, "nobody is an enemy, not a Waata, not a Rendille, not a Samburu. You must lead the people. You make the head [those in front] slow down and the tail [those behind] catch up. You must wait and make them meet together. You make things straight." Hearing this, I thought of the mythical crossing of the parted lake, with the camel calf at the head of the line and its mother bringing up the rear.

Galgalo made a habit, when I visited, of fishing a tattered Swahili Bible and a pair of ancient black horn-rimmed glasses from his kit. He would sit on his bed and read. He often read aloud. I think he wanted me to know that he was a Christian. No doubt he assumed that, since I was white, I also was a Christian. I did not encourage or discourage these Bible readings. He seemed to want me to know that, like me, he knew how to read. Perhaps it was also his daily habit. He held his body differently when he read. He sat on the raised pallet inside the tent, crossed one leg over the other at the knee—as I imagined Bwana Haylett had—and gazed down at the book through the lower half of his bifocal lenses. It was a sort of performance. If I did not notice him, he would read aloud to make sure I noticed. He never brought out the Bible when other Gabra were around. He never read in the better light outside the tent. I think what led Galgalo to read the Bible so conspicuously in my presence was his desire at these times to connect with me and distance himself from others in the yaa. In Kassam's (1987) account of the 1986 *jila* transition ceremonies, she writes that Galgalo, then in the process of becoming a d'abella and abba dibe, tried the patience of younger men by insisting on a lengthy Christian prayer meeting outside the nabo. I did not know about this when I was in the field, or I would have asked him and others about it.

There were several other Christians in the yaa, mainly old men, who knew Father Tablino. Tablino and his confrere Father Bartolomew

Venturino used to make regular visits to the yaa, bringing presents and sometimes offering livestock to residents who had lost their animals in one mishap or another. But in the past ten years, as the priests grew older, these visits were fewer and fewer. Except with me, in the privacy of their tents, I saw no public expression of Christianity or Islam in the yaa.

Once, late in my fieldwork, while Galgalo and I waited by the corrals one evening for the camels to return, he asked whether I would wear Gabra clothing when I returned to the United States. By then, except for a brimmed hat to keep the sun off my face, I was dressing pretty much as a Gabra: I wore sandals made of castoff tires, baggy muslin shorts, and a fringed sheet for sleeping. I carried a wooden staff and, on long journeys, a spear. I told him that these things would look out of place in my country. They would not always be practical. I explained that it was often too cold in the United States to wear sandals and shorts. He nodded that it was so. He said, *Arbi laf olu fakata*, "The elephant looks like where it spends the day." Elephants have the habit of covering themselves with dirt, so they look reddish in places with red soil and blackish in places with black soil, and so on. The proverb was the Gabra equivalent of "When in Rome." I thought it was interesting, in this place where ethnic identity is worn on one's sleeve, that the implied injunction was to *look* rather than *do* "as the Romans do." I laughed and nodded. *D'uggum*, I said, "That's true."

Earlier that day I had learned another proverb: *Gurra gaf jirani gaf duan d'agan*, "A man's story is told after he dies." Galgalo and another man, Ali Roba, the two oldest residents of the yaa, were sitting off by themselves. When I joined them, Ali Roba asked me whether I knew the proverb. Just before that, some younger men elsewhere in camp had insulted Galgalo. The two elders were now comforting each other. They said they felt old and useless, "like two giraffes (*satowa*) in a flock of sheep." The incident illustrates the complexity of old men being at once central and marginal, weak, and frail.

There had been a visitor, a Gabra man from a development organization, who sought the yaa's cooperation on a veterinary project at Torbi. The man, as was customary, had brought tobacco to share with the d'abella. Galgalo brought the tobacco to the shade, where the men were playing a board game called *sadeka*. He held up the package, told the men about the visitor, and invited them to come share the tobacco. The men were thick in their game. They ignored Galgalo. He repeated the invitation. One of them, Mamo Dido, a hayu from a neighboring camp, asked Galgalo what else the visitor had brought and wondered whether Galgalo was hiding it in his tent. This accusation was motivated by an event of the week before. I had arrived at the yaa with the usual tobacco and coffee beans, but this time I had also brought a rather larger amount of tobacco, tea leaves, and sugar, a gift from Father Tablino, who had asked me to carry the gifts for him to the yaa. The elders quickly distributed the sugar and tea leaves among themselves so as not to have to share it with neighboring camps. Of course, the neighbors heard about it and complained.

Galgalo was angry with the hayu's accusation. "You are always first when it comes to sharing things," Galgalo said. "But where are you when there are decisions to make?" He told Mamo that, as hayu, he should be living inside the yaa, not outside. Mamo responded that he lived nearby, where the yaa could easily call him. Galgalo was not satisfied. "When someone asks you where you were when you sat on the *barchuma* [the stool, symbol of power], what will you say?" The hayu now accused Galgalo of being old, moved by anyone's words, talking too much. The others laughed. No one looked at Galgalo. They all kept their eyes on the game.

The abba dibe said nothing. He waited a few minutes. The men continued their game.

Galgalo stood and walked off toward his tent. He sat in its shade and began hammering at a new camel bell with his adze. Ali Roba, who had been snoozing under his sheet beside the men playing sadeka, rose to his aging feet and hobbled over to Galgalo. It was the first and only time I heard anyone ridicule the old man. After a while Yara and I followed. We found them talking quietly. Galgalo said that when someone moved away from the yaa, he left a gap in the circle. Ali Roba said the gap was like a death. In either case, he added, you do not notice someone until he is gone: *Gurra gaf jirani gaf duan d'agan.* I was uncertain whether they were speaking of people, like the rude hayu, who had moved away from the yaa, or themselves.[15]

Wario Elema

Galgalo Shonka, abba dibe of Yaa Galbo, was a special case from the center of Gabra society. Wario Elema was a special case from the beer huts and relief lines of the settlements, the margins of both nomadic and settled communities. Wario was my closest Gabra friend. It was an unlikely but not surprising friendship.[16] I was a foreign ethnographer who had shown up one day to learn about Gabra culture. He was the village drunk. It took me a while to understand what he might have seen in me. As for him, when he was sober, Wario was a good companion. He was bright, quick to understand new things, and good at explaining them to others. He had a gift for languages. He had gone to high school, had traveled to Nairobi, had been to Mombasa. He had seen the ocean.

The first time I saw Wario was at the Catholic Mission at Maikona. I was sitting on the front stoop of the dispensary with a few boys from the mission primary school. They were teaching me words for parts of the body: head, eyes, ears, nose, mouth, that sort of thing. There were a dozen or so others, mostly old men and young women with babies, waiting to see the nurse. Wario came and sat with another man at the other end of the porch.

Everyone else was talking or listening to someone else. Wario was not talking and did not seem to be listening to anybody either. His neighbor was telling a story to someone else farther down. Wario gazed out at the plains shimmering in the heat beyond the church, and every now and then he tossed a pebble the wind had blown onto the porch back into the yard. His lack of engagement made him stand out. An air of absence gave him a presence.

Three or four days later he turned up for work with Yara, my research assistant. Yara pulled me aside and said Wario wanted a job with us. I told Yara I didn't have money to hire another assistant. We went back, and Yara drew Wario aside and, I guessed, told him there was no chance for work. But when Yara and I set off to visit a nearby camp, Wario tagged along. I was nervous that Wario believed he had a job after all, or might have if he was persistent. I told him I was sorry but I couldn't hire him. He shrugged his shoulders. What could I do? If he wanted to tag along, who was I to stop him?

Wario would show up several days running and then disappear, sometimes for weeks. Usually when he disappeared like this he was drunk somewhere in the settlement. I saw him when he was like this. At those times his eyes were red and gummy and his mouth was full of spit and he couldn't finish a sentence or hold a gaze. I wouldn't see him for a few days, even a week or two. Then, his clothes wrinkled and dirty from sleeping on the bare ground, he would turn up. He told me he had nothing else to do: there was no regular work to be found in Maikona, and spending time with us was more interesting than doing nothing. So we became friends, and he became a presence in my fieldwork.

What interested me about Wario and other young men like him—guys who had had some mission schooling and spent most of their time in towns, the dusty settlements near the wells of the Chalbi Desert—was the sense I had of them, and they of themselves, of being on the margins, unattached. Wario's drunkenness, however, was exceptional. Alcohol was a growing problem in settlements and towns, but most young men I knew were sober. What made them marginal was not alcohol; it was their apparent lack of integration in either nomadic or town institutions. The very few with regular jobs tended to invest in livestock to supplement their income and insure themselves against unemployment and old age. In this way they straddled the nomadic and settled worlds but remained fully in neither. They were the lucky ones. Most of them were unemployed.[17] They got by on what family and friends shared, what they could pick up in day labor, and what dry maize and beans the government and churches distributed as relief.

They were educated: they had at least some primary school, many had been through high school, and a few had even been to college. Most guys in town between fifteen and thirty years old spoke three languages with some competence: Borana, their mother tongue; Swahili, the national language; and English. A few also knew a little Rendille, Samburu, or Somali that they had picked up from friends in school. They wore trousers and T-shirts, wristwatches that rarely worked but looked smart, and sunglasses. Hats were popular: Muslim skullcaps, floppy green safari hats, colorful baseball caps that advertised athletic teams, reggae stars, or construction equipment. Hats, T-shirts, watches, and sunglasses were urban adornments. They distinguished those who wore them from nomads. But they were expensive and rare, and so they were loaned around among friends.

The young men preferred to wear anything on their feet but sandals made of old automobile tires. These "Firestones," as they were sometimes called, are worn by most Gabra, all nomads, and rural poor throughout East Africa. Young town men liked to wear shoes with a modern, machine-made look. If they had any choice, they wore canvas athletic shoes, rubber flip-flops, or leather street shoes. Wario, who was employed for several years as a social worker for a non-governmental aid organization until he was fired for drunkenness, wore a pair of leather shoes when I met him. But these threatened to fall apart after a few weeks of walking with Yara and me across the lava rubble of the Chalbi plains, and he was soon wearing tire sandals.

Wario was a tall, spindly twenty-eight-year-old. He had a long face, a high forehead, and dark rosewood eyes. The eyes were richly grained:

engaging, kind, unaggressive, and sad. He was thin as a tent pole and his clothes flapped against his bones like canvas sheeting in the wind. He wore his curly hair long and unkempt. He had let the nails on his pinky fingers grow an inch or more beyond the fingertips, an affectation I saw among others in town. The long nails, they said, looked modern and stylish. For someone from town, Wario seemed unusually keen to learn about nomadic life, and he did not assume, like so many schooled Gabra, that he already knew all there was to know. Other Gabra enjoyed his company when he was sober, though they were quick to tell me behind his back that he was a drunkard and not to be trusted. Wario liked to accompany Yara and me on our camel safaris to the nomadic camps, to sleep on the ground with us, to drink soured camel's milk, and to listen to old men talk beneath the shade of acacia trees.

Wario had been abandoned as a boy by his father and reared by his mother. This was a central fact about him, one that he regarded as having shaped the trajectory of his life. Indeed, one can see him again and again in the accounts that follow create problematic separations and attachments with others, including his distant father.[18] After we had known each other for six months, I asked Wario if he would tell me about his childhood. One day when Yara was off doing census work, Wario and I found some shade and privacy and talked.

He was born 250 kilometers southeast of Maikona, near Merti. Back then, in the 1960s, in the first flush days of peace following independence, many Gabra lived with their animals in the Merti area along the banks of the Ewaso Ng'iro River, far south of their present region. The peace did not last, however, and by the end of the decade the area was a war zone. It lay within a wide swath of northeastern Kenya claimed by Somalia, and in the late 1960s Somalis began fighting Kenyan soldiers over the territory. Opportunistic bandits, hiding in the bush and exploiting the chaos, raided nomadic camps. In the ensuing tumult Gabra and Borana camels and cattle were lost or stolen, and their owners were killed, absorbed among the bandits, or chased north toward Marsabit or south toward Isiolo.

Wario's family was among those who trekked to Marsabit, the district seat. His father, Elema Tura, got a job with the administration police, a post somewhat like deputy sheriff, largely on the strength of his having been a colonial soldier fifteen years before. Wario remembered that his parents were already fighting with each other in Merti, and when they moved to Marsabit and later Maikona, their troubles grew worse.[19]

"My father wanted to marry another wife. In Merti, the animals were not there. Even my mother was telling him, because of her children, and her children were very young, and without animals, without any hope, it would be very hard to maintain another family. But when he came to Marsabit, and he got employment, he was ready to get a second wife. So in Marsabit there was this family problem.

"We ended up coming to Maikona, because my father was transferred from Marsabit to Maikona, and the family stayed here. And then while we were here he married the second wife, this woman he is now staying with. She was already married before but her husband died. My father became her friend and decided to marry her.[20]

"When we came here, I attended nursery school. My two brothers were ahead of me. They were boarding, in standard one. Here at Maikona. In fact, I was not of the age of attending nursery school, but I have to go, I have to get food, because it is being given at the school. My mother did not have anything at all. My father, he was not caring for us since we came to Maikona.

"He just went without giving the mother anything, and he was earning, administrative police. My mother has to struggle now. She took us to school purposely at first to get food from school, and she goes and collects firewood and then she brings and then she sells to people. She buys us things like tea, sugar. By then it was not cheap. Then she was buying us these things through her own ways. And we stayed for almost two years, something like two years, here. And my father was mistreating us."

"In what way?" I asked.

"Our houses are close to one another. They are *marara* [wattle and daub] houses. It was sort of round, shaped like *mina dasse* [tent]. And my father has built a very big marara house for his second wife. So we are almost living close to one another. The house is not there now. Our houses were close to one another. Sometimes we might come at night after school, and there's nothing that we eat at home. My mother has maybe gone for firewood in the morning. She has only bought us tea leaves. This is not enough to provide us with what we need. And my father was employed, and he was drinking, slaughtering maybe goats, celebrating. Friends would come to his house, while we sleep hungry in my mother's house. So there was such mistreatment. And then my mother said, she said, 'We have to leave, because we cannot survive in this condition. He celebrates with friends while we are suffering.'"

I asked whether he remembered his feelings.

Figure 11. A permanent house at Maikona. The tent pitched beside it is used mainly as a
kitchen but on ceremonial occasions becomes the ritual center of the household.

"At that time I was very young. But I could see what was happening.
Because my mother usually at night she calls us together. 'Do you see what
your father is doing?' She was putting something in us that you have to
remember these things. I do remember how things were going. Because I
can see when they are celebrating, we have to sleep without food. In fact,
by then I was younger, I couldn't have bad feelings against him, something
like that. But I grew up with that feeling, feeling that my father has done
something bad when I was young. And then my mother told us, 'Now we
have to leave.'"

Wario's mother, Gumato, had five children: Katelo, the eldest son, followed
by son Diba, daughter Bonu, Wario, and finally Isakho, a baby boy born
after the move to Maikona. Their mother managed to get Katelo and
Diba enrolled at the Catholic boarding school in North Horr under the
sponsorship of a German teacher named Hildegard Helmer. So the two
boys went to North Horr, leaving their mother, Wario, his sister, and the
youngest brother behind in Maikona.

"Then one night, my mother woke me up. I was young but I still could
remember that part of the whole thing. She told me, 'Wake up, let's go.'

I couldn't realize, but I would have to follow her. So she told me, 'Let's go.' I waked up. It was past midnight. It was in the dark, but there was moonlight. So we went to a hotel [tea shop]. There was one hotel here in Maikona. It belonged to another mother called Fatuma. She's now staying in Marsabit. Fatuma Yataani. So she took me there, she bought me some *mandazi* [a kind of fried bread] with the money she got from her logs, which she sold during the day, and then she put the mandazis in sort of a plastic bag. She bought a lot of mandazis. By then mandazis were very cheap, only five cents, so she bought many of them. She put them in the plastic bag, and then she told me, 'Let's go.' I didn't know where we were going. But Bonu remained behind. She had not remained in our home but she was staying in one of my aunt's here in town. My mother couldn't go back at night and call her. The two of us, we left, together with my other brother, who was very young. My mother was having him on her back. We just left in this way.[21]

"Walking. At night. In fact I even remember the way that we passed. We went between the *konon* [the escarpment beyond the wells from the settlement]. We climbed up where there was a path people followed when they were headed to Kalacha. So we followed that path with our mandazi and nothing more. Our house is closed. There was no *shao* [canteen for water]. But my mother knew there were other villages which were not far. So we went, walked the whole night. Walking. Because she was now to walk according to my steps. I can't walk fast because I was very young."

Eventually they came to the camp of Gumato's uncle, her mother's brother. They rested two days. The family gave them milk. At night, while the others were asleep, Wario's mother fed him the remaining mandazis. After two days they resumed walking. They rested at other camps on the way and eventually reached Kalacha, a settlement like Maikona, about halfway to North Horr. They rested at Kalacha. Gumato bought more mandazis, and they set off on the final leg of their journey to North Horr. The entire trek was about eighty kilometers as the crow flies across shadeless, stone-strewn, hard-scrabble plains. It is less than a two-day jaunt for a Gabra adult, but an epic journey for a five-year-old boy.

They found Wario's brothers at the mission school in North Horr. The eldest, just twelve years old, went to Hildegard and told her about his family's problems. Hildegard paid some men to build a marara house for their mother and enrolled Wario in school. The mission gave them clothes and food. Gumato again cut and sold firewood. With the money she earned, she bought wholesale tobacco, tea leaves, razor blades, and cloth. She traveled on foot as an itinerant merchant among nomadic camps north of North Horr and sold the goods out of her backpack. Because the mission gave her food, she was able to save the money and buy goats and sheep. I never met Gumato, but according to Wario and others I spoke with, she prospered in goats and sheep, eventually left the mission, and was now spending nearly all of her time in arjalla (camp for goats and sheep) near Lake Turkana, where she tended her own animals.

Meanwhile, news came from Maikona that Elema had taken his daughter Bonu away from her aunt's and was making her tend his own herds of goats and sheep. "He was treating her the way he was treating us. He doesn't give her food. When they eat nice meat, she is being prepared [maize-meal] porridge. But she can't leave him." Months after arriving in North Horr, Wario's mother began to plan her return to Maikona to fetch her daughter.

"My mother now, after we had stayed and we settled for some time in North Horr, and she had no problems, she arranged how she is going to pick Bonu. She knows that if she came and tried to get Bonu, my father will not accept. So she was now trying to plan stealing her, abducting her, and taking her back. My father had some few goats that he had bought from this and there. And Bonu, in the morning, instead of going to school, she was forced to look after the goats. In the morning she was following the goats, then she come back in the evening. She was just in this life of suffering, without food, without clothes.

"So my mother came on a truck, up to the Gamura area [an oasis an hour's walk from Maikona]. Then she footed from there, knowing that now there were some villages next to Gamura. She passed to these. She say, 'Where is that? Where is that? Do you know where Bonu is?' And then she was told, Bonu is looking after goats. She said, 'Where do these goats normally go for grazing?' She was told where these goats are going for grazing. She spent that day at the village, and then next morning, because the goats were going this side for grazing, she started moving, finding for goats, until she got Bonu. Then she found her, and told her, 'OK, now forget about these goats. You just come. Let's go.' She left the goats behind there, and she took Bonu, and they started footing to Kalacha and then to North Horr. So all of us have now joined."

I asked Wario if his father came after them or demanded that they, or any one of them, return. Wario said no, even though the elders might have sided with Elema and insisted that his family go back to him. Years later, Wario's father sent word to his sons that he wanted to come live with them, that he did not want to die alone. Katelo, the eldest, went to Maikona and brought his father back to live in North Horr. The reunion lasted less than a week. Elema slipped off one night and returned to his second wife, a woman who had never borne him children. He remained with her thereafter. That act, his leaving his sons, changed the moral calculus between Elema and his family. But that episode came much later.

The parallels between Wario's and Galgalo's lives are as striking as the differences: both struggled with prolonged separations from their fathers, but in Wario's case, that separation was early and permanent. It skewed but did not preclude his ability to use Gabra myth and lore as narrative anchors for his life. In fact, I think that one reason Wario was drawn to me was that through me, or traveling with me to visit Gabra elders, he could identify with a Gabra oral tradition denied him by Elema, his father.

Elema was not tall. His head barely reached Wario's shoulder. But he managed somehow to seem larger than his son. He was stout, barrel-chested and muscular, bulkier than the typical skinny Gabra. He had a large gray beard that jutted out from his chin and exaggerated the size of his face. He wore a wide white turban around his head. He reminded me of Sinbad the Sailor. What stood out most were his eyes, which were pale for an African, almost blue, with a yellow streak running through the irises. He held his eyes wide open, so you could see the whites all around. His nostrils flared. He was intense and intimidating. The first time I met him, I was talking with a Konso blacksmith who had set up his goatskin bellows beneath a tree. Elema came, greeted the group, squatted beside me, and told me to come with him. *Kot*, he said. "Come." We walked off twenty or thirty feet. He told me he was Wario's father. He asked if Wario was working for me, if I was paying Wario money. I told him no; I didn't volunteer that I sometimes helped Wario with a little cash. He considered that for a moment. Then he stood and left. That was the sort of man he was—abrupt, direct, full of himself.

Elema was abba olla, father of a camp, and Olla Elema always seemed to pitch its tents about an hour's walk from Maikona, near enough to make daily visits to the wells and town, and far enough away to be close to pasture. It was a strange encampment—the least friendly I ever visited. I sent word several times that I was coming to talk with Elema. Each time we showed up, however, the village was all but empty, its residents off taking care of business. This in itself was not unusual: Gabra are busy.

But it happened again and again, so that even Yara wondered whether they were avoiding us deliberately.

It turned out that Elema and others in the olla belonged to the Ayana cult. The word *ayana* can be glossed as "spirit," and in ordinary usage it refers to days of the week, which are thought to have special energies, or spirits, associated with them. Ayana, as I understood it, was a mix of Islam and spirit possession.[22] Ayana had been criticized by missionaries, particularly Anglicans, as "devil worship." Some cult members were known as healers, and sick people would ask them to exorcise their illnesses. One former member, an Anglican convert, told me that usually the healer would demand goats to be slaughtered at each stage of diagnosis and treatment, and that in the end the patient would remain sick, rid only of his goats. On the other hand, I heard stories of people with debilitating illnesses, such as madness and blindness, who were miraculously cured. I also heard that Ayana followers practiced nightlong rites of dancing and drinking blood. Everyone seemed to agree that Ayana was rare among Gabra but more common among Borana.

After his own investigations, Yara found out that people at Olla Elema assumed that because I was white, I was a missionary come to trouble them about their beliefs and practices. He eventually convinced them otherwise, or at least enough that they agreed to talk with me.

Elema and two other men in his village, both Borana, sat in some shade cast by a single spindly acacia sapling one afternoon and spoke with Yara and me. They said they were Muslims. Yara had advised me not to ask about Ayana, so I did not. Instead, I told them generally that I was interested in learning about Gabra traditions. Elema then launched into a long angry tirade against the younger generation, the generation of his sons, who he said were abandoning Gabra traditions. Elema did almost all the talking. The others nodded and agreed with him. He said Gabra traditions were eroding, and that failure to observe tradition was bringing drought and disease and misfortune. He blamed mission schools. Schools, he said, gave children new ideas and drew them away from the camps and their father's control. He said Christian churches and employment in towns also exposed people to new ideas and divided their loyalties and commitments.

He illustrated this by telling me how people were forgetting to tie a sheep in front of the house on mornings after the new moon. "Nowadays," he said, "there's nothing like that. Nobody said do not do that. But people do not do these things." He said the same was true for putting qumbi over one's eyebrows at new moons and gathering one's animals together for sorio sacrifices. Sons, he said, do not respect their father's wishes. "Sons say: 'What is Waaqa? Show us Waaqa!' Or they say: 'What is sorio?' They refuse to come home for sorio or to accept a bride engaged by their fathers." He pointed at Yara and said Yara came from an important Alganna family, but that neither Yara nor his brothers knew anything about Gabra tradition. Tradition, he said, was being lost.

I had heard much the same from other elders. What made Elema's diatribe interesting was that it came from Elema, a man who I knew did not practice any of these traditions himself. I knew because none of them may be practiced if a man's firstborn son is not also present, and Elema's firstborn was estranged and living in North Horr along with the rest of his family. Moreover, as a Muslim, Elema was not supposed to practice "pagan" Gabra rites.

Why was he so critical of young people? It could be that he told me what he thought I wanted to hear. It could have been a performance for other elders in his camp. It could be that his remarks, though superficially about the erosion of tradition, reflected anxieties about his own estrangement from his sons. He lamented that people did not perform the very rituals he himself did not perform, and the reason he did not perform those rituals was he had chosen not to live with his sons. Elema was curiously Gabra and not Gabra; he was born Gabra and lived like one, but he could not practice the rites that are distinctively Gabra, such as observing new moons and slaughtering Sorio Nagaya. These practices, more than the more common material facts of nomadic life, distinguish Gabra from their Somali, Borana, and Rendille neighbors. There are different levels to being Gabra, and the oppositions characteristic of Gabra identity play out in different ways at different levels. Elema was a sort of inside outsider.

As we saw in the last chapter, the distinction between inside and outside is important in this nomadic society, where the boundary between them is constantly negotiated. That someone could be both in and out is not strange. In the next chapter I discuss outcasts, who are banished even though they continue to live with their families. Elema was not formally outcast, but his separation from his sons did cut him off from ritual practices and, as I will show, from traditional jural processes as well.

Wario's separation from his father separated Wario from other Gabra at the same time as it exposed him to another universe of attachments. "The only part that has been missed," he said, "is some of the traditions, for example.

Like sorio. We never had sorio in our family. Never. Because our father is not there. But he's not dead. So we can't practice it when he's not dead, when he's alive but not there. We never had *mora*, like when a son is born, to slaughter *elemo* and *korbes*.[23] No member of our family had that, that is my brothers and my sister, no one of us. Because the father was not there, all of this because the father was not there. We never had things like sorio or Almado or Sadeta, nothing. Because he wasn't there. Apart from that, except for those times, we don't see that we are missing anything. We know that these occasions are happening, the sorios are happening, because we go and attend other people's sorio, celebrate as they do. The only difference is that we don't do it ourselves, because our father was not there."

Wario, a Catholic, converted to Christianity as a pupil at the mission school. His mother, like his father, was a Muslim. He spoke of religious conversion as though he had swapped jobs, changed clothes, or moved from one place to another.

"My mother told us, for our own survival, we have now to become Christians. We have to be Christians so that we should be accepted by Hildegard, because she was a Christian. She was not discriminating on any religion. She does not say this is a Christian, this is a Muslim. But it is good that we should become Christians so that she would accept us more closely than when we are Muslim or when we are, let's say, following *ada* Gabra. My mother did not join [Christianity] because most of the time she was away. She's trying to struggle for her own, for us. She is already grown up, she's an adult. But for us, we are children. Sometimes we can even look at people as they are slaughtering sorio. But if we are Muslims, we can't go and celebrate this. People are celebrating it, eating meat, and we as children sometimes we can go and look at these things and feel bad. Now our religion does not allow us to eat this meat. So to avoid all these things, we ended up in becoming Christians, in order for us also to participate in the sorios that are being carried out by the others, when we go back to the villages, or when the sorio is being done. We participate also because we are now Christians, in a way that we don't avoid these traditional sacrifices."

I asked how he related to Gabra outside the mission.

"With me they were just behind the fence.[24] They were just next to us, close to us, because once we leave there, once we are out of that mission in the reserves, we are Gabra. We stay together with them. If they celebrate sorio, we are a part, a part of them. They don't say, 'No, because you are

Catholics or because of religion, you cannot come to sorio.' Nothing like that. So though they are not staying with us there (at the mission), they are apart from us there, we are always together, even in practicing tradition. We are always together. I don't see that they are far away from me, they are close to me, even in those times. People accept us, because it is not our fault that our father was not there. We go to other people's sorio, celebrate as they do. The only difference is we don't do it ourselves, because our father was not there."

There are recurring themes of groups and space in Wario's stories. Wario's becoming a Christian, his mother thought, would make the mission woman accept him "more closely." Hildegard may not have discriminated between Muslims and Christians, but Wario did—among Muslims, Christians, and traditional Gabra—at least enough to calculate his advantage under the circumstances. His mother wanted her sons to be able to negotiate as many worlds as possible. The mission fence divided two worlds with a porous boundary that allowed Gabra to be Christians on one side and Gabra on the other; Gabra were not "far away" but "close to me." Like their father, Wario and his brothers could not slaughter sorio themselves in his absence. But as children, they would not have performed sorio themselves anyway, for sorio is fundamentally the right of a husband and father. They were all inside outsiders; the distinction denoted by the mission fence was not absolute.

Nor were Wario's feelings about his father absolute. Like so many oppositions in Gabra society, love and hate formed a peculiar alliance. I thought it was understandable that Wario would dislike or even hate his absent father. What was curious to me was the way he also valorized him. Wario told me stories, with admiring tones and elaborations, about Elema's adventures. A man can achieve celebrity by killing an enemy or a dangerous animal such as a lion, elephant, or rhinoceros. Elema, among other exploits, once killed an elephant. His feat is now memorialized in men's songs. Wario told me the story, which I paraphrase.

Elema had a friend, Isakho, who asked Elema one day to join him for tea at Isakho's lover's tent. Isakho's lover was beautiful. The young Elema was handsome. The woman looked at Elema with interest while she was making tea, and Isakho noticed but said nothing. When they had finished tea, and in the presence of the woman, Isakho told Elema that he could see that the woman, his lover, liked Elema. But, Isakho said, Elema had done nothing to prove he was a man, that he was worthy of the beautiful woman: he had never killed a large animal like an elephant. Isakho suggested that they go together then and there to hunt elephants. If Elema proved himself by killing an elephant, Isakho said, he would leave his lover and make way for Elema.

Elema, according to Wario, was annoyed that his friend would say all this in front of the woman. He felt that he had no choice now but to go with Isakho to hunt elephants.

In this part of the world, if one wanted to find elephants he would go to Marsabit Mountain, which is where Isakho and Elema headed, armed with their spears and their small, leather-encased, wooden canteens, or *shao*. On the way they met some other men who were also going to Marsabit to hunt elephants. Among the men, Isakho was the most experienced: he had killed elephants before, as well as lions and men.

After two days of walking, they reached the forest on the mountain. They soon found a herd of elephants. Several men who had accompanied them panicked at the sight of the elephants and fled. Elema stood firm. A young elephant, little more than a calf, ran past him, and Elema threw his spear and hit the calf but did not kill it. The calf cried out and dashed deep into the forest. Meanwhile, his friend Isakho had killed another, full-grown elephant.

Just about this time the grandmother of the calf came rushing at Elema for revenge. Elema, without a spear, had nothing to do but run. But as he turned he met friend Isakho behind him with another spear, and Isakho bolted forward and thrust the spear deep into the large female and killed it. He knew from experience where to plant the spear. Then the two men set out and found the calf and killed it. So Elema and Isakho returned from the hunt successful. Elema had killed an elephant, the only one he would ever kill, according to Wario, and though small, it was an elephant, a praiseworthy achievement. Isakho, however, stayed with his lover, the beautiful woman, by mutual agreement.

Wario told me that several years later, when his father was a soldier for the colonial government in the early 1950s, Elema fought in a battle with some Dassanetch who had raided Gabra livestock near North Horr. The Dassanetch are regarded as fierce and merciless enemies; I heard many independent reports of Dassanetch raiders entering villages and killing everyone, including old men, women, and children (see also Hodson 1970 [1927]:59–61).

When the Gabra soldiers met the Dassanetch, Wario told me, several of the Gabra fled, wanting no part of the fight. Elema held his ground but kept his head low. Both sides were fighting with rifles. Another soldier, Dub Sharamo, managed to sneak around the Dassanetch flanks and kill two Dassanetch. When he scrambled back to Elema's station and told Elema what he had done, the report moved Elema to the point that he lost his mind. He whooped and he stood up and he charged toward the Dassanetch without cover. Dub had to chase after him and beat him over the back with his rifle to stop him, knock him down, and protect him from the Dassanetch bullets. Elema's response was characteristic of brave men. Many times I saw men who were singing war songs suddenly convulse, whooping and grunting, falling on the ground, or bolting off in an irrational way, even into a boma's thorny fence. This sort of behavior, Gabra say, indicates bravery. The British promoted Dub Sharamo, not for saving Elema but for holding his ground against the Dassanetch. He was given a medal of honor. Elema was also remembered in songs and stories for his bravery. Wario told me this as a funny story that nevertheless documented his father's courage.

Wario and other young men lamented that opportunities to prove their valor by killing elephants and lions were scarce, in part because the Kenya government had become vigilant about protecting wildlife. Nowadays, they said, men in nomadic camps made raids against Rendille, Somali, Burji, or Dassanetch livestock instead of killing elephants. Even if they did not kill a man and seize a trophy on these raids, they might bring back animals which they could give to relatives, friends, and lovers, and in that way they could gain a reputation. Men in towns, who were not used to traveling far across the stones without food and with little water, and whose lives did not center so much on animals, distinguished themselves in different ways. They talked about how much schooling they had, or how far they had traveled, how many languages they spoke or how many places they had seen. Those fortunate enough to have found employment or succeeded in business gained prestige through gifts of store-bought items, cloth, and jewelry instead of stolen camels. All these facts distanced them from other Gabra, but the experiences also enabled them to relate to a Gabra-typical life course: like their nomadic brothers they had gone outside, albeit a different sort of outside.

Wario told me about a high school trip he once made down country much as other men told me about hunting giraffes or elephants or going on raids to steal enemy livestock. Although the elements differed, stories of this sort all had a similar script-like structure: they began at home or camp (or, in this case, school); young men gathered, decided where to go, and then left, usually to some place far away; on the journey they met hardships; the hardships might be so severe that some cowards among them turned back; they arrived and found (or did not find) what they were seeking; they also found something unexpected, something that made the story unique; and the story ended with some sort of moral, a lesson learned, or an expressed desire to repeat or not to repeat the adventure. What was important was that the men left home, experienced something strange far away—outside the normal arenas of life—and returned to tell about it. The essential trajectories were the departure and the return.

"We left Marsabit with the school administration truck. It was new, it was from Japan, it was contributed by Japan, and we were taken with this truck from Marsabit to Isiolo. We were sitting in the back. I think we were almost around forty or fifty. We had form fours and form threes [school grade levels]. We are the form fours, and there were also some of the form threes who joined us. We left together. We reached Isiolo at around seven in the evening. That was our first time to see Isiolo."

On the way, they passed Laisamis and Merille, towns like Maikona and North Horr, settlements of stockless pastoralists. In Isiolo they spent a trying night reckoning with mosquitoes, which bit through their blankets and kept them awake. Marsabit is too high for mosquitoes, and the Chalbi is too dry for most of the year. Next morning they all saw the snow-covered peaks of Mount Kenya. It was then that they knew they had come to a different place than they had ever seen.

"In the morning we passed through Nanyuki [at the foot of Mount Kenya], but we didn't stop. We were to be in Nairobi that day. We had no time to stop. When we reached Naro Maro [another town near Mount Kenya], there was rain. It was terribly cold. The truck was open. It was hard for us to sit in the back of that truck. It was very cold. It was raining. We couldn't even look at the mountain because there were clouds and there was a lot of rain. At least we passed by it.

"We reached Nairobi in the afternoon, and we stayed in another school. They were ready for our visit. This was now our first time to see things like TVs. Directly our teacher took us to where the school was, and we were in the school compound. The school compound was fenced and it was already dark. There was no way we could see what was outside. From inside the school compound we can just see tall buildings. But the area was dark because there were dark clouds. We went in the school and then we were shown where to sleep. It was even our first time to sleep in a storied house, this tall building. You have to go upstairs to spend the night. We were shown the dorms. And then there were these toilets that they use, this one they use where you pull this thing down and the water comes down. None of us is used to these things. It was hard for us to ask those who were already there, those who were employed there, to say, how is this toilet being used? So just among our students there are those who had been to Nairobi, so they were showing us how these things are being used. They are going from one room to another, showing the students how these things are used. So we saw how it is used.

"Then we went back to see TV. It was our first time. In Marsabit, there was nothing like TV or videos, nothing like that. So the pictures, the way people were acting inside there, and how that small box was bringing all those things into our view was wonderful. While it was very strange, it was very nice. It was a color TV. It was a nice program. I don't remember what now. It was a sort of drama that we were seeing, something like that. The only thing that I can still remember are the clothes that those people wear. Especially women. Trousers. High shoes. It was very strange, because we had never seen such things in Marsabit: women wearing trousers. Such things! The type of clothes that these people wear was not something that we have ever seen."

Nor was the food at supper. Pastoralists of northern Kenya are accustomed to eating meat and milk, and those who go to school also get used to maize and beans. But down country, in Kenya's lusher highlands, students are often fed stewed greens in addition to maize and beans. That night's supper consisted of greens and chicken, the latter served as a special treat. The boys from Marsabit managed the greens, which were strange but edible. They could not swallow the chicken. Gabra do not normally eat any sort of bird; chicken is not considered food. The Gabra boys refused to eat it. The kitchen managed to cook some beef for them, but only after their teacher, a Goan from India, tried to coax them into eating the chicken. "Why don't you eat?" Wario remembered him asking.

"We said, 'No. Our tradition does not allow us to eat. So we can't eat.' It helped that there was a Borana teacher with us. He said, 'No. If they are not willing to eat this, we have to adapt, so don't force them.' Then we were prepared beef. The others took their supper and we waited. We had our supper separately from the others, only the Gabras."

That night, he remembered, everyone went to sleep early. They had slept poorly with the mosquitoes the night before and had spent two arduous days riding in the back of the truck. The next morning, the boys came down to a breakfast of boiled eggs.

"Boiled eggs! For the breakfast. They come with boiled eggs. Again, not one of us Gabras could eat. We said, 'No. These ones we are not taking.' We were given bread instead. The others ate eggs with bread; we ate bread. So it is within this trip that we ended up eating hens' eggs and these types of things."

How long was it before they ate chicken and eggs?

"Two days. We started eating after two days. We started eating eggs. Just one person was trying to see how it tastes. So when one tried, others said, 'OK, let me also try a piece of it.' So it was tasting very nice. It was good. We ended up eating. That was my first time to eat eggs, in Nairobi."

They spent several days in Nairobi, visiting museums and libraries, government office buildings, pharmaceutical companies, and soft-drink factories. They had seen many of these things in photographs or read about them in books, but seeing them at first hand made an impression. Wario said the city made them feel backward.

"But still we feel that where we come from is sort of a reserve, a reserve to these places, sort of like a village outside, and this is the center of where life is, where everything is being done. People are busy with big machines, making drugs. But in our country, people are looking after goats, something like this. So we are finding that we Gabra are more or less in a reserve. We are not in Kenya. We find we are not even in Kenya. This was the real Kenya, Nairobi, when we were in industry."

The boys journeyed to Mombasa and then to Malindi, a coastal town midway on the route north to the Somali border. Here, much to their surprise, they found people who spoke their own language, Afan Borana. These people were mostly Orma, who spoke an Oromo dialect very similar to Gabra. The Orma had migrated into this area from Ethiopia and northern Kenya over the past three centuries.

"When we came down off the truck, our teacher told us, 'OK, let's have soda here.' So we went into the big shop. When we came in, the person heard us talking in our language and he greeted us in Borana language: *Babaro? Nageni badada?* Just like up here. Although his dialect was a bit different, we can clearly get what he was saying. He greeted us. It was very strange to us. Then he said, 'Where are you from?' *Esa duftani?* We said Marsabit. He was trying to get news of people living in Marsabit. He said,

'How is Marsabit? How are the people in Marsabit? How is the Borana there?' He was asking us these questions. So we thought that maybe this one must be someone who was staying around Marsabit area, and must have come this side because he was employed, something like that. Then he told us, 'OK, you get free sodas and biscuits.' We were provided free.

"Some of us went outside. There was a sort of wall in front of the shop. So we were sitting on benches and drinking soda and people now, some of them, were coming close to us. And then we hear that they are talking the same language. They come closer, closer, until they come now where we are, and then they asked us, 'Where are you from?' We said we are from Marsabit. 'Oh, you are from Marsabit.' They told us, 'We are Oromos.'[25] Some of them were saying they are Oromo. We are the same people. They started giving us fruits now because they had a lot of fruits. Almost each and every woman was carrying a basket of fruit on her back, giving us bananas, oranges, mangoes, lemons, all of these things. Coming now, crowding, almost from everywhere. They were telling us, 'Give us news about Marsabit.'

"We gave them news. And we asked them how they happened to come here. Are all these people in the same tribe? They told us the majority of the people here are the Oromo people, or the Wardaa people, and the Wardaa and Oromo are almost one. They spoke the same language. So they said, 'Our origin is from Marsabit area, almost the same as Borana, though we are now staying here.' They also said there are parts of Borana who came from Merti area, who are living also here. They told us a lot of stories about where they come from, how they happened to be there, what they do there. They asked us also about our place. What do we do here? We told them here we are keeping animals. We don't grow these fruits that you grow here. We only keep animals like camels, cows, goats. So they also get a lot of news from us, and we gave them a lot of news. They gave us everything we wanted. Free.

"In fact, even lunch, we took there, from the person with the shop. He arranged for a meal for us. We had lunch at his home, with his family, all of them talking the same language. So we stayed together for the day. We didn't want to leave. We didn't want to go back to Mombasa."

I asked if there were any Gabra in Malindi.

"No. We never saw any Gabra. But they told us, you are the same tribe, you are welcome. This is your home. So they received us as if we are part of their own tribe. In fact, it was very nice. Except for the language, there was nothing similar. The way they dress is different from the way we dress.

It was only the language. It made us feel that we were at home, because staying in Nairobi we have not met anybody of our tribe. On the way we have not met. But this time it was as if we were home. We found almost everybody talking our language. It was so good. And they were very kind. I hope one day I'll go back."

The journey distinguished Wario, much as many other sorts of stories I heard distinguished others: stories about raids made against Rendille or Dassanetch enemies, or Galgalo Shonka's stories about life with missionaries and in the British army. The story's exotic content was the very stuff that made it familiar: Wario had done something—and something strange—to make him credible as a young Gabra man. His adventure was a distinguishing and transformative experience not unlike my own experience with fieldwork.

Back in Maikona, Wario's life was complicated, connected yet somehow also disconnected. His plans for his own livelihood were vague and prone to fade away. Throughout the time I knew him, he was surviving on relief food along with what his extended family shared with him and what he could pick up here and there in day labor. When I occasionally needed extra help, he worked for me. At first he talked about wanting to save enough money to buy a loading camel or donkeys to carry and sell retail goods such as tea leaves, sugar, cloth, and tobacco to nomads. Some of the most successful shopowners in town had made their start this way. His own mother had done the same to raise money to buy goats and sheep. But after a while Wario stopped talking about that plan, despite my offers to help him raise the initial cash. Then he talked about trying to find a job with a non-governmental organization in Marsabit. He asked me if I would inquire around for him, and I did. The news was never good; jobs were scarce. On the other hand, Wario never followed up, as I advised him, to visit the organizations so they would know him and his interest. One day toward the end of my stay, he asked me if I would give him my camera. People in town always wanted pictures of themselves. He thought he could take photographs of people and sell them at a profit. I told him I could not give him my camera, which had been a present from my wife. Instead, I gave him, as planned, a parting gift of cash that was more than enough for him to purchase a modest camera for himself. As far as I know, he used the money to live on and to drink.

Wario was forever borrowing money from others, and because people knew he was my friend, they sometimes came to me to ask me to pay his debts. Several times I mediated disputes between Wario and them, getting both sides to agree on some sort of terms. Once a group of elders called me to a meeting beneath a shade tree. They told me a man had brought a debt case to them against Wario, and he had asked them to ask me to settle it. I told the elders that I was not Wario's father, that I was not responsible for his debts. Normally, in this sort of situation, a father would be called in and they would negotiate what was owed, and the father would either pay or make his son pay. The father, as long as he was alive, was technically responsible for his son. The elders knew that Wario's father would not accept responsibility. They agreed that I was not responsible. But they pointed out that I was his friend. They thought that, since I was a white foreigner and presumably wealthy, I was in a better position than Wario to settle the debt.

They asked the man to find Wario and bring him to the meeting. The man refused; he said Wario had been abusive the last time they talked. I told them I would find Wario. When we returned, Wario said he did not have any money to give the man. He said if he got some money, he would pay, but he could not pay what he did not have. The elders accepted this. But they also thought that if Wario got money he was as likely as not to spend it. At the time Yara was away on family business, and I had some transcription work I needed done. I drew Wario aside and proposed hiring him for a week. He agreed. When payday arrived, the man Wario owed showed up with Wario, and with Wario's permission, I paid the man what he was owed and gave Wario the balance. I did not see him the next week, and people told me Wario was drinking.

None of Wario's problems was made easier by drink. Wario told me he had little if any control over his drinking. If a friend said "Let's drink," he drank. He denied, when I asked, that getting drunk was a way to soothe his many personal sores and sadnesses. In fact, he said, he felt better sober than drunk. For Wario, drinking was intimately associated with being close to other men. Oddly, as much as drink estranged him from others, he believed that it connected him: he drank, he said, to be social, to feel one with his friends.

Wario had failed to get a seat at a college or university after high school, but he was bright and had good clerking skills. He moved to Maikona and got a job at the Christian Children's Fund, a mission-associated agency providing services for local children. At the time there was a small drinking establishment serving beer and sodas in the settlement, a place frequented by men lucky enough to have cash. The bar was a palm-thatched mud hut on the edge of town, with a low wooden door and a single small window like a porthole on the side. The size of a closet, the structure served for storage; customers drank outside, sitting against its walls.

"It was when I was in Maikona after finishing school. It was just, you know, friends. Most of the time we were together with teachers [at the primary school] and the CCF [Children's Fund] workers. So when we go out at night to visit one another, stay together, they take us to where the bar is, and they buy for, let's say, all of us, and then they told me, 'You also have one.' In fact, I had not had before, even in North Horr or in school in Marsabit. I didn't know about this. I was just drinking sodas. So those friends of mine told me, 'Take, it's good.'

"This night I taste, and then, when I drink one, I think I have to be carried away from there. I'm flat, completely drunk. One bottle. The first time. So the next week—we are going on weekends—we come to the same place. Then my friends buy me one again. This time I find that I am not as drunk as the other time. It continues. It continues, until myself when I started finishing one, I wanted to do with two now. I ended up in getting two.

"So it was from this time, going with friends, going to the bar, that I started using the habit of drinking. And lastly I started even buying myself. That drinking two or three is not enough, so I ended up in drinking four or five, buying for my friends, my friends buying for me. We came up with a sort of group, the same group. We started drinking. Not enough. I am meaning, if I drink one I see I need another one. So it's not enough. I have to add one. So if I drink one I say, no, not yet, I have to add one more. By then I had the third one. Until I see that I am drunk. That's the time I see that it's enough. So we go.

"But lastly [the bar having gone out of business], there were no beers, and there was no way. When we come together and talk and discuss things, the best way of doing that normally is going to the bar and staying together and doing nothing. But these times, there are no beers. What to do? You have to buy *changaa* now.[26] We buy changaa, mixed with sodas, and then we come together. We drink mixed with soda. And we talk and discuss many things, every issues. We, together as a group. Coming together and talking. What is the meaning of the work, anything concerning life. Coming together and talking.

"To me the first time when I started [drinking] it was just as a coming together with friends and talking and discussing. That is when I started it. As I go, as the years go, as the days go, I found that my drinking has changed. I start drinking more and more, the more I stay, the more I drink. So it also completely changed my life from when I was not drinking or when I was drinking for the sake of coming together as friends. Because later I happened to go even alone and drink. This time I was not discussing anything, but just to drink. So it changed my life."

Wario told me countless times that he was going to quit drinking. Sometimes he would last several months without alcohol, and during that time he would tell me that he was happy, that he preferred being sober to being drunk. He once went to the government hospital in Marsabit with chronic intestinal problems. We both thought he had amoebic dysentery. A health worker checked and found no amoebas, but he told Wario that his liver was fragile. He told Wario that drinking alcohol would eventually kill him. But as surely as the moon waxes, Wario drank again. I asked him one time whether he thought he drank to ease the pain of his childhood, the rejection of his father. He said no. When he was sober, he said, he didn't experience pain or discomfort. "I end up drinking because friends or something like that, somebody makes me to drink. They say, 'Come on, let's go, let's have a drink. Let's talk about something important.'"

Neither Wario nor his father, Elema, was typical. Gabra have long been strangers to alcohol; as far as I knew, the nomads did not even have a word for "drunkenness" and borrowed instead from Swahili or Amharic. Alcoholism was a worsening problem in towns owing to the new availability of cash, spare time, and the raw material for alcohol: surplus relief maize. Still, it remained rare. Likewise, few men that I heard about abandoned their families the way Elema had. If anything, the reverse was more usual: a man might ignore a wife who failed to bear children in favor of one who did.

I have written about Wario and Elema not because they were typical, but because I think their lives illustrate some of the common complexities of social inclusion and exclusion: being inside, among Gabra, and being outside, alienated from Gabra. These complexities, unlike alcohol, are familiar to these nomadic pastoralists. Sedentarization, of course, has given them new kinks. Wario and Elema were socially outside and inside at once. One reason Wario befriended me, I think, was that I was an outsider, like him, who nevertheless identified with insiders. I spent my time with Gabra elders, learned about and participated in traditional ceremonies, and walked long distances like a Gabra with camels. Wario, who had been to high school, visited Nairobi, and seen television and industry, ridiculed traditions and nomadic life. He told me that daubing one's forehead with blood at sorio was silly, primitive, and superstitious; however, he never failed to step up to the sacrificial goat and put blood on his own forehead. Perhaps by sharing my journey to learn about *ada*, tradition, he sought some affirmation of his connection with the Gabra community, or some small vindication against his rejecting father.

When Wario was employed, he gave his father money. I asked him why he did that, since his father had given him so little. Wario said he did it because Elema was his father. It was during the time of Wario's employment that Elema sent word to his eldest son in North Horr, asking to come home. He said he did not want to die alone, without sons. Katelo came to Maikona and took Elema back to North Horr. Elema stayed six days. In the end, he grew lor.esome for his second wife, who had refused to go with him to North Horr. Wario told me that once his father left Katelo, Wario stopped giving him money. "He was rejecting us all over again," Wario said. "If he doesn't want to stay with my brothers, he is rejecting me also." Wario and his brothers washed their hands of Elema.

Toward the end of my fieldwork, Elema complained to elders that his sons were not helping him as he thought they should. He asked the elders to forward his case to the yaa, the final authority in such matters. But the yaa refused to hear the case. Elders there said that Elema had left his sons, and as long as he was away from them, he was outside the bounds of tradition. If Elema wanted his sons to help him, they said, he had first to return to them. Then, and only then, would they ask his sons to care for him.

Implicit in the yaa's decision was the notion of a jural boundary inside which Gabra rules and customs apply, and outside which they do not reach. The yaa has no jurisdiction, for instance, over Rendille or Borana. It has jurisdiction over Gabra. Elema's refusal to live with his sons had placed him outside the community. He was now an outsider, though he continued to live inside: he owned camels, goats, and sheep; he slept in a dasse tent; he dressed in the clothes of a nomad; he invoked Gabra tradition in lamentations against his sons. On the other hand, separated as he was from his sons, he could not practice any of the ceremonial forms that signified someone was Gabra. He could not slaughter a goat at sorio or tie a sheep in front of his tent at the new moon. He could not wear qumbi on his forehead or carry his stool to pray at Almado, or even assume his role as father at his children's weddings. He was outside, no longer a member of the group, no longer subject to its sanctions or deserving its privileges. He was isolated, self-banished, alone. His sons had gone to school and lived in settlements of North Horr and Maikona. They wore trousers and shirts and street shoes. They slept in marara houses; they owned few if any animals; they knew more about life in Nairobi than about life in the yaa. They were inclined to snicker at traditional beliefs and practices.

Nonetheless, Elema's sons had not rejected their father. They were inside, members of the group, subject to its sanctions and deserving of its privileges, if only because, unlike their father, in this one important respect, they were blameless. Elema's sons had gone "outside" and lived several removes from traditional nomadic life, but they remained "inside." Their father stayed "inside": he lived as a nomad; he lamented the passing of Gabra tradition. But he stood "outside."

I asked Wario what he thought about his father's complaint against him and his brothers. Wario thought for a moment. He cleared his throat and spit on the ground. He said he had heard about his father's complaints. He said that Elema, having left his sons, might as well be in fora, in the camel camps. One may not lodge a complaint against his family from fora, he said. He must be at home. "He can say what he wants to say when he is at home," Wario said. "Now he is in fora. He should not shout like that from the wilderness."

Conclusion

The stories of Galgalo and Wario reveal some of the complex ways in which two different men experience the oppositions of separation and attachment, association and estrangement, marginality and centrality. Galgalo spent a long youth oscillating between living with his family and living away, first as an Anglican mission houseboy and later as a Kenyan soldier. His stories focus on matters of separation and attachment: his father's journey to dig a well; his mother's reunion with her husband; the Gabra flight from Samburu; the Gabra alliance with Borana; the separation of Gabra from Borana at the time of Kedi Guura at Lake Turkana; their eventual reunion but their perpetual separation from those caught on the opposite side. Even the tale of the Samburu cow that refused to graze for want of its calf evokes the problem of separation and attachment.

Wario, by contrast, contended with a father who abandoned the family. He negotiated opposing connections to the Gabra community and the Catholic Church. Whatever the reasons for his alcoholism, he understood his desire for drink as a desire to connect with other men, to lose himself in a group of fellow drinkers. Elema, though immersed in nomadic life, was distanced from traditional institutions by his voluntary estrangement from his sons. Wario, though outside nomadic life, was attached to its institutions, a member in good standing, because he had not rejected his father.

This chapter forms the center of a three-part elaboration on the complex work Gabra do with oppositions such as separation and attachment, inside and outside. In chapter 2 we saw the way Gabra reverse concepts of space, seniority, and ethnicity to make sense of complex and ambiguous experience. In this chapter, we have seen how those experiences play out in the lives of two very different men. In my view, the materials in these chapters are much the same but are described at different levels.

In the next chapter, we turn to the cycle of rituals surrounding marriage to see how salient oppositions in Gabra life are formally evoked and managed on another level, through symbolic reversal and juxtaposition. The marriage chapter is the final panel of what amounts to a descriptive triptych. After it, we will have sufficient background to make sense of d'abella, the men who are women.

4

Weddings
A Marriage of Outside and Inside

Who is this coming up from the wilderness
leaning on her beloved?
—SONG OF SONGS 8:5

The ideal is to return home, for "the only place one never returns to is the
womb."
—E. J. KRIGE AND J. D. KRIGE, *The Realm of a Rain-Queen*

I DEVOTE A CHAPTER TO MARRIAGE because the Gabra weddings that
I observed contained idealized images of male and female roles, shifting
social boundaries, and the complex relations between domestic centers
and wild distances.[1] It was the ritual context in which Gabra thought
most clearly about the central issues of this discussion: separation and
attachment, inside and outside, masculinity and femininity.[2] What follows
is a description of the basic elements of marriage, from engagement to
its social consummation. My account follows the chronological order of
events.

At key junctures, Gabra juxtaposed, divided, and united aspects of
masculinity and femininity, moments of aggregation and dispersion, and
movements toward inside and outside spaces. They told me that marriage
formed a unity of opposites: *lami toko*, "the two are one," or *chufti
tokuma qaba*, "they make one." The marriage cycle seemed symbolically
to represent and resolve tensions between opposing dispositions that could
not be fully resolved in ordinary life.

The Moral Significance of Marriage

Weddings enjoyed a special status among Gabra rituals. For one thing,
they occurred at the most auspicious times of year. The weddings I saw

125

were more elaborate than others and contained elements—echoes—of the others. Marriage was the premier gateway to adult social legitimacy. One might forgo many cultural forms in Gabra life and still be a Gabra in good standing; marriage, however, was not one of them.

A basic assumption was that all persons eventually marry. That someone would never marry was unthinkable, absurd. After thirty years of missionary work among Gabra, the Roman Catholic Church found many converts, but only one man had become a priest—and most Gabra thought he was strange.[3] They said it was only a matter of time before he came to his senses, left the church, married, and became a father, in their sense of the word. An unmarried person was not a person. He or she had no dependable access to traditional shelter, could not participate fully in feasts and sacrifices, and could not have legitimate children—that is, heirs. (Father Tablino wrote me in 1998 to say that the priest had left the ministry and married.)

A man might marry late. Men often did not marry until their late thirties or forties. I attended the wedding of a fifty-seven-year-old man who was marrying for the first time. He came from a poor family. As a youngster he had migrated away from Gabra south to urban Nanyuki to work as a night watchman. Years later, his father's brother's son tracked him down and all but dragged him back to marry traditionally. The brother's son explained that the family's reputation would have suffered if his cousin were "lost," never married, and that he would have had trouble arranging the marriages of his own sons and daughters. Women generally married soon after their circumcision, or clitorectomy, which is performed around the onset of puberty, between age thirteen and eighteen. I have heard of women marrying as late as their early twenties, but I never heard of an unmarried woman much older than twenty-five—except an outcast.

Marriage outside Gabra tradition was not fully recognized and gave the couple ambiguous status. Marriage was understood as a sort of birth, and failing to marry properly made a couple and their children illegitimate. But an improper marriage, such as an elopement or Christian marriage, might be redeemed if the husband paid bridewealth and the couple performed the traditional ceremonies. Failing to marry was another matter.

Sexual contact between a man and unmarried woman—by definition, a girl, *intala*, whatever her age—resulted in banishment. It was considered the worst crime in Gabra society, easily comparable to murder. And banishment was the most severe punishment. The two were cast out, *chabani*, broken from the whole. What banishment entailed was different for men and women. A girl who was no longer virginal was usually taken by her father or a brother to Marsabit or Kargi and married off to a Rendille man. Gabra said that Rendille, whose unmarried girls were sexually active (Spencer 1973:44; see also Beaman 1981, Roth 1993), did not care if their brides were virgins. Rendille, they said, liked marrying Gabra girls, for whom they did not have to pay bridewealth.

The offending male was banished within: he did not need to leave, but he could never again take part in Gabra rituals. He "cleansed" himself in a ceremony during which he burned his clothes and crawled into and out of a hole dug in the ground, a sort of burial and rebirth; this allowed him to marry another girl and have legitimate children. He or his family also had to pay a fine to the banished girl's family. In the final analysis, his crime was taking property.

I heard about outcast men going mad. I knew one who became a murderer, and others were not at all surprised by his career. I knew another outcast, an elder, who became wealthy and influential, though still *chabana*. His brother's son had to stand in for him as his daughter's "father" at her wedding. Thus a shadow lingered over an outcast and his family.

On the other hand, despite severe concern about the virginity of unmarried girls, women once they married had considerable sexual freedom. They were expected to have extramarital affairs. A woman's husband did not like it. She would keep her affair a secret from him, just as he kept his affairs secret from her. But her right to take lovers was culturally endorsed. Men and women alike told me that all self-respecting women had lovers, or "friends."

Uncircumcised boys, like girls, were not supposed to have sex, but there was no punishment that I know about if they did. Nonetheless, I never heard of a boy having sex. Women said the uncircumcised penis was dirty and ugly, and that boys—even uncircumcised young men in their teens and early twenties—were undesirable as sexual partners.

Once circumcised, however, men were expected to pursue love interests among the wives of married men. Marriage transformed both bride and groom into new sorts of persons, but the transformation was marked in opposite ways: by sexual freedom for the bride and by new responsibilities for the groom (Kratz 1995, Spencer 1988).

The vast majority of Gabra marriages were monogamous (see Torry 1973:310). When men did marry a second or third wife it was usually because the first marriage failed to produce a son (yet recall the case of

Wario's father, in the previous chapter). In these cases a man returned to his first wife's family to ask for one of her sisters. Polygynous husbands were expected to care for wives equally. I knew several women who were abused and abandoned by husbands in favor of second or third wives, but this seemed rare. There was no formal mechanism for divorce.

Separation was vigorously discouraged by elders, but spouses did abandon each other. Men, whether widowers or estranged from their wives, could remarry, though people I asked said families were reluctant to engage a daughter to a divorced man. Women widowed or estranged could never remarry traditionally. Some settled in towns and married within another tradition, such as Islam or Christianity, or they simply declared themselves married to a partner. These marriages were not recognized by elders.

Marriage, as we shall see, represents a series of significant changes in attachments and separations between individuals. The bride parts with her family and joins another, while the groom leaves behind his bachelorhood to become a responsible elder and eventually a father. The bride's and groom's families form an alliance: each gives and receives livestock, so herds mingle. In-laws observe relational avoidances, which simultaneously separate and call attention to their new and enduring intimacy. The ceremonies serve to spell out and rehearse these new relations.

I shift now to "ethnographic" present tense to mark that I am making generalities. The use of past tense would have made the description that follows sound like a discrete event. In fact, it is a composite based on more than half a dozen marriages that I saw in part or whole. It is also based on interviews with others about marriages they had witnessed or participated in. The patterns I describe were prevalent at Gabra weddings at the time of my field work. They have no doubt changed and will continue to do so. There is nothing essential or eternal about them, though Gabra elders always spoke of them as both essential and eternal to Gabra identity.

Engaging a Bride

A groom's first marriage may occur in only three of the twelve lunar months: Somd'era Qara, Somd'era Ege, and Yaaka.[4] These are "camel months," which means they are holy. All Gabra, many of whom are scattered in the various livestock camps, are supposed to gather in main camps in these months for Sorio Nagaya sacrifices. It is only at these times that camels may change hands or be branded and castrated, and that loading camels may begin training. It is in these months that young men and women are circumcised. It is during the waning moon of these months that Gabra perform a special sacrifice, *Sorio Hamtu*; this usually involves the slaughter of a camel, and it ends the time of mourning for dead fathers and grandfathers. Weddings are celebrated the same day as these sacrifices—three or five days after the full moon. It is also during these months that wedding engagements commence. Camel months are times of social *aggregation*, but they are also times of important transitions, when *distinctions* and *divisions* regarding camels—which are, or certainly represent, members of households—are effected, and when *separations* of marriage and death are formalized.

Engagements may last years. Children, particularly girls, are sometimes betrothed before they can walk. Parents might even discuss the possibilities of marriage between yet unborn children, though this was unusual. In any case, the parents of the prospective bride and groom take the lead.[5] Gabra men may not marry until their mother stops bearing children, that is, until she reaches menopause. Later we will see how the groom's mother passes a metaphoric torch of fecundity—bearing sons—to her own son on his wedding night. If a son should marry while his mother appears still young enough to bear children, she is supposed to sit on a sharpening stone or a sadeka board, after which, it is said, she will have no more children. A younger brother may not marry before an older brother.

The preferred bride—especially for a firstborn son, or *angafa*—comes from the groom's mother's family and is ideally his mother's brother's daughter. Despite this ideal, I was told that the relation between a man and his mother's literal (in the English-speaking sense) brother's daughter was too close for marriage. Rather, Gabra seemed to prefer the classificatory equivalent—say, a mother's father's brother's son's daughter, or someone more distant.[6]

There is a fair amount of flexibility allowed in the search for an appropriate family. If the prospective groom's parents fail to find a suitably distant matrilateral cross-cousin, they look elsewhere within the mother's natal clan or *milo*. In one sample of twenty-four firstborn males, Torry (1973:300) found that 64 percent had married daughters from their mothers' clans. Gabra acknowledge that they may opportunistically explore affinal alliances in other clans or even other phratries. What is most important, they say, is that the prospective bride or groom comes from a "good" family: one that has observed traditions and has had none of its members lost or outcast; one whose men are successful at, or at least conscientious about, animal husbandry, and whose daughters have had no

trouble bearing children. Gabra clans are strictly exogamous. Gabra phratries, on the other hand, are semi-endogamous. Everyone I asked told me
that marrying within the phratry was ideal.[7] Phratries divide into moieties,
but it is not always clear how moieties structure marriage patterns.[8]

In-laws

Marriageable families are called *halkuma*, a noun that connotes legal or
right order, moral propriety. In-laws are *sodda* (subject to ritual avoidance),
a word related to *soda*, which means "fear" or "respect," as well as being
the general term for "salt." There are complex lifelong avoidance rules
between the husband and some or all of his brothers on the one hand
and the wife's mother and several of her female relatives on the other.
Participants in these avoidance relations vary slightly from phratry to
phratry and even from clan to clan. For example, in Galbo clans, the groom
and his next younger brother, and perhaps their youngest brother, "avoid"
the bride's mother, the bride's mother's eldest (or, if she is firstborn, her
youngest) sister, the bride's father's eldest sister, and the bride's father's
eldest brother's wife. As a married man or woman, one may be involved
in multiple sets of sodda relations with different in-laws of one's own
and one's married brothers and, if one is female, sisters. Notice that the
relation applies between males of the groom's family and females of the
bride's family. Gabra emphasize respectful relations with sodda affines.
They may not utter each other's names—even if the name happens also to
be that of a different person and the in-law is not present. They may speak
with one another but not look at one another. When they visit, they meet
on opposite sides of a tent wall. If one should accidentally say the name or
catch the eye of the other, then he or she makes a gift of tobacco to the other,
or they exchange gifts of tobacco, to restore the respect between them.

The sodda relationship plays along the divide between social attachment and separation, nearness and distance; it calls attention to the strong
connection between in-laws through their enforced separation. The sodda
relationship exaggerates the divide between in-laws already separated by
family, generation, and gender, and through their forced non-interaction
it unites them.

Once I was at the Gamura spring with a group about to migrate with
goats and sheep across the Chalbi Desert. I happened to be carrying the
spear of a friend, Abudo Halake. As I walked past his mother-in-law, an
ancient woman who knew me, she joked about the "large" spear in my

hand. Playing along with her innuendo, I asked if she would like the spear, and she said yes, so I gave it to her. All of this was in fun. Women do not carry spears. Then, curious about her reaction, I told her that the spear was Abudo's. She mocked an expression of fear and quickly passed the spear back to me as if it were a snake. There was no damage done; she laughed with the other women as I walked away. But even surrogates must be avoided.

Payments

Engagement payments (*marra*), like bridewealth, are standard. Additional gifts may be requested, given, and haggled over, but engagement payments always involve tobacco and coffee, small livestock, and cloth, just as marriage payments involve camels, cloth, and additional small stock. The process begins when the prospective groom's mother or father expresses interest by taking a token amount of tobacco and coffee berries to the parents of the prospective bride. The gift is called *kutu*, referring to the small triangular cloth bags used for carrying one's personal tobacco. The word is a variation on the verb *kuta*, "to cut or break," and probably refers to the prospective break between the daughter and her family. Interestingly, *kutu* is also the word for a little boy's penis. Thus kutu, the gift, may also be metonymic for the son expected from the marriage. For Gabra, marriage is first and foremost a means to obtain sons.[9] The acceptance of kutu indicates that the bride has not been spoken for already, is available, and it establishes a promise between the families. Subsequently, the groom's parents begin taking marra to the bride's parents. One marra consists of two leather bags containing tobacco and coffee beans—several pounds of each—and perhaps cloth, sugar, and tea leaves. Tobacco and coffee are not only social lubricants but also are shared in ceremonies; they suggest the group's collective relation with Waaqa, the Gabra divinity, who is said to enjoy nothing so much as the sound and aroma of frying coffee beans.[10] The bride's family may also ask for and get a male goat or sheep with each marra. Altogether an engagement requires eight marra, which may take several years to pay. The first set must be sent in one of the three camel months; the last is given when the groom's family shifts to the bride's camp for the wedding, also in a camel month. After the first payment, the groom himself may take some or all of the remaining marra to his future in-laws. These are substantial investments. If the bride's parents renege on the engagement, marra must be repaid.

Bridewealth, or *qorata*, consists of three camels: two young males (*gurbo*) and a young female. The first male camel is *gurbo esuma*, from the term for the bride's family, and is turned over to the bride's mother's eldest brother. The second is *gurbo chulu*, referring to the material used for making mats for the tent, and belongs to the bride's mother. The female is simply called *orge*—female calf—and belongs to the bride's father, or by some accounts to the bride's eldest brother (Torry 1973). The family may delay paying the female camel, but the two males are a minimum payment due on the wedding day. Along with each male camel goes a substantial length of heavy muslin cloth, a yard wide and at least five forearm lengths long, which is divided between the bride's father and her maternal uncle. At the very least, the payment to the bride's mother's brother ensures an enduring relationship between a husband and wife's families: the marriage of a sister today will reap multiple rewards in future. Each cloth is tied with small bundles of tobacco and coffee beans, held in place by a strand of *ergumpsa*, the strips of bark with which women weave water and milk containers. In addition, the groom's family gives a number of sheep and goats for ceremonial sacrifices as well as to feed the wedding guests. On the wedding day, they send containers of milk and oil to the bride's family. The qorata, like the marra payments before, emphasize social ties; they aim to strengthen bonds between in-laws. But affinal ties always lie across a shadow of separation.

Preparations and Prayers

Eventually the parents agree on a wedding month, taking into account not only the new couple's needs but also the availability of family and friends, who will contribute to the wedding and invest themselves in the couple's future. Early in the appointed month, the groom's people move to the bride's camp. By "people" I mean the groom, his parents, his siblings including married brothers and their households, and perhaps extended family. The groom's family moves to a place near the main camp of the bride's family—anywhere from a ten-minute to one-hour walk away. Then, on a propitious day, the groom's camp joins the bride's camp. They load their camels and approach the bride's camp from the east. In this largely flat and vacant landscape, the bride's family will have seen them coming for some time. When they are within calling distance, the groom shouts out four times: "Woowi! Woowi! Woowi! Woowi!" It is the call one might use to get the attention of a distant bull camel or d'abella. Now, however,

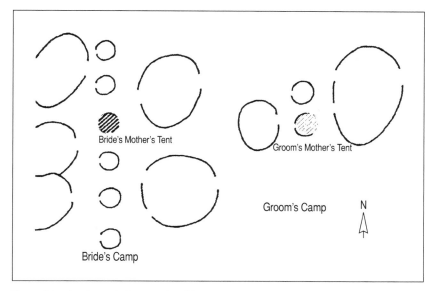

Figure 12a. A schematic layout of wedding camps.

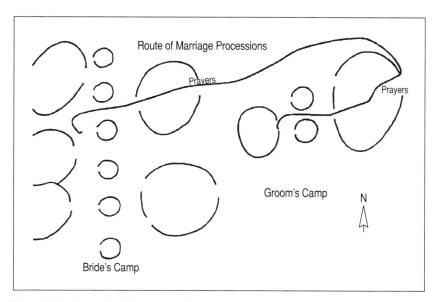

Figure 12b. Route of wedding processions.

it signals the bride's father that the groom and his family have arrived.
The bride's father and the abba olla, the father of the camp, walk out and
show them where they should pitch their tents (see diagram, Figure 12a).
This is typically a stone's throw east of the main camp's line, lateral to the
bride's mother's tent and her father's corral.[11]

A week before the wedding—on the twelfth or fourteenth day of the
waxing moon—the families of bride and groom perform a series of prayers.
The ceremony is called *eba mora*, literally "blessing of the fat of the
stomach." *Mora* denotes a length of white fat attached to an animal's
peritoneum, a symbol of bounty and fecundity. *Eba mora* denotes the
male goat sacrificed when a son is born. A strand of mora fat from this
goat is worn by mother and newborn son on the day of his birth. Thus,
the term *eba mora* refers at once to the groom, for whose birth a goat was
slaughtered, and to the son anticipated from the groom's marriage. There
is no mora for a newborn daughter. I also heard the ceremony called *eba
qarqara*, "blessings, or prayers, of assistance."

In the morning, before the camels are sent to graze, four d'abella and
four exemplary women, ideally with young infants on their back, gather
at the groom's father's house.[12] The women should be married, should be
mothers of firstborn sons, and should never have suffered stillbirth or lost
a child in infancy. The d'abella and women all carry ceremonial staffs and
small branches of *mad'era* (*Cordia sinensis*), a ritually important fruit-
bearing tree. These green branches are called *sarmuche*, and Gabra recognize a similarity between waving the twigs and the characteristic waving
tail of a pregnant camel.[13] Two of the women also carry containers of milk.

The d'abella and women escort the groom's father through his camel
corral to its external gate, the door through which the camels leave for
grazing (see routes diagrammed in Figure 12b). The father stands at the
corral's exit, facing out; the others stand outside, facing in toward the
father. The groom may or may not be present. The corral exit is the point of
contact between the household and the rest of the community, the boundary
between inside and outside. Now the d'abella say prayers and the groom's
father says a prayer, and if any other man stands with the father, he too
says a prayer (Figure 13). Then the d'abella and women leave the groom's
father and walk around the north side of the corral over to the bride's
father's corral. Here they meet the bride's father, her eldest brother, or
both, and again they say prayers.

The prayers of d'abella involve mysterious words that people say they
do not understand. Many of the words are names of sacred places. The

Figure 13. Four d'abella, wearing white-plastered turbans, pray outside a camel corral at a wedding. They wave their staffs (*ule matari*).

translation below involves my informants' and assistant's best understanding of what the words probably mean. There is a certain amount of uncertainty to the entire translation; question marks indicate greater uncertainty. The prayer that elders who are not d'abella say, which follows, involves ordinary words and is relatively easy to translate. Prayers mainly declare that Gabra are people of peace and ask Waaqa to send rain and peace. Entire prayers are said in turn by individuals, with others answering in chorus after each line with *la* or *nagah*. The prayers are then repeated by different individuals an even number of times, with eight being ideal, though I have heard prayers repeated from four to eighteen times, depending on the number of men present and the significance of the event.

EBA MORA (Galbo phratry)
(Prayer of *mora* fat by d'abella)

Jil' dure, jil' dure
(feast of [?wealth], feast of [?wealth])

Bar nabiye, bar nabiye
(season of [?peace], season of [?peace])

Agon birri, dursen birri
([?] [birri = riches])

Nabiyele
(?even peace)

Nu d'ur ol
(guide us, be in front of us)

Qaliti
(high priest [word is fem.: ?wife of high priest])

Nu d'ur ol
(guide us, be in front of us)

Omato
(creation)

Nu d'ur ol
(guide us, be in front of us)

Forole
(sacred place name)

Nu d'ur ol
(guide us, be in front of us)

Magado
(sacred place name)

Nu d'ur ol
(guide us, be in front of us)

Eleya
(sacred place name)

Nu d'ur ol
(guide us, be in front of us)

Maero
(sacred place name)

Nu d'ur ol
(guide us, be in front of us)

Qulqulo
(purify, a prayer)

Nu d'ur ol
(guide us, be in front of us)

Wojera
(place name [Wajir, connection with Somali])

Nu d'ur ol
(guide us, be in front of us)

Sabaqo
(fold in d'abella turban)

Nu d'ur ol
(guide us, be in front of us)

Sabaq diib
(one hundred turban folds)

Nu d'ur ol
(guide us, be in front of us)

Melbanna
(sacred place name)

Nu d'ur ol
(guide us, be in front of us)

Melbaris
(?season of health, a prayer)

Nu d'ur ol
(guide us, be in front of us)

Dawiti
(sacred place name)

Nu d'ur ol
(guide us, be in front of us)

Dadiye
(?lead, walk slowly)

Nu d'ur ol
(guide us, be in front of us)

Dada ol
(stay in peace)

Nu d'ur ol
(guide us, be in front of us)

Dada gal
(return in peace)

Nu d'ur ol
(guide us, be in front of us)

Duke dadis
(camels play in dust)

Nu d'ur ol
(guide us, be in front of us)

Arbad ol
([?go forth with milk] [*arba* = elephant])

Nu d'ur ol
(guide us, be in front of us)

Arbadan gal
(?return with milk)

Nu d'ur ol
(guide us, be in front of us)

Gamad ol
(be happy going out)

Nu d'ur ol
(guide us, be in front of us)

Gamadan gal
(return happy at night)

Nu d'ur ol
(guide us, be in front of us)

Miju olii, miju gal
(be filled [satisfied] going out, be filled coming home)

EBA MORA (Galbo phratry)
(Prayer of *mora* fat by other elders)

Jil' dure, jil' dure
(feast of [?wealth], feast of [?wealth])

Nu wor nagaya
(we are people of peace)

Ka alkan nagaya
(whose night is peace)

Ka guya nagaya
(whose day is peace)

Ka mirgi nagaya
(whose north is peace)

Ka bitan nagaya
(whose south is peace)

Ka wari nagaya
(whose evening is peace)

Ka ware nagaya
(whose animals graze early in peace)

Jilti jil robaf nagaya
(the feast is a feast of rain and peace)

Hori bula
(multiply and live long)

Halkum kajela
(wish for good in-laws)

Kosi qumbi
(animals [their dung] are myrrh [sweet smelling incense])

Angafaf manda tula
(accumulate sons)

The prayers ask for peace, well-being, and fecundity. They attend to sacred places (the d'abella prayer) and, ordinary practices (the prayer of other elders).[14] Note the opposition between leaving and returning in the d'abella prayer—"be satisfied going out, be satisfied coming home"—and in the elders' prayer, with its related oppositions between day and night, north and south, evening (returning from grazing) and morning (leaving for grazing). These represent the antinomic moments of Gabra life, which are evoked throughout marriage ceremonies (see Kratz 1994:166). The oppositions articulate with each other: north, as I have said, is ordinarily a direction of dispersion, and south, a direction of return and aggregation. The same is true of day and night, morning and evening. These are critical aspects of ordinary life, each of which evokes moments of coming together or dispersing, each as important as water and grass. And as they do for water and grass, elders request Waaqa's blessing for the going forth and coming back. From the very start of the marriage process, elders ask families and participants to associate the ceremonial and the ordinary, to think about them together.

After the prayers, the d'abella and women proceed through the bride's father's corral to his tent. They place their sticks and branches atop the tent and enter. Many ceremonies involve placing ritual objects such as these atop a tent; this confers a blessing on the house, much as placing these objects upon a sacrificial animal confers a blessing on the animal and links the animal to the event and the owners of the objects. Inside the tent the ritual party say more of the same sort of prayers and drink fried coffee and hot milk, all of which was supplied earlier by the groom's father.

During the prayers, d'abella remove their sandals. This is normal: men should remove the back strap and partly step out of their sandals when they pray; it suggests one's nakedness and purity, as well as one's intention to stay for the prayer. After coffee, the d'abella's sandals are all set in a row at the threshold of the tent door. The bride's mother turns the sandals to face into the tent, then away from the tent. At each turn, d'abella say prayers, blessing the moments of going forth and returning, and the bride's mother inside the tent answers the prayers while she anoints the sandals with oil. Finally, the bride's father gives the men and women tobacco as a blessing. Time and again, the sandals serve as metonyms for people, as well as for the acts of coming and going; sandals embody the ambivalence Gabra feel for separation and attachment, because they signal both moments at once.

The parties now reverse the order of their procession. They step out to the exit of the bride's father's corral with him and say prayers there. Then they proceed to the groom's father's corral, where they meet him and say prayers, and finally they go through the corral to the groom's father's tent, ending the journey.

The wedding month is marked by the arrival of the groom and his family at the camp of the bride's family. At the same time, others who have been away for weeks or months arrive for sorio sacrifices, as well as for the wedding. Weddings prompt social gatherings and occur in months that are independently times of social gathering. Yet in the midst of the community's aggregation there occurs a major separation: the bride's move from her family to her husband's. Running through the joy of gathering is the sadness of impending departure.

Wedding Day

The wedding day is the third or fifth day after a full moon, depending on the day of the week: Mondays and Thursdays are especially good days, and Tuesdays and Saturdays are particularly avoided. It is curious that Gabra hold weddings an odd number of days after the full moon, when auspiciousness is usually counted in even numbers. Gabra I asked immediately recognized that holding a ceremony on an odd-numbered day was a problem that needed an explanation. Their solution was this: three or five days added together with the customary three hearthstones of the new household make an even number, six or eight, which is auspicious. They pointed out that Rendille hold weddings on the tenth day of the waxing moon, and that Rendille hearths have six, not three, stones, making an even number, sixteen. It also could be that Gabra hold weddings on the third or fifth day to suggest the separation of the bride from her family.

On the morning before the wedding (which begins that afternoon, since the Gabra day begins at noon), the bride's father shaves the crown of his daughter's head, or a token part of it, and sends her out to look after his camels. He tells her that that night she will marry, and he tells her to spend the day in peace. Young girls, and sometimes boys as well, wear their heads shaved except for a ring of hair, like the brim of a hat or a laurel wreath. This tonsure, called *gamme*, is a sign of childhood. When a man marries, he is said to "cover" the bride's gamme, first with the *hagogo*, the white shawl worn for a year by the newlywed bride, and later by her growing hair. A married woman does not cut her hair again, but plaits and braids it, until her husband's death, when she shaves her entire head.

As the animals go for grazing, the bridewealth animals, which will soon be handed over to the bride's father and family, remain behind. It is at this time that (pro forma) negotiations resume. As I said, the content of bridewealth is fixed. The engagement is finished; the wedding is all but a done deal. Nonetheless, the bride's father now sends word that he does not like the looks of the camels being offered. "They look sick," he says, or weak, or skinny, underfed. "What if they die?" he wonders. These questions both are and are not serious. They are taken seriously by elders who gather and look at the camels and deliberate. Usually they say that whether the camels live or die is up to Waaqa, and that all that matters now is whether they are alive when handed over. On the other hand, the bride's father's questions are not taken too seriously because everybody knows he is supposed to wonder whether the camels are good enough for his daughter, regardless of how healthy they look. At every turn until his daughter is handed over in the small hours of the next morning, her father resists the marriage, hesitates, appears to change his mind—all of which tends to increase everyone's estimation of the bride and helps to manage his own ambivalence about her imminent departure.

March of the Wedding Camels

At last, the bride's father agrees. The wedding camels, accompanied by a separate camel loaded with milk containers and any goats and sheep that are part of the procession, now assemble in front of the groom's father's corral. They are joined by the groom's father and the groom, standing inside the gate, and by two or four d'abella and two or four exemplary women with infants just outside the gate, facing the groom. The elders say prayers. The ceremony mirrors the one that occurred a week before; one ritual rehearses the other, and both rehearse events in ordinary life, since it is normal for fathers to say prayers for their sons and animals each morning as they leave the corral and set out to pasture.

The procession, led by a boy driving the camels, now moves to the bride's father's corral, where more prayers are said. The groom and his father remain behind. The camels enter the corral and will remain here without grazing the entire day. The loaded camel and the wedding party move on through the corral to the bride's mother's tent. Women from both camps unload the milk containers; the d'abella and select women place their ceremonial sticks and mad'era branches atop the tent; and all enter or sit on stools just outside the tent. Again, echoing events of the week before, they say prayers, drink coffee, and anoint sandals.

One of the sheep sent along with the qorata, a ram, is called *elemo moila*. The bride's father slaughters this ram in front of his tent. In some clans, the carcass is tossed into the tent by four unmarried men. Unlike other sacrifices, moila blood is not allowed to flow freely on the ground; instead, it is confined to a space by mounded gravel and is removed, along with the wet dirt, so neither groom nor bride will have contact with it. The bride's father cuts strips of skin from the ram's forelegs and penis and makes bracelets for the d'abella, the man who held the ram's head for slaughter, the bride's mother, and himself. In some clans, the ram's sacrifice signals the beginning of sodda avoidance relations between in-laws. Some milk from the loaded camel is given to local Waata in return for blessings.[15]

The rest of the day is spent drinking milk and tea, chewing fried coffee beans, eating meat, and visiting. Guests contribute milk for the festivities.[16] Late in the afternoon, the camel that brought milk that morning is loaded with the empty containers and sent back to the groom's father. By then, the bride's father will have entered his wife's tent, sat on his stool, and with a staff, lifted one of the mats on top of the tent, and shouted the name of the mother of the *gurbo chulu*, the bridewealth camel linked with the marriage tent. This is done to show that the camel's ownership is known, that it is *halala*, owned outright by the groom's father, free for him to give, and not a stray, stolen, or borrowed beast.

Marriage Tents and Wedding Corrals

When the harshest heat of afternoon has abated, the families perform two interrelated ceremonies. In the first, women of the bride's camp dismantle and rebuild her mother's tent and pitch the marriage tent for the first time. In the second, the groom, at the adjacent camp of his father, is shaved, dons new white clothes, and sets off barefoot with an axe to collect thorny branches for a symbolic corral. Only women take part in striking the mother's tent. Soon after the women start on the mother's tent, the men at the groom's camp, a stone's throw away, begin to shave the groom; in this part women are not involved. These activities last several hours until dusk. They start separately, with different genders and different people in different places. Eventually they come together in an expression of union between bride and groom and their families. Now, instead of surrogates such as sandals, the entire community disperses and aggregates, first separating into distinct, gender-specific activities, and then gathering so that the practices overlap, making a whole of the parts.

The tent (mina dasse) that the women build is much more complex than a canvas tent. Setting one up and taking it down require considerable effort and knowledge (see Prussin 1995). The tent's frame is an intricately latticed hemisphere made of more than a hundred curved and tapered wooden struts and poles. Each piece has its own place and purpose. Using lengths of rope and thong and strips of cloth, women weave the pieces together into something like an overturned basket or primitive weir. The swift Chalbi wind requires that the frame be braced and anchored, especially at the rear, windward wall, with rocks, stakes, and posts. Over the frame they lay thick mats woven of sisal fiber, each the size of a throw rug, about a meter square. The mats are called *dasse*, and the tents themselves are known metonymically as *dasse*. Women lash the mats to the top and around the sides of the dome. The vertical fibers on the outside of the mats are long and thick, like bristles on a heavy broom. They serve as thatching and protect the dark interior from sun, wind, and, somewhat less effectively and less needfully, rain. The women also tie cow skins and cloth around the sides for added protection and decoration. Each tent is about two meters tall at the center, and three to four meters in diameter. A woman's tent grows as her marriage matures, and it shrinks as her daughters marry and her daughters-in-law need larger tents. Setting up and taking down her tent, a ritual performed again and again throughout a woman's life, becomes a sort of kinesthetic mantra by which she continually re-creates home, a domestic place, in the wilderness.[17]

The women dismantle the mother's tent, piece by piece, piling poles and ropes, mats and skins, on the ground. The mother sets aside some poles and mats from her tent with the new poles and mats that she and others have made for the bride's tent. The rest she will use to rebuild her own, now a little smaller than before. The women take the poles and mats for the bride's new tent and set them up within the thorny walls of her father's camel corral—but only tentatively. Before they finish, they take the tent down again. Again they gather poles and mats under their arms and march in single file from the bride's father's corral to the groom's father's corral, where they finish setting up the tent for the duration of the wedding. The march of the tent, like the march of the bride the next morning, is a mirror image of the march of the wedding camels earlier in the day. The interlude at the bride's family corral is, among other things, a gesture of tenderness. It expresses the family's reluctance to let her go. In the end, though, they relent and pitch the tent in the groom's camp. Even here, the bride is not far from her parents. Gabra expect the bride and groom and the groom's family to stay with the bride's family for a year. Often they stay longer.

The Groom's Journey

While women take down the mother's tent and set up and tear down the bride's tent in her father's corral, the groom has also been busy. He sits at first in the shade of his father's tent and bathes his body, shaves his head, and wraps himself in new white cloth and a ceremonial turban called *rufa*.[18] Then, clean and shiny as a newborn, carrying for the first time the ceremonial accouterments of a married man—a stout wooden staff (*ororo*), a ceremonial whip (*licho*), a ceremonial stick (*ule ejarsa*), an axe (*d'agera*), and a woven milk container (*chicho miju*)—he sets off barefoot with three unmarried men to chop branches from two particular kinds of trees. Just as the women build the marriage tent, the groom and his men will now build a symbolic corral.

This is not to be an easy journey. Trees do not grow everywhere on these dry, sun-scorched plains, and there is often a lengthy search for the ritually required species. The trees must be *wara* (*Commiphora candudulla*) and *d'ad'acha* (*Acacia tortilis*). Both have thorns and are commonly used as fencing for corrals. In this case, however, the trees must be virginal, never before having been cut for branches, so they are doubly difficult to find. There is an emphasis throughout the ceremony on newness and perfection: the witnesses to the marriage, the four d'abella and four women, must be exemplary citizens; the groom is shaved, like a newborn, and clad in new cloth; the groom and his companions search for trees that have never been marred by another hatchet; the materials for the marriage tent and its contents are new, or made to look new, and anointed with oil to make them shine like something new; and the bride herself must be virginal, her head shaved at least in token part, and her body clad in new clothes.

The plains over which the barefoot groom searches for his branches are strewn everywhere with sharp igneous rocks and boulders. The groom's journey is painful, and meant to be so. At each chosen tree, the groom mumbles brief prayers and makes small offerings of coffee beans, milk, and tobacco (Figure 14). Then, with the axe, he trims branches from the trunk. Each of the four men carries back two or four small branches from each tree.

The groom's ritual journey for branches is repeated each time the couple has a son, establishing a connection between marriage and reproduction, as well as between men and the male space of corrals. When a son is born, his father and three others, who are friends, brothers, or even older sons, journey away from camp to make offerings and chop branches from d'ad'acha and wara trees. They carry these back to camp, and the father places the branches, along with his axe, between the two legs of his marriage stool and ties the stool atop his tent, where it must remain until the family moves again.

The Unity of Tent and Corral

By the time the groom and his friends return, the women should still be dismantling the bride's tent at her father's corral. The men's arrival signals the women to hurry up and bring the tent to its destination. The men now lay the branches in a circle within the greater circle of the corral. If the

Figure 14. On the afternoon before his wedding, Ukura Yatani, an official in the Kenya government, makes an offering of coffee at a young acacia tree before chopping off branches. He and his companions will carry the branches back to the wedding camp to build a symbolic corral.

groom is *angafa*, the firstborn son, this circle will be in the senior northern half of the corral; if the groom is *manda*, born later than the family's angafa, the circle will be in the southern half. The branches form a symbolic corral within the actual corral. The ritual performance re-creates what men do each time they move camp—chop thorny branches and drag them back to build new corrals. The ritual evokes a practice of ordinary life, and the oft-repeated practice continually evokes the ritual.

The women will build the new tent, not within the line-up of the camp, but in the circle of branches in the groom's father's corral. This indicates the new couple's liminal position in the community; only later, after they have grown accustomed to each other (and the bride to her new family), will they move the tent into the camp line. It also suggests that the male sphere, the camel corral, encompasses the bride and the marriage tent. It links the fertility of camels with the desired fertility of the couple. And, since she replaces them in the corral, it links the bride with the bridewealth camels.

The groom sits within the corral on his new *barchuma*, the married man's stool, a gift from his father, to watch the women approach and make his new home.[19] The women, each carrying an armload of tent material, leave the bride's father's corral through its outside gate. They march in single file to the north of the groom's camp and enter through the outside gate of his father's corral. Their path reverses the route taken by qorata, the bridewealth camels, earlier that day, and it charts the route the bride will follow in the dark hours next morning.

On arrival, the women are expected to taunt the groom. The bride, of course, is absent. Having spent the day looking after her father's camels, she does not return until after dusk. In the marriages I saw, older men warned the grooms that women would insult them. Indeed, the women would ask the groom what he had ever done to prove himself worthy as man, husband, and father. What gave him the right, they wondered, to sit on a barchuma? The groom is not supposed to be defensive. The grooms I saw either laughed and made wildly exaggerated claims, or turned the tables and pretended to instruct the women about how to set up the tent, something they clearly knew nothing about. The point does not seem to be to humiliate the groom. But, in a humorous way, the teasing warns him that he will now be subject to women's judgment and possible scorn.

The women lay poles and mats in a circle on the ground on top of the thorny branches fetched by the groom's party. Everyone now gathers to watch as the groom's family blesses the tent and the symbolic corral beneath it. First the father takes a wooden bowl of fried coffee beans and oil (usually clarified butter) and passes around the outside of the circle, using a ladle to sprinkle the oily mixture on tent and branches. He repeats a short prayer: *Afan wol d'agaha. Ak dansa wol intaa*, "Understand one another. Stay together well." Then the groom's mother does the same, except that she passes around inside the circle; mothers, unlike fathers, may enter their son's tent. The mother's prayer is *Hora darara. Afan wol d'agaha*, "Get fruits (children). Understand one another." Sometimes the groom's brothers too perform this ritual; the eldest remains outside the circle like the father, and others go inside.

One implication of rules about who may go in the circle of tent parts and who must stay outside is that the poles and mats, though they have not yet been constituted as a tent, already function as one. This is not because the circle consists of tent parts. It is because the parts describe a circle, and the *circle* signifies home, just as the circle of branches signifies the corral. I have already discussed, in the context of masculine and feminine objects, the contrast between the straight shapes of thorns and spears and shepherds' staffs and the circular shapes of tents and milk containers. Placing the poles and mats on the circle of branches links tent, *mina*, and corral, *mona*. These are the spheres of women and men respectively. They also represent, because they define, inside and outside spaces. Here then is a key instance in which these opposites are brought together. Each space is a center of reproduction: the tent, the place of human sexuality and childbirth; and the corral, the place of livestock care and reproduction. The tent customarily sits at the very center, constituting the middle of camp. It is a center of comings and goings. The corral is also a center, but it is always off to the side: if the corral is at main camp, then it sits either east or west of the line of tents, marginal to their centrality; if the corral stands alone in distant fora, then it is by definition on the very margins of sociality, far away from the central camp. Yet the corral's encompassment of the marriage tent and its encompassment of the family's wealth—as well as the fact the family meets the community and outside world at the corral door—suggest that the corral is a center of centers, and its thorny walls are the mobile boundary between domestic and otherwise. All this points to the complexity of Gabra oppositions; tents and corrals are *both* central and marginal to each other. Each is encompassed and encompassing.

Women now erect the bride's tent (Figure 15). There is an order to its construction that recapitulates social priorities. The women first erect the back wall, *boro*, the strongest part of the tent. Then, as they elaborate

Figure 15. Women at a wedding set up the bride's new tent.

the framework into a dome, they construct the raised pallets, the couple's beds, in the rear of the tent and tie these into the side walls. As they continue to build the framework, they leave an opening in front for the door. Finally they tie mats, skins, and cloths to the frame. The process is more easily described than executed. A pair of women may work three or four hours to set up a tent; it takes a team of eight or ten about an hour.

The greatest attention and strength are accorded to the private, rear, domestic half of the tent. The tent, as I noted earlier (and see the analysis by Prussin 1995, 1996), has two halves: a front public half (*bad'a*) and a rear private half (*dinqa*). The practice of reinforcing the rear against the destructive winds also serves to reinforce Gabra associations between the tent's strong, durable foundation and the family's procreativity. The rear of the tent houses the marriage beds, where children are conceived and delivered. It is the location of the family's prized possessions. The bias toward the rear is suggested not only by the priority given its construction but also by the placement of *chicho miju*, the family's milk containers, which are given to the couple at their wedding. The chicho hang inside on the rear wall and form a sort of mantle, or altar, between and above the couple's beds, at the point of greatest strength. The rear is also where women make offerings of milk and *gale* branches at new year rites of Almado. A number of practices thus reinforce associations between the place and ideas of strength, centrality, and certainty.

The Wedding Fire

As women pitch the tent and the groom sits on his barchuma and "supervises," his three companions fetch firewood.[20] The men will build a fire in front of the marriage tent. This is a significant reversal. Except in the satellite camps, where there are no tents, Gabra rarely build fires in the open. The only other occasions for this are when a son is born, to burn the umbilical cord; at his circumcision, to burn the foreskin; at the new year feast, Almado, to burn symbolically the past year's sins; and perpetually in the nabo (ritual center) of the yaa. The wedding fire remains kindled for four days outside the tent, after which it is moved into the tent.

The outdoor fire made by groom and companions evokes the fire of fora camp. In this way, the "outside," represented by the young unmarried man, fresh from fora, is brought at first near and eventually into the "inside," represented by the young woman, the marriage tent, and the socially central main camp. Building the fire outside the tent locates it first and foremost in the male sphere, within the mona (corral), and outside the female sphere. But the ritual collapses the opposition upon itself: fora, an outside space, is brought into the main camp, an inside space, but within the encompassing mona, a space that is both outside and inside. The poles fall into one another.

When sufficient firewood is ready, the groom and his companions use two firesticks (*uchuma*) to make the fire.[21] Fire is a symbol with ambivalent connotations. Fire suggests life. The tools that make fire are among the sacred objects of the olla yaa; the nabo fire there is the absolute center of the yaa. If the tent is the center of social life, the hearth fire is the symbolic center of the tent. Not incidentally, fire is made through the almost sexual interplay of two sticks, rubbed against one another. Gabra told me that they saw an analogy between fire, the product of rubbing two sticks, and life, the product of "rubbing" two bodies together. But fire is also destructive. A fire can easily incinerate a tent and kill those inside it. Fire is proverbially one of the "three worst enemies"—the others being water and women (worst because against them there is no revenge). The men use dry elephant dung for tinder and the groom's mother's right sandal as a platform for making the spark. The uchuma sticks must be new, and they will thereafter remain in the husband's kit. They are made of a special wood, mad'era (*Cordia sinensis*), which is also used to make the husband's staff. There are no elephants on the arid Chalbi, but they do roam the forests atop Mount Marsabit in the distant southeastern corner of the region. They are quintessentially wild and dangerous. Fetching elephant dung requires that someone in the family or a friend make a journey before the wedding. The use of the mother's sandal ensures that she is nearby. It also suggests something like the passing of a baton in a relay: a son may not marry and become a father until his mother has reached menopause. The mother passes her "fire" to her daughter-in-law through her son. The sandal anticipates the couple's childbirth, when the husband's sandal will be used as platform for cutting the child's umbilical cord.

With the fire lit, the women and men separate. The women return to the bride's camp where they spend the night visiting, singing songs of children and lovers, and looking after the bride. The men meanwhile gather around the groom, who sits on his stool in the husband's position, outside and to the north of the tent door. They spend the entire night singing songs of war and raids and distant fora. Most weddings occur several days after the full moon, so a nearly full moon rises an hour or so after twilight and lights the night's activities until dawn.

Wedding Songs

Women sing different kinds of song at weddings. All women and girls of both camps—except the bride—may participate, gathering in the bride's camp, in front of her mother's tent, where the bride waits out the night. One genre, called *amasso*, consists of songs that relate women's experiences in childbirth and their attachments to their sons. Another, called *karile*, comprises love songs that describe women's attachments to lovers. Women sing songs at weddings not about husbands but about the other men with whom women may form attachments once they have married: sons and lovers. As far as I could tell, there is no reference in these songs—certainly no emphasis—to relations between wife and husband. Advice on domestic affairs is passed along privately to the bride by her parents and friends. It is not a subject of the wedding songs.

Men also sing several types of songs on wedding nights. Again, men of both camps, though not usually the bride's father or her eldest brother, gather around the groom in his camp and share in this singing. Principal among the song genres are *gob* and *labu*. Both recount male exploits in fora, on raids, and at wars. Gob songs tend to be imagistic narratives; they tell stories and describe scenes. Labu name famous individuals and celebrate their specific achievements; such fame usually stems from killing an enemy or a dangerous beast such as a lion or elephant. The emphasis of these songs is bravery, courage, and exemplary performance. Again, as far as I could tell, there is nothing in them about marriage. What women's and men's wedding songs express instead are ideals related to the female and male genders, including illicit romances between them. A wedding, a union between sexes, is an opportunity to remind everyone of gender ideals.

Men's Songs

The groom opens the singing with this verse:

>   Groom: *Korbes buku*
>   (The he-goat rolls in the dust)[22]
>
>   Others: *Awe! Awe!*
>   (Hey, hey!)
>
>   Groom: *Ka kale bubuka*
>   (The one like a kidney rolls in dust)
>
>   Others: *Awe! Awe!*
>   (Hey, hey!)
>
>   Groom: *Ka arba funchan*
>   (The one like elephant pees)
>
>   Others: *Awe! Awe!*
>   (Hey, hey!)
>
>   Groom: *Funchan d'adu*
>   (Pees to challenge others by his deeds)
>
>   Others: *Awe! Awe!*
>   (Hey, hey!)
>
>   Groom: *Ali gallo, tapa iyolen galte.*
>   (Ali, child, who has gone to play, come home. The time for playing is over.)
>
>   Others: *Woo woyo. Si barbad'an gala.*
>   (We look for you. Come home.)

My informants said the words of the opening song are sung because they have "always" been sung: they are tradition. They were unsure how some of the words related to marriage. They did say the part about Ali returning from play refers to the groom's new responsibilities as *abba wara*, father of the household. I would add several observations. Rolling in dust, for instance, is something livestock do that seems to give the animals pleasure; the image is one of exultant, even virile liveliness. The elephant possesses strength and wildness. Dry elephant dung is used to kindle the marriage fire, which represents hearth and domesticity, the antithesis of wildness. The image of the elephant urinating as a challenge links elephant and camel. Bull camels periodically enter musth, a time of vigorous sexual interest in females and violent antipathy toward anything else, especially other males. At this time, usually during rainy seasons, the bulls urinate on their tails and fling the urine onto their backs. This makes their rumps black as tar. The behavior—along with the black smudge—is called *d'adu*. D'adu is a challenge to other bulls. Male elephants exhibit the same behavior. In fact, men challenge each other in a rhetorical exchange, a verbal donnybrook, also called *d'adu*; in it they declaim their deeds and demand that others do the same.

The opening song suggests that the wild, untamed boy—that is, the elephant, the virile male—is being called in marriage back to the hearth fire, the seat of social and domestic order.[23] As is often true of Gabra images, there is no neat opposition between domestic and wild. Fire may be domestic, but it also evokes danger and emotional volatility; fire is never completely tamed. Building the marriage fire outside rather than inside the tent, as well as kindling the fire with elephant dung, reminds everyone of the dual symbolic value of fire, and by extension of marriage: like marriage, fire incorporates domestic and wild elements, masculine and feminine sensibilities.

The singing continues until just before dawn; I collected hundreds of verses for these songs, and even those are a tiny sample. Their number seems to be endless. Verses are often improvised around themes, with only slight variations from line to line, building on key words and phrases. The *gob* that follows suggests something of the spirit and form of these songs. The songs are sung loudly, and the pace is pulsatingly quick. The singing seems to create a deep unity among the men. One man sings—it is more like a shout—the first line of each couplet; the others answer in chorus with the second. The lead normally shifts every two lines. The men sit huddled in a tight circle around the groom, each wrapped in white cloth, their staffs and spears jutting out from the huddle like bayonets above a parade. The central image of this song is *hand'ar*, or fringes, hundreds of which are tied by hand into every man's cloth as decoration. As Kratz points out, the ritual experience has as much to do with "engrossment, doing, feeling, and social interaction as with cognitive understanding" (1994:286). The men sing about a unity of fringes and, as they sing, form a huddled unity themselves.

> *Wa aah hand'ar yase aha*
> *Wa aah hand'ar yase*
> (Wa aah like fringes aha
> Wa aah like fringes)
>
> *D'iro d'iro d'iron yate*
> *Eh, hand'ar yase*
> (Men men men went away
> Eh, like fringes)
>
> *D'iron yate d'iron ate*
> *Hand'ar yase*
> (Men went, men fought
> Like fringes)
>
> *Goli arba d'iro woli ate*
> *Hand'ar yase*
> (As elephants, men fought together
> Like fringes)
>
> *Wolin yate eh d'awi batee*
> *Hand'ar yase*
> (Together they moved as a wave
> Like fringes)
>
> *Wolin yate eh wolin yate*
> *Hand'ar yase*
> (Together they went, eh, together
> Like fringes)
>
> *Ahatun arba eh jirman yate*
> *Hand'ar yase*
> (Elephant fighters, eh, went with spears
> Like fringes)
>
> *D'iro d'iro oh d'iron yate*
> *Hand'ar yase*

(Men men, oh, men went
Like fringes)

Ahatan arba eh fila bore
Hand'ar yase
(Elephant fighters, eh, at first light
Like fringes)

Fila bore eh boru loltee
Hand'ar yase
(At first light, eh, they fought this morning
Like fringes)

D'iro d'iro eh d'iron yate
Hand'ar yase
(Men men, eh, men went
Like fringes)

In songs of this sort, men linger over and explore single themes, ideas, or images, and repeat them over and over, as if savoring them. In this song it is the image of fringes, and large groups of men acting concertedly—like fringes. In others the image might be cowards hiding in trees, or strong men running across waterless plains, or brave attacks on enemy villages at dawn. I heard heroes compared to hyenas or elephants, and the number of men on a raid to drops of rain in a storm.

What is the significance of fringes? Almost all men carry a large white cloth of muslin fabric over their shoulders. They use it as a wrap against the evening chill, as a cover against the afternoon sun, and as a bedroll at night. They tie hundreds of tiny fringes at each end of the cloth as decoration and to keep it from fraying. Each tassel is four to six inches long and made of only four to eight threads, so the fringe is as fine as a horse's mane. Men take care to ensure that fringes on a cloth are the same length. There is an esthetic uniformity in fringe, like the legs of dancers in a chorus line. Women never tie fringe on their clothes, but men take pleasure in tying the fringe and having the ornamentation. Fringes are a common image, and a common metaphor for like things moving, or standing, concertedly: the thousand legs of a herd of camels, the trunks of trees in a forest, the tall grass in a meadow, and in this instance, the running troops of an attacking army. Fringes have the property of being simultaneously many and one, for their uniformity expresses unity. Unity suggests concerted behavior, conformity. The association between fringes and social conformity is underscored early in child development: elders punish children by "spanking" them with the relatively harmless gathered fringes of their white cloths.

The men sing into the night. There may be fifteen or twenty men, depending on how many live in the surrounding camps. Now and then someone rises to stir the fire. The fire is off to one side; the groom, not the fire, is the center of attention. A few ancient men, thin and brittle as wind-fallen branches, may lie down on skins and sleep for an hour, but even they soon resume singing. The groom alone is enjoined to stay awake all night, but there is manly pride taken by all those who manage to last the night. Singing thus becomes an endurance event, an act of strength and fortitude, like the raids and hunts the songs describe.

Periodically one of the singers enters a "trance" state, which Gabra call *iwachis*. This expresses itself in a range of behaviors from trembling to violent convulsions to irrational dashes into the void. I have heard of men falling into fires and have seen them run square into trees and lacerating thorns. Many carry spears, so their wild behavior is also dangerous to others. Those who experience iwachis are said to have been moved by the songs and the singing. The songs' images of brave men rushing off to war make the singers want to do the same.

There is something hypnotic about the intense, numbing rhythms of the songs and the tight synchronous movements of the men. They rock their bodies back and forth and roll their heads with the quick rhythms. My impression was that the singing men seemed to "lose" themselves in song, that they ceased to experience themselves as separate selves, and that for some this loss induced a sort of convulsive vertigo. I was far too self-conscious to experience iwachis; if anything remotely like the trance crept upon me, I always chased it away simply by paying attention to it. The men I asked who had experienced iwachis said they had no memory of it.

Iwachis seems close to Katz's (1982) account of *kia*, the "boiling" of *num*, an inner spirit, among Kung trance-dancers (see also Kratz's account for Okiek, 1994:266). Unlike Kung, Gabra do not associate the altered state with healing power. In its extreme form, iwachis resembles an epileptic seizure; it seems painful and unpleasant, and men recovering from it are dazed and disoriented for half an hour. Men moved by iwachis are said to be brave. There is status in succumbing, but even greater status in experiencing iwachis without losing control. The man who remains seated, who represses his inclination to run and limits the outward expression of iwachis to a slight trembling, is said to be very brave indeed.[24] As the group sings, the men form a unity that is broken by the individual experience of iwachis, itself an expression of personal rather than collective valor and achievement. Even in song, the tension between self and other persists.

Women's Songs

While the men sing in the groom's camp, the women are singing and dancing in the bride's. In contrast to men, who sit on stools, women stand. They stand and dance in a close circle, elbow to elbow, facing one another. A girl in the center accompanies them by jangling an old iron cowbell. The women link arms or embrace shoulders. They dance on cow skins laid out on the bare ground as a colossal drum. Each woman places one foot forward, which she uses to beat time on the skins. If the wind is right, one can hear the women's pounding feet for miles over the stony plains. They stand in place. The dominant movement is vertical, but the dances are subtle, involving nuanced rolls of head and shoulders.

The women take turns leaping into the air, in pace with the songs, pushing off their neighbors' shoulders for extra height. When the normally reserved women gather like this to sing, it is one of the rare moments they seem to abandon themselves to joy. Women dance when a son is born and when a daughter, whose birth is not celebrated with dance, marries. Their faces—eyes closed, mouths half-smiling—are ecstatic and serene at once, like someone who has found a sweet spot in time. As they leap, they extend their necks as far as they can and thrust their heads forward as if to earn an extra inch of height. A long neck is beautiful. The dancing gesture imitates the long-necked gerunuk (*gugufto*), the ballerina of desert antelope.

Some women's songs sound much like men's camel songs, celebrating the looks and manners of favored animals. Others address child-rearing. One, which I was unable to record (but see Tablino 1999), spoke of grown children running and cutting the roots of trees with their feet, as they once had cut their umbilical cord and later would cut the shoulder strap of their mother's dress. Again, feet are images of separation.

Women also sing *karile*, sweet poetic songs about illicit lovers. They would normally be afraid to sing such songs around men, but the cover of the wedding crowd gives them courage. I did not record karile at weddings, though I heard them sung. What follows is a song recorded by my wife, Carol Young Wood, which was sung for her by woman friends, and transcribed and translated with permission.[25]

> *Ada, chari tiya wori chari tiya*
> *Chari tete unda nagaya damte gurra*
> (My love, you are far away in the hills
> Send me news of your peace)

> *Ada, chari tiya me hache robdon michicha*
> *Chari korma gaala deroye tesita*
> (My love, on hills of white stones and grass
> There you watch the tall bull camel)

> *Ada, dera gaala waderi taro manye*
> *Kara dera demi waili bora kawe*
> (My faraway love, the camel is hobbled
> My brown love, with only rifle for company)

> *Ada, guya jila gallen uluko*
> *Mormi dale kiya me garte gugufto*
> (My love, the fruits of ceremony are at the door
> Has my long-necked lover seen the gerunuk?)

> *Indalu indalchu dahachi kotan mani?*
> *Ind'aqu inqabu garachi, mani tola?*
> (What use is my barren belly?
> If I cannot go, what good is it?)

> *Ada, wan megado kad'acha futi qabdi*
> *Nagadachat koton arr harka na qabdi*
> (My love, if you beg for megado, you get it
> Today I am begging for you)

> *Ada, wor dira kara ya fages*
> *Naga, dale kiya, nam dugat odes*
> (My love, the roads of town go far
> Someone brought me good news of you, my sweet)

> *Sotowa sindal' kun derini mani?*
> *Wolin indalane wotun jalatin mani?*
> (You are no giraffe, how then so tall?
> We were not born together, why all this love?)

> *Inqabad' gaala ka tulu koret iye*
> *Sinqabad' kula me hayo one chibra*

(The forgotten camel climbs the hill and shouts
I forget you, too, a mother's heart defended)

Ada, guya jila mormi licho jila
Dassa guya jila agartan na ila
(My love, the day of ceremony, the whip's long neck
The ceremony is good, for my eye has seen you)

This is rich love poetry. Note its images of separation, loneliness, and longing. The woman's lover is far away; she longs for news of him. He stands alone on a knoll, perhaps a rifle or spear in hand, watching a solitary bull camel. Of course, men are seldom alone in fora camps: they enjoy the company of their fellows, and the herds they watch are numerous. But the song imagines the lover's solitude and isolation. Life in the camel camps is synonymous with isolation and loneliness, regardless of the social reality of the experience. The reference in the sixth verse to megado, a salt mined at a sacred crater in the distant north and used as flavoring with chewing tobacco, contrasts the easy accessibility of the white salt with the inaccessibility of the brown lover. In the end, there is good news: the lover has come back for the holiday, probably Sorio Nagaya, a thrice-annual sacrifice for which every Gabra is enjoined to return home. But even this is bittersweet: doubtless the singer's husband also will return, so she might see her lover but not touch him.

The complexity of the oppositions evoked by men's and women's songs demands further elaboration. Compare, for instance, the images of fellowship and camaraderie in the men's song above with those of loneliness and separation in the women's song. Of course, women also sing songs of camaraderie and men sing of loneliness. The songs I have used as examples are characteristic, though: men's songs, of collective adventures; women's, of isolated men and women and their particular deeds. The point is that these songs imagine men *both* as anonymous fringes among a collectivity of men and as isolated heroic figures atop windswept hills. Gabra ideas about gender draw on a basic contrast between distant wild isolation and close domestic sociality. But it would be a mistake to assume an invariant analogy, that male goes with outside, wildness, and isolation as female goes with inside, domesticity, and sociality. It is seldom if ever so neat. As the men's song suggests, though the heroes are "outside" in the wild distances, they are anything but isolated or lonely: they are as numerous as fringes. And, as the woman's song suggests, though she dwells at main camp, at the domestic and social center, a woman is as lonely as she imagines her distant lover to be. Similarly, the image of the wild, isolated male does not displace but rather complements the image of the politically and ritually driven, social male. Male gender ideology encompasses lonely distances and public centers.

The Bride's March

During the night, while the men and women sing, representatives of the two families continue pro forma negotiations, usually near but outside the bride's father's tent. The point again seems to be to express reluctance to give the bride away on the one hand, and eagerness to have her on the other. The groom's people visit the bride's people and ask them to hand her over. The bride's people delay. In fact, the transfer is not supposed to occur until *bakalcha*, the morning star, has risen about ten degrees above the horizon, usually around 4 a.m., an hour or so before the first light of dawn.[26]

Shortly before the transfer, the bride's father visits his daughter, and much as he shaved a token part of her *game* (tonsure) the day before, he now combs her hair and offers her advice. Women have already anointed her with oil and dressed her in new clothes. Her father covers her head with *hagogo*, the white cloth of the newlywed bride. He advises her to obey her husband, to live nicely with him. He sends the bride's procession forth: a line of women with the bride holding onto the back of a woman in the middle.

About the time bakalcha is observed, the singing, grown lazy in the small hours, begins to build energy and volume. Gabra deny a connection between the men's and women's songs. They are separate performances; however, each side can hear the other. The songs mingle, all the more as the bride emerges from the tent and the women and bride begin their procession to the groom. As they approach, the separate songs form a choral unity, a bizarre and dissonant fugue, which however unintended is nevertheless expected as an integral part of the emergent experience—like the cacophonous cries of opposing mobs. As they came to the groom's camp the afternoon before with the tent, the women now come with the bride, who is carried like a baby on a woman's back, covered by a white cloth. The bride is not at the front nor at the rear, but hidden within, at the middle of the procession. The women lift their voices. The men shout. Divisions between families seem to dissolve: the contrast now is between women and men. It is as if each side wants to drown out the other. The women march slowly, reluctantly, through the pale opalescent moonlight.

They reverse the path of bridewealth. They start at the bride's mother's tent. They march through the bride's father's corral. They march north of the groom's father's corral. The men's and women's songs merge. The noise fills the spaces, building to a crescendo. Inside, the men sing-shout, and their seated bodies rock. Outside, the women sing-shout, bearing the bride. The groom's father pulls aside the thorny branch that fills the doorway to the corral, and the women enter, going around to the feminine south side of the new tent, where they come at last to a halt. The singing suddenly stops.

The Groom Asks for Gifts

A complete shift of mood and purpose occurs. Out of the silence, still at the very center of the crowd—the men remain seated, and the women beside them are standing, witnessing—the groom asks his father, his brothers, his uncles, and his friends for camels. *Abba,* he says in a whisper, the appropriate tone of important discussions, *gal' na ken'*, "Father, give me camels."[27]

They have gone from raucous singing to serious silence. They have gone from boyish enthusiasm to mature seriousness. Where before they were a relatively undifferentiated, exclusively male group, they are now mixed company, men and women. They turn from the romance of hunt and battlefield to the business of negotiating wealth. The groom's social ties, their strengths and weaknesses, are made plain, public, and utterly specific. In a sense, the social unity of the singing in the night is handed over to the groom in the form of livestock, a unity embodied by camels living within his corral. The father knows his son's request is coming and has made his plans. He gives his son a camel, or several, or he gives the future offspring of camels. The groom turns to his brothers, who have their own animals in their father's herd. *Gal' na ken'*, he asks of each. They may give a camel or promise one to come, say, from the marriage of a sister. Female camels are better to receive than male camels, since females make more camels. But a young male can be traded for a female calf, and though it is more trouble, in this way it too can make more camels. The groom turns to his uncles. He turns to men of his clan. He turns to men of his wife's clan. He turns to friends of his father. *Gal' na ken'*, he asks each. And they give, or they make excuses. Some claim poverty. Or they declare they have more sheep than camels, so they give him sheep. Someone may give a cow. Others, perhaps from the bride's father's village, say they do not yet know him well enough, but they encourage him to ask later—say, next year—when they will know him better.

I once saw a wedding where the groom, a man named Yataani Boru, failed to request camels from one man, Guyo Adi, a distant relative, who had expected to be asked. When the asking was over, Guyo spoke out of the darkness. "Why didn't you ask me?" he said. "I have camels. I was going to give you a camel. Do we mean nothing to each other?" Guyo made a speech and demanded that the groom ask him for a camel. So the embarrassed Yataani asked. Guyo said that since he had not been asked originally, he would not give a "living" camel, but one "on the way," that is, the next pregnancy of a particular female in his herd. He urged Yataani to "try his best" to ask him for a "living" camel in the coming year. I doubted Guyo's sincerity. I did not believe he was hurt because Yataani failed to ask him for a camel. It seemed to me that he was getting symbolic credit for saying he would have given a camel without having to give one in fact. Others, however, saw no duplicity: they said Guyo was expressing love for Yataani.

Entering the Tent

The wedding party—the groom and bride, along with a young girl and boy as attendants—now step into the tent over a milk-filled milking bowl, or *gorfa*. The girl came with the bride from her camp. The boy, who is supposed to be a friend of the groom, carries the groom's stool inside, and doing so seals a special friendship between them. Thereafter the boy is supposed to have free sexual access to the wife, which is probably why grooms seemed always to pick very young boys for this job. The girl is a friend and comfort for the bride. For this first night and the next three, the couple have these two round-the-clock companions. Everyone I spoke with said the couple waits to consummate the marriage until after these four days. When the bride is very young and recently circumcised, it may be weeks before the couple has sexual intercourse. They are supposed to use this time to get to know each other slowly and quietly in the company of others, easing the initial shock of married life. It is possible that they had not seen each other before, probable that they had not spoken.

In Gabra clans with explicit Rendille origins, the groom now emerges from the tent for one last ceremony. He must pass back and forth under the belly of a standing male camel. Then he goes back into the tent, accompanied by three d'abella, and they exchange prayers with four d'abella standing outside and to the rear of the tent. The groom's passage beneath the camel is dangerous and is approached by the groom with considerable anxiety. The thought is that if the groom has been a good man and has done nothing to merit ostracism, such as having sexual contact with a girl, the camel will stand still. If he has been a bad man, however, and has done something very wrong, the camel is likely to kick him. I never heard of a camel kicking a groom, which is surprising, since I never met a camel that would not kick someone trying to pass beneath it.

Next morning, several hours after sunrise and just before the animals are sent to pasture, the groom ritually slaughters *elemo chibra*, a ram (or, in some clans, *gurbo chibra*, a young male camel). *Chibra* refers to a married woman's plaited hair.[28] He may also slaughter a young female sheep to "clear the ground of women's footsteps" from the night before. These are the groom's first sacrifices at his new home. The bride does not cook the meat, which is prepared instead by the groom's mother or some other woman. The bride does no cooking in these first days. Indeed, except to relieve herself, she remains secluded inside the tent. The groom also remains close to the tent, and if he steps away, he should always take along his ritual wedding accouterments.

Four Days Later

On the morning of the fourth day of marriage,[29] bride and groom are visited by two d'abella and two women, upstanding members of the community, like those who blessed the families the morning before the wedding. The men wash the groom's hands and he theirs. The women wash the bride's hands and she theirs. They use a gorfa full of water and milk, four pellets of camel dung, and sometimes coffee beans. Then, inside the tent, the men kindle a small fire with the groom's firesticks and elephant dung, and four times the groom smears the hot ashes on his hands and right thigh. The bride does the same. These acts were described to me by Father Tablino and Gabra informants; I did not witness them myself. During the ceremony the elders bless the couple, praying that they will have sons.

On this morning, the wedding fire, which has smoldered all the while outside the tent, is brought inside for the first time, and the bride cooks her first meal for her husband as *had'a mana*, mother of the house. It consists of *buluqa*, a hot mixture of just about any foodstuffs available—milk, oil, herbs, tea leaves, sugar, coffee beans, and grain, rice, millet, or corn, if there is any. Buluqa is a drink of plenty, a liquid cornucopia. On this day, the bride and groom's chaperones, the boy and girl, go home. This is also the day that the bride's mother visits and advises her daughter.

That evening, the bride fries whole coffee beans and mixes these with hot milk and butter, and the couple in full marriage regalia visit her parents with the mixture, as a sort of toast to the marriage. The bride now and in the coming weeks makes formal visits to members of her family to ask for *barito*,[30] gifts to the couple, usually in the form of sheep and goats. Like the groom on the wedding night, the bride seeks to translate the collective enthusiasm for the new link between the families into tangible livestock.[31]

After a week, or a month, the next time the encampment shifts location (or longer, if the husband is away), the couple move their tent from corral to village line, in the appropriate position north of the groom's father's tent. At this time the groom places the two firesticks on either side of the corral's doorway, a separation of sticks otherwise united. Women strike the tent and load it on two or three camels. Then the bride is put up on the lead camel and handed another woman's baby, ideally a firstborn son. This is extraordinary; except for babies and invalids, Gabra do not normally ride camels. The ceremony anticipates the couple's own children. The groom walks in front, spear in hand, followed by a woman, not necessarily his mother, who leads the camels out of the corral and around to the place where the bride and other women rebuild her tent. The firesticks are replaced together in the husband's kit within the tent. Around a year after the wedding, in a propitious camel month and on a propitious day, the bride removes her hagogo, the head shawl of a newlywed.

Marriage is slow business. Gabra spread the ceremonies out for weeks, from wedding preparations to the four central days of marriage, from the transitional weeks spent in the groom's father's corral to the bride's year-long time of wearing hagogo. Marriage occurs in stages, during which the two families rearrange their many social ties and cleavages.

Conclusion

This chapter is an overview of Gabra marriages as I saw them between 1993 and 1995. It is not exhaustive. I sought to convey details of the process as well as its choreography. In light of my larger project, I focused on moments in marriage that seemed to address the separation/attachment problem, within the family, between marrying in-laws, across the broader Gabra community, and between the genders. What emerges from this description are a series of structural parallels between the oppositions masculine and feminine, separation and attachment, dispersion and aggregation, and outside and inside. But these parallels are not all transitive or symmetrical.

Men and woman are associated with *both* separation and attachment. Separation and attachment occur outside as well as inside. There are, however, persistent biases: masculinity, for instance, is more closely linked with separation and the outside than is femininity. Such biases tolerate a certain amount of symbolic slippage in the represention of oppositions. One has to forge some sort of attachment with in-laws, but they must also be kept separate, apart, other. A young man has to cut himself off in the fora camps, but while doing so, in obeying a social expectation and family need, he maintains ties to the community.

Symbolic compromises bridge the gaps between opposite poles. The tent, a defining representation of main camp, is set within the corral, a defining representation of fora, the satellite camp. The wedding fire, kindled with elephant dung, an image of the dangerous distances, is built atop the mother's sandal, an expression of the domestic center. Between families, sodda relations of fear and respect express closeness through imposed distance. Gabra take the oppositions of masculine and feminine, separation and attachment, inside and outside, and rearrange them. In doing so, they make sense of the ambivalence generated by the impossibility of finally, forever, making a choice between irreconcilable opposites. By representational fiat, they resolve in symbol what they can never quite resolve in fact.

5

D'abella
Men Who Are Women

They grew one body, one face, one pair of arms
And legs, as one might graft branches upon
A tree, so two became nor boy nor girl,
Neither yet both within a single body.
                    —OVID, *Metamorphoses*

THE PRECEDING THREE CHAPTERS have shown how Gabra life is informed by oppositions in the daily and seasonal alternations between pastures and camps, in complex understandings of space and hierarchy, in the constitution of ethnic and moral boundaries, in the construction of selves, and in the performance of rituals. We have seen that the relationship between opposing poles is complex; Gabra do not seem to see polar opposites as discrete and separable, but as entangled with each other, twined like the interlocking branches of a wind-gnarled tree. In this chapter I return to the d'abella, the men who are women, to show that in them too, opposites come together in one place. I first set out the facts about the d'abella—some I have already mentioned, others new. Then I offer a series of structural and poststructural analyses and interpretations. There is no simple explanation for understanding these men who are women. There are several related and interlocking interpretations that together form a complex explanation.

A Tent Full of Ambiguities

D'abella are a tent full of ambiguities. They are men who are women. They are central but somehow marginal. They are ordinary, involved in the usual affairs and activities of mature adult men with families; but they are special as an elite priestly class of elders. They are feared, and they must not travel at night because someone who met them unexpectedly might die from

166

fright. They are, however, often old and feeble. They have the kindness and power to offer sanctuary to rogues and scoundrels, but their curses drive the cursed insane and may even be fatal. Others approach d'abella with respect and humility, but children are unafraid and meet them like equals. They are senior, but associated with the left side, the south, the feminine, the junior dispositions. They represent the entire community, but the rules governing their behavior prevent them from doing or saying things common to the rest. They are marked like no one else by special clothing, prayers, language, and greetings. They are the first to pray, the first to eat, and the last to leave. Ask anyone, and she or he will say that the most important people are d'abella. But question the d'abella themselves, and they say they have been stripped of power. "Our time is finished," a d'abella once told me. "We have nothing left but prayers."

Of course, there is more to them than prayers.

Sacred Turbans

As I have mentioned, d'abella wear special clothes, most notably a brilliant white-plastered turban, or crown, called *hitu*, or *dubo*, or sometimes *korma*,

Figure 16. Elders rest in the shade outside a friend's tent, drinking a kind of yogurt (*ititu*) from specially woven containers (*chicho*).

which means "bull."[1] The hitu is the most important element of the
d'abella's uniform. I once saw a d'abella clad in blue jeans and a button-
down shirt, which d'abella are not supposed to wear; however, he wore
the hitu, so everyone recognized him as a d'abella, albeit a curious one.
Had he worn all of the d'abella's customary clothing and ornaments but
not the hitu, he would not have been recognized as a d'abella. Some men I
know in towns told me that when their time came to be d'abella they would
probably not do so; to wear the turban at civil service jobs or in mercantile
shops would be awkward, they said, and a d'abella may not wear the turban
at some times and not others. One can recognize a d'abella from a distance
because of the hitu, and the white turban is thought to contain some of his
powers.

I have already described the lore about how the hitu came to Gabra
from Somali, and noted that to this day the cloth for making it comes
from a Somali lineage, which offers it to Gabra at the time of initiation
in ritual exchange for a young male camel (see Schlee 1994). The story
underscores a link between d'abella, as an institution, and Gabra origins;
the hitu represents a Gabra past, and therefore it represents tradition,
or law (*ada*). Somali traders bring the cloth just before or during the
month-long rites of Jila Galana, the ceremonies of the return home, which
culminate with the initiation of a new generation of d'abella (see below,
and also Kassam 1987, Tablino 1989, Schlee 1990, Stiles 1991). Anyone
unable to participate in the migration receives the cloth and other materials
from members of clans associated with the hereditary ritual figures called
qallu.[2]

The cloth is heavy cotton with a coarse weave, not unlike the cloth
used for making plaster casts to set broken bones. It is folded and rolled
into a hollow cylinder about two centimeters thick (as thick as a thumb),
twenty centimeters tall (as tall as a fez), and the diameter of its owner's
head. Wild burrs bind the layers of cloth together, and the last wrap is
stitched in place by thorns—d'abella wear the resulting prominent seam
on their left. The external surface of the turban is then plastered a brilliant
white with a mixture of milk, water, and the white clay (*boji*) dispensed by
qallu. The result is as white as chalk. I never touched a hitu; it would have
been wrong, even dangerous, for me to do so. But my sense from having
watched d'abella put them on, take them off, and set them down—not on
the ground, of course, but on some respectable structure such as their
sandals—was that they are as heavy as a crown, a burden.[3]

Lion's Skin and Porcupine's Quill

The inner folds of the turban create wallet spaces for d'abella to hide private and sacred objects. These are formally supposed to include the following four items: chunks of *megado*, a salt Gabra chew with tobacco, which is white, and therefore pure as milk; qumbi (myrrh), a reddish resin from a local tree, used in ceremonies, chewed and affixed to men's eyebrows on ritually significant days such as mornings after new moons (interestingly, d'abella do not do this, though they share qumbi with others who do); a small patch of lion's skin; and a piece of porcupine's quill.

D'abella are ambiguous figures, but their ambiguity has a certain form suggested by the opposition of these objects. White megado opposes red qumbi, as white and red are opposed colors, each with a constellation of symbolic referents such as milk and blood, life and death, peace and violence. The lion's skin and porcupine's quill are also opposed. The skin is red; the quill, white and black. Lions are violent animals, much feared, and there are many kudos to the man who kills one. Porcupines, on the other hand, are passive, harmless creatures, whose skin, in a sense, just happens to have "teeth." I knew men who carried a lion's tooth or claw as a talisman, so I wondered why d'abella used the pliant piece of skin, rather than the more representative tooth or claw. It could be that there was more skin and fewer teeth and claws to go around. But every lion has twenty claws and, according to Gabra lore, thirty teeth (I have not counted them myself), so every lion killed would yield fifty objects. Gabra have killed many lions in the area in the past century, and their teeth and claws have a long life. It could also be that the piece of skin is like *medicha*, a strip of skin customarily cut from a slaughtered animal and given as a bracelet to the person in whose honor the animal was killed. In this sense, the skin represents both the animal, the sacrifice, and the owner of the sacrificed animal. The skin is a perfectly intelligible representative of the whole. Conversely, I wondered why d'abella favored the sharp hard quill for their turban, not the softer fur or skin beneath, or that of some other animal more easily opposed to the lion. Except for the troublesome quills, the porcupine is much that the lion is not: slow, peaceful, nonpredatory. Why then have Gabra selected its hardest, most aggressive part?

D'abella and others told me that lions are violent and aggressive and that porcupines are peaceful, docile, and slow-moving. None could explain why the lion's skin and not its claw was stored in the folds of the turban, or why the porcupine's quill and not its skin. The objects, I think, represent symbolic reversals in the opposition between lion and porcupine: it is the soft and pliant, not the hard and violent, aspect of the lion represented by the skin, just as it is the hard and prickly, not the soft and passive, represented by the quill. The objects refer metonymically to the animals themselves, of course, but also metaphorically to their opposite: the quill of the weak porcupine points, if not directly to the lion, then to the idea of aggressive defense; likewise, the pliant skin of the lion suggests its vulnerability, its weaker opposite. What d'abella preserve in the turban is symbolic complexity—a complexity that would have been lost with a lion's claw and a porcupine's (or some other weak animal's) skin. The complexity is significant, given everything else we know about d'abella. Each pole of these oppositions—lion and porcupine, skin and quill, masculine and feminine—encompasses another opposition: the violent is also pliant, hard is also soft, aggressive is also peaceful, peaceful is also aggressive.

D'abella Dress and Accouterments

In addition to the hitu, a d'abella customarily wears a wide white cloth as a kilt or sarong about his waist, and over his shoulder a larger white cloth with angel-hair fringe at both ends. The kilt replaces the more usual *gombora*, the baggy hand-stitched muslin shorts. Unlike other men's clothes, which are embroidered with colored threads, the d'abella's clothes should be plain and white, signifying purity.[4] A string of square, sky-blue beads hangs about his neck, and a plain iron bracelet (called *d'iro*) dangles on his left wrist.[5] Many also wear ear and finger rings and other bracelets and necklaces, but these are not characteristic of d'abella. I knew several d'abella who wore ivory *arbora* bracelets on their upper right arm, signifying that they were heroes who as younger men had killed enemies and brought back the severed penis and testicles as a trophy (*misa*).[6]

D'abella's sandals are also distinctive. Ideally, they are made entirely of skin, as all sandals were before rubber tires arrived in the area. Now d'abella typically wear tire sandals, or *kope tairi*, like virtually all other Gabra. But d'abella often affix leather medallions the size of silver dollars onto the straps of their sandals, a gesture to the old-fashioned design. The thick leather of the medallions is cut from the hide of buffalo or giraffe, wild equivalents of domestic cattle and camels. The medallions, which like hitu are emblematic of d'abella, and the sandals themselves are called *gange*, or "mules," after the infertile hybrid of horse and donkey.

Gange is a curious name for something closely associated with d'abella, who are agents of fertility.

Like all married men, a d'abella carries a stout shepherd's staff, called *ororo*, which stands at least as tall as its owner's armpit, the better to lean on; this is made of wood from a ritually significant tree, mad'era (*Cordia sinensis*). A d'abella should not carry a spear, though I knew several who did. In fact, one was a Kenya "home guard," a deputized civilian, and he carried a government rifle to deter livestock raids. When I asked about the rifle, he grinned sheepishly and acknowledged that as a d'abella he should not carry it—but then he said, invoking a cross-culturally familiar logic, that the rifle helped keep the peace, and that probably made it all right.

D'abella own ceremonial objects, which they keep inside their wives' tents and bring out at weddings, new moons, birth and naming ceremonies, and sorio sacrifices. These include a wooden bowl (*kore*), wooden cups (*budunu*), and a wooden spoon (*moqa*) for serving coffee (*buna*), a ceremonial drink of whole berries, fried in butter to a blackened crisp and served in sweetened milk after prayers and as a blessing.[7] Another is a ritual stick called *ule matari*. The stick, prepared for a man's initiation into d'abellahood, is shorter by a third than the ororo staff and is adorned with long strips of skin (medicha) from sacrificed cows and sheep (never goats or camels). The first strips come from the bulls slaughtered on the owner's first day as d'abella. Each strip is less than a centimeter wide and about a meter long. They hang like a beaded curtain from the middle of the stick. As the skin dries, it twists and spirals down its length like a pipe cleaner. D'abella bring their ule matari to ceremonies to hold and wave while saying prayers and to draw along the backs of sacrificial animals as a blessing before slaughter. The d'abella collect medicha strips at each sacrifice over which they officiate. The ule matari of some are hung with hundreds of medicha. If a d'abella for some reason has not brought his matari stick, he may use his ororo staff cloaked in his fringed white cloth instead. The ule matari is not supposed to touch the ground, and it should not be handled by anyone except the d'abella, his wife, and their eldest son. It is stored by his wife at the back of the tent, along with the couple's milk containers.

Avoidances

D'abella say that they have "nothing left" but prayers. They are indeed excluded from many things. Though they are first to pray, and though their blessing is essential for judgments by the generationally younger grades of qomicha and yuba to be final, few become active participants in these debates. They are advisers, not decision makers. They pray for a peaceful outcome, and bless it when it occurs.

They are not, as I said, supposed to wear shorts or embroidered cloth. They are not to walk through a moving herd of animals, dividing what was otherwise whole. They are not to dig or even to look into a hole in the ground, which might make them think of graves and death and thereby cause a death by their thoughts. They should not walk in front of other men, but behind. "D'abella are like the fathers of the community," said Ali Roba, the father of the *abba magalata* ("father of the horn") at Olla Yaa Galbo. "They bless others. They go behind and let others go ahead."

They are associated with the left and the south, the feminine directions, and with the association comes a certain marginality: they are last to bless a sacrificial animal and thereby glean its blessings; they are last to anoint themselves with its blood, and then, like women, they must do so on the left shoulder, not on the forehead. They do not wear qumbi, the waxy reddish resin chewed and affixed to men's eyebrows after new moons. They do not slaughter goats, but sheep, which are feminine.[8] Like new mothers, recently circumcised boys, and honeymoon couples, d'abella may eat only meat that was slaughtered by humans, and not that killed by drought, disease, accident, or other animals. A d'abella may not wear the customary bracelet made of the scrotum from a sacrificed goat, worn by a father for four days after a son is born. He may not participate (except to pray) in *korma*, a communal sacrifice involving a male goat and all-day singing meant to revive men's spirits.

The exclusions that set d'abella apart from others extend to ordinary language. We saw in the last chapter that the language of d'abella's prayers and songs is peculiar, different from that of ordinary prayers and songs. Their everyday speech too involves the omission of certain common words and the substitution of others. The substitutions—many of them euphemistic—distinguish d'abella from others and create an air of ceremony about daily interactions with them.[9] These words are *afan seda*, or "language of respect," about which people say, *Waan jechu malte, injenne*, "You don't use the word, but cheat and use another." The words are as important for what they do not say as what they do. For example, instead of *worana* (noun, "spear"), d'abella say *d'ae* (verb, "strike"; also sometimes "deliver," as in a birth). Instead of *bila* ("knife"), they say *qencha* ("fingernail"). Rather than *kala* ("slaughter"), they say *gololcha* ("feed"). Rather than *dua* ("die"), they say *gabbad'a* ("grow fat"), *godana* ("move camp"), *rafa* ("sleep"), or *jara* ("age").

D'abella say *d'amsa*, a special word for meat, instead of *fon*, the ordinary word. They say *gange* ("mule") instead of *kope* ("sandal"). They say *anan dimo* ("red milk") instead of *d'iga* ("blood"). A d'abella "makes a swamp" rather than urinates; he "grows big in health" rather than becomes sick; his stomach is "cold" rather than upset. When a d'abella asks someone to shave his head, he does not use the word *hada* ("shave") but says *Koti, na mudi*, "come, anoint me." When he asks for *megado*, a powdery salt chewed with tobacco, rather than say "Give me some megado," he says *Hala te na elm*, "Milk your camel for me." Likewise, when he asks for *riga*, a toothbrush stick, rather than ask the giver to "break" a piece he asks the giver to "milk" a piece for him. Not only should d'abella use the special vocabulary; others should also use it when addressing d'abella.

D'abella thus avoid words associated with violence and death—cutting, bleeding, dying, separating, slaughtering. This is consistent with another d'abella avoidance, not separating or dividing flocks of sheep or processions of camels. The d'abella's role is to promote peace and unity, not death or division. There is also the sense that d'abella should not say certain words for fear that the utterance would cause the denoted events to occur. D'abella, as I said, have mystical powers: their curse is effective, their wishes bear fruit. When d'abella emerge from initiation, they should avoid eye contact with others who are not d'abella, because their powers as d'abella are new and still beyond their control: an inadvertent gaze might harm someone. When a d'abella loses something—a sheep, say—rather than consult a diviner (*ibiftu*), who might tell him where it was, he removes his sandals and sprinkles tobacco on them, all the while wishing for the sheep to return, and soon it will.

D'abella are supposed to say blessings—things such as *ilman d'ungat*, "kiss a son"—rather than to think or say potentially harmful words, such as "spear" or "knife," "slaughter" or "death." If d'abella were to say such words, they might set in motion unintended events; their words might cause harm and division, rather than peace and unity.

D'abella Are Bulls

I have said that d'abella are men who are women. Before I say more, I want to note that they are not unequivocally feminine. D'abella are also

korma, bull camels, much as their turban is also called *korma*. A number
of features link d'abella with masculinity: they are, after all, senior men
at the same time that they are women. These features include a litany of
rights and behaviors, not only of the d'abella toward others, but also of
others toward d'abella.

Gabra have two sorts of wooden stools—*barchuma*, owned by married
men, and *kara*, owned by women. Both are made by men, who alone
may carve wood; each is made from one piece of wood. The barchuma is
masculine. It has two wide legs, like the prongs of an electric plug, and a
bowl-shaped seat. It is often adorned with strips of medicha from animals
its owner has sacrificed. The kara is feminine. It has three splayed legs
and a flat triangular seat, and it is lower to the ground than a barchuma. It
is a functional object, unadorned, with no ritual significance. Women sit
on kara when they tend the hearth fire and cook. When visitors gather at
someone's tent, men sit on whatever is available, barchuma or kara, but
d'abella may sit only on barchuma, in deference to their seniority and their
masculinity. Other men, even older men, will yield their seats to d'abella
and sit on the ground or squat on a stone.

D'abella are "bulls." When people hail them from a distance, they
should shout "Owi! Owi!" instead of calling the d'abella's name or some
other exclamation. "Owi!" is the call for a bull camel, much as "Soo-wee!"
is the standard call for a pig in some parts of the United States. At marriages
in certain Gabra clans, a young male camel (*gurbo*) is tied up with special
rope, called *erara*. The rope is wound like a ribbon around its hump and
under its belly, and women gather around the camel, holding the rope, to
sing and dance. Afterward, lengths of this rope are given to d'abella, as
the senior men, the bulls, to use as *jilba*, a rope that hobbles a camel's
knee but is also tied as a collar around the neck of the herd bull; the jilba
signifies the bull. When a young man has killed an enemy and brought
back a trophy, his maternal uncle (*abuya*) should give him a young female
camel, which thereafter wears the jilba of a bull—an instance, analogous
to d'abella, of changing genders. The gift camel is *sarma*, a word that
connotes fear or respect.

At Sorio Hamtu, a sacrifice to mark the end of a year's mourning for a
dead man, the sacrificial animal is always male, a goat or a bovine bull for
a married man, and always a bull camel for an active or retired d'abella.
People identify the sacrificial animal with the dead man. Several times
I saw a dead man's wife and daughters begin to wail when they saw the
camel brought for slaughter, as if it were their husband and father having

to die all over again; the man's harried sons, struggling with the reluctant camel, would shout at the women to be quiet, telling them that the camel was not really their father.

As senior men, d'abella are first to pray, first to eat, first to sit. They enjoy privileges over other men and women. They are senior elders, not women—not women in any ordinary sense.[10]

D'abella Are Women

different responsibilit

A woman once told me, when I asked, that d'abella are not *like* women. They *are* women, she said, nothing more: *D'abella isini challa.* It is a significant distinction. D'abella do not behave like women or dress like women. They are not transvestites or homosexuals. They continue to have sexual intercourse with their wives and lovers. They behave as fathers to sons. They are heads of households, owners of livestock. They are not thoroughly women, not fully women; they are "women only," women by name, by strict definition. They *say* they are women. Others refer to them— not always, but formally and at ceremonial occasions—with the feminine pronoun: *isini* ("she"), not *inni* ("he"). And elements of their dress and behavior and value in society are understood as feminine, as "belonging" to or "on the side" of women.[11]

D'abella squat when they urinate and do not hold their penises, as if, like women, they did not have them. An offense against a d'abella is punished as an offense against a woman: the fine for striking a woman or a d'abella and drawing blood is one heifer (*rada*), which might be paid with its equivalent, a large cloth, then also called *rada*. I have already indicated a number of prohibitions for d'abella that are the same for women: not eating meat from animals killed by natural causes, not wearing sacrificial blood on their forehead, not using red ceremonial paint, not affixing qumbi to their brows.

D'abella are marked as feminine by their association with the left or south, *bita*, in contrast to the right or north, *mirga*, which is associated with men and masculinity. D'abella tie their cloths on the left side of their body. They wear the seam of their turbans on the left. They take sorio blood on the left arm. They receive tobacco from someone with the left hand, not the right hand. While they eat the meat of the right side of a sacrificed camel, the camel is slaughtered facing east, so it is actually the south, or left, side of the camel that they eat. An old Gabra informant, Waticha Boranticha, who was generally thought to know and care more than others about "tradition" (and who despite being more than ninety years old belonged to a set of men who had yet to become d'abella), said that d'abella are "denied" (*dida*) the right side; they are limited to the left, he said, like women.

The whiteness of cloth and turban links them with femininity, though the link is oblique. People say white is feminine, a color for women, while red is masculine. Women do not now wear white cloth, but dark colors such as red, orange, and blue. A widow shaves her head and wears a white cloth turban (*sure*) for up to a year after her husband's death. Similarly a bride drapes a white cloth (*hagogo*) over her head for up to a year after marriage. White signals milk, purity, peace, and life. As I said, a d'abella once explained to me that white was senior to red, because white was the color of living animals such as sheep, goats, and even camels, while red was the color of blood and meat, which came after and was dependent on the white animal. Women and d'abella wear white ceremonial paint (*shila*) at new moons, but they may not wear red ceremonial paint (*walmale*). Of course, just as women need not be left-handed to be associated with the left side, they need not wear white to be associated with that color, or for white to be a feminine color. They are white by oppositional analogy: red signals violence and blood, which are associated with masculinity, while white signals peace and milk, which are associated with femininity. Just as there is no steady alignment between sex and gender, there need be none between gender and its many associated signifiers. D'abella are white, and this fact links them with femininity, fertility, purity, and peace.[12]

D'abella are supposed to smell good: they perfume their clothing with incense on the *mano* structure at the rear of the tent just as women perfume their clothing. Smelling good is the same as being healthy, clean, and pure. One does not ask a d'abella the common greeting whether he is strong—*Faya?*—but whether he smells good—*Urgoftu?*; this is also what one asks a mother of her children: *Ijole urgoftu?*

A further connection between d'abella and women is the notion that children are not supposed to fear d'abella, even strange d'abella, just as they are not supposed to fear women, though they often fear strange men.[13] D'abella are in this sense like mothers, belonging to a class of individuals whom children do not fear, because children see them as locations of safety and comfort. Indeed, much as mothers serve as sanctuaries for their children, d'abella serve as sanctuaries in the wider Gabra society: a man pursued by enemies has only to touch the cloth of a d'abella, or grab a support pole within a d'abella's tent, to find protection and an advocate for mercy.

I once saw a man use the privilege of sanctuary against a d'abella. The d'abella, Mamo Dido, then *abba uchuma* or "father of the firesticks" at Olla Yaa Galbo, had brought a complaint against a *jalaba* in the Maikona area. The jalaba, an appointed representative of the yaa, had allowed a Gabra man to be beaten by Kenya police; he had in fact taken the case against the man to government authorities instead of to Gabra elders, and later had threatened to beat the older Mamo when Mamo was sitting as an elder in the subsequent case against the jalaba. These were all serious charges, complicated by others against the same jalaba. In a meeting that lasted most of a week and involved more than a hundred elders, including emissaries from the yaa, the jalaba was fined a dozen cattle, which he was to pay to Mamo and the man who had been beaten. While the elders were discussing the fine, the jalaba sneaked around the circle of elders and, when the d'abella Mamo was not looking, touched Mamo's cloth and begged for mercy. Others at the meeting, many of them d'abella, insisted that the d'abella Mamo must show mercy, though he did not wish to, because the jalaba had touched a d'abella's cloth.

Although d'abella are sanctuaries, locations of comfort and succor, they are also feared. I have said that d'abella should not walk at night because someone surprised by them in the dark might die of fright.[14] Women are not supposed to walk at night, either. I suspect that it matters whether the d'abella or woman is walking alone, since meeting anyone alone after dark on the desert is disconcerting—it happens so rarely. Gabra say that a solitary d'abella or woman might be confused for a witch (*murma*). Accusations of witchcraft, which as far as I could tell were rare (see Baxter 1972), seemed to single out solitaries, a man or woman living apart from others, who were thought to have supernatural powers to harm others. Thus, d'abella and women are sanctuaries, but they may also frighten people. They arouse ambivalent feelings, depending on context and purpose.

Perhaps the strongest link between d'abella and women is their shared participation in matters of reproduction. D'abella are secluded after their initiation to d'abellahood as mothers are secluded after childbirth. In both cases, the seclusion is called *ulma*. There is thus an explicit analogy between the d'abella's migration for and participation in the Jila Galana initiation rites and women's bearing children. They are both acts of procreation: one serves to bring rain and peace, the other to bring children. Gabra say d'abella "give birth" (*d'ala*) to tradition (*ada*). D'abella remain secluded in the nabo enclosure at the center of the yaa camp for four days and nights; women and infants remain secluded in the tent for up to seven weeks after childbirth, emerging only to relieve themselves.[15] In both cases d'abella and women eat special foods—milk and fatty soups for d'abella but no meat; fatty soup, milky tea, and blood for women, but no fresh milk or meat for the first four weeks. During ulma, d'abella and women should think about life, never about death. Infertile women, as well as women who have not borne sons, take their problem to d'abella, who spit on the women's hands, pray over coffee, and bless the women, rubbing their breasts with oil. I knew several women who said that d'abella had given them children in this way. Almost every Gabra I met, when she or he learned that my wife and I did not have children, advised us to seek help from d'abella, and we would surely get a son.

D'abella are seen to have special reproductive powers: not only do they have some direct influence over women's fertility, they also have the power to reproduce the rain and peace which are the *sine qua non* of all life. Robert Paul (1996a) has described how men in many societies monopolize cultural reproduction and insist that cultural reproduction is more important, more essential, to the reproduction of life than sexual reproduction, over which women are preeminent.[16] In Tibet, for instance, "the ideology of (Buddhist) religion places its asexual, cultural mode of reproduction above the sexual one, which in turn is understood to be controlled by the symbolic activities of the monks" (Paul 1996a:20). In Gabra society, the "monks" are d'abella.

Jila Galana, Symbolic Reversals

There is an episode during the Galbo phratry's Jila Galana migration to Forole that offers insights about the symbolism of the d'abella. The "ceremonies of the return home" are a series of initiation rites that culminate with three events: the constitution of a new generation set (luba) of political leaders; the installation of a new generation of d'abella; and the retirement of the previous d'abella.[17] The migration is years in preparation; the trek itself lasts several months. There are other ceremonies within the series more pertinent to the initiation of d'abella than the one I recount here, but none stands out in Gabra memories more vividly or as more representative of the whole than this one. The following episode reveals how Gabra manipulate symbols of separation and attachment, outside and inside, toward a synthesis—a synthesis that, I go on to argue, is also embodied in d'abella.

Toward the end of the cycle of ceremonies, the pilgrims camp at Qiti, a mountain near Forole, the ceremonial transition grounds of the Galbo phratry. The series of rituals leading up to the final ceremonies is now beginning to quicken. That night groups of young men set out to distant mountains in the north to collect white soil, or boji, for the new d'abella's turbans, and red soil, or walmale, a ceremonial paint. Meanwhile, young women walk to Ele Dimtu, a mountain to the east, to collect the burrs used to bind the cloth layers of the d'abella's turban. Once again, women are linked with an image of unity and aggregation.

Early the next morning, everyone leaves the main camp. The young men who will constitute themselves as luba and become qomicha during this migration—that is, the sons of men who will become d'abella—take four male goats (and others as needed) and climb to the top of Qiti to slaughter the goats and eat their meat. The rest—who may include several hundred men and women—pack portions of their tents and other goods and move with camels toward the base of Qiti.

Below the mountain they make camp at the site of an abandoned encampment (*ona*; Figure 17 shows a different abandoned campsite), a ceremonial camp used in just this way in previous ceremonies. This itself is extraordinary, since Gabra do not normally settle in abandoned campgrounds; there are strict rules against doing so. The fact that they settle at the old camp indicates the special circumstances of the moment. During Jila Galana, they are explicitly returning to an ideal, original, and therefore former state. They speak of following the footsteps of their ancestors. This is the first of several reversals in the day's events: they turn what would otherwise be a mistake into a rule, a part of the program.

At the ona, the abandoned camp, they find a stone nabo built in time immemorial, presumably by Waaqa. A nabo, as I have said, is an enclosure used like a mosque for worship.[18] Near the center of the nabo, beside its western wall, the abba uchuma or father of the firesticks kindles a fire. Then all the men build a huge corral with thorn branches in a wide circle around the nabo. In an even wider circle around the corral, women locate their separate campsites beside ancient stone hearths (consisting of three stones each), which are also thought to have been placed there by Waaqa. Near each hearth they pitch the few poles they have brought from their tents and drape these with cloth and skins. The structures are more windbreaks than tents, like the *gosse* of fora camps, providing only a little shade and relief from the incessant winds. They thus assume new positions in an old place; they fit what they are now into what they were before.

Figure 17. After a Gabra camp moves, only a circle of stones remains. An abandoned campsite (*ona*) may not be used again.

When the men have finished the corral and the women have lit their fires from the central nabo fire, the men move in groups from hearth to hearth to drink coffee prepared by the women and to say prayers. Prayers finished, the men now go to milk their camels. The men have put all their animals inside the large corral, but each clan has a separate door, and each man enters through his own clan's entrance. The arrangement is reminiscent of fora camps, and it reverses the practice of main camps, where every owner has his own separate corral. This is the second reversal: turning main camp into fora camp.

At the beginning of the day, a senior descendent of Boru Umuro, a lineage in the Barawa clan, sits on the ground by the fire in the nabo. Boru Umuro is a mythical figure. His ancestry is unknown. Years ago, they say, he was found living alone on Mount Forole. Gabra saw him, sought him out, and after much effort, convinced him to come down the mountain and join them. Now the man from Boru Umuro, who in antiquity sat alone on the edge of things and was beckoned to come join the others, sits alone in the center of things, and it is the rest who join him. This is a third inversion: taking someone from outside and putting him at the center.

After the men have milked their camels, they bring bowls of milk to the nabo. Each offers the descendant of Boru Umuro a sip, takes one himself, and pours the remaining milk on the man from Boru Umuro. Interestingly, at sorio sacrifices, the sacrificial animal is also offered a sip of milk in just this way before it is slaughtered. Each of perhaps a hundred or more men does this until all the milk has been poured over him, and the milk lies in a massive puddle on the ground, and the man shivers with cold from evaporating milk. The shivering is important; all the various accounts I heard of this event emphasized that he shivered.[19]

Then the man from the family of Boru Umuro stands and mixes the white milk with the red soil called walmale, collected by the young men the night before from a distant mountain, and makes a paint (*shila*), which he smears on everyone, men and women alike. He smears the paint on the faces of the men and on the left arms of d'abella and women.

The day's ceremonies end late in the afternoon when the young men, who have held separate ceremonies and eaten meat at a nabo on top of Qiti, blow the horn, the yaa's magalata, and signal everyone to pack their things and return to the tents at the main encampment.

Let us review the reversals mentioned so far and add several more. The participants have turned a mistake into a rule; they have turned the main camp into a fora camp; they have taken someone from outside and put him at the center. Moreover, as it is the young men atop Qiti who signal the return, rather than the older men below, they have reversed normal relations of authority. Similarly, since it is older men and women who dwell in this ritualized "fora" camp, rather than young men, who typically occupy fora, they have reversed the normal distribution of people. Among the many rigors of life in fora is the cold men experience when it rains. In the night without shelter there is nothing to do but sit shivering in the wind and rain, when it falls, and wait for day. Rain at this time is both a blessing and a curse. When day comes they can milk the camels and drink the milk and sustain themselves against the cold. Now, however, the descendent of Boru Umuro sits shivering in a rain of milk in daylight. His relief comes with close of day, when the young men blow the horn and all return to the olla. So here at Qiti, night becomes day, rain becomes milk, black (*guracha*, the color of clear water and rain) becomes white (*addi*, the color of milk), old becomes young, and olla, or main camp, becomes fora, or satellite camp.

The most common opposition in Gabra experience, as I have said from the beginning of this discussion, is between coming together and dispersing. Gabra gather at the olla, the main camp, where tents are pitched and their mothers and wives dwell; they separate by and large into the many satellite camps for camels and other livestock. The satellite fora camp is the prototype for dispersion and separation. What Gabra pilgrims do at Jila Galana is *gather* Gabra from throughout the region to enact a moment that best represents their *fragmentation*, their separation from one another. Now, however, instead of shelterless hearths and shivering men representing the wilderness, these very features represent Gabra unity, the phratry's collectivity.

But the events in the ceremony are not quite as tidy and symmetrical as my description and analysis so far have made them seem. What I have suggested is that Gabra perceive a number of oppositions that might, for the sake of discussion, be reduced to an opposition between olla and fora, such that olla is pleasant and desirable and fora is unpleasant and undesirable. In the ceremony, they convert olla into fora and fora into olla. I have implied a Durkheimian basis for the inversion, which perhaps imbues the unpleasant and socially fragmented with aspects of the pleasant and social. What Gabra are doing is actually more complex.

For example, the difference between olla and fora is not as absolute as it seems. This is not to suggest that the difference between them is fuzzy: Gabra are clear about what is olla, or main camp, and what is fora, or satellite camp. Rather, what is true of the one, in terms of social dynamics, daily experiences, and ceremonial sanctity, is also by and large true of the other. Fora is more isolated than olla, and its hardships more severe, but men are not alone there, and among them there is a complex set of social relations. Just as olla has an abba olla, or father of the encampment, fora has an abba fora. There are tasks to be done, decisions to be made, and conflicts to resolve, and the men perform these various tasks according to procedures—models, if you will—that are also true of olla. In fact, young men describe their time in fora as training for their subsequent roles in olla. Although fora life can be unpleasant, young men are usually glad to go and sorry to leave the relative freedom they enjoy there. They are, in fact, ambivalent about both places; each has advantages and disadvantages. Moreover, though Gabra may not perform rituals in fora, all their rituals concern camels, so life in fora, removed as it is from ritual performance, is nevertheless lived most intimately with the subject of ritual. If one dwells at the altar, missing the service may not be terribly significant.

Another disturbance in the symmetry suggested in my analysis above is the location of the young men during the ceremonies at Qiti. If Gabra were simply reversing roles between old and young, the young men might have remained behind in the main camp while the older men and women left for their "fora." Where did the young men go? Even farther away from the olla than the elders, to the very top of the mountain. They have gone, as young men usually do, to an even more remote and isolated place than the rest. The symmetry of reversal would appear to be badly skewed. In going to the top of Qiti, however, the young men have gone to a place that Gabra regard as close to the sky divinity, Waaqa. The tops of mountains in this landscape have little utilitarian value for pastoralists and their herds, but they have supreme religious significance. By going to the mountaintop, the young men draw close to the source of life itself. The location may at first seem symmetrically off, given the scheme of reversal, but it is actually dead on, given Gabra cosmology. Just as fora orbit distantly around olla, everything revolves around Waaqa. By going to the top of the mountain, close to the divine force in the universe, the young men have left one olla, one center, for an even more potent center.

If the divine is a distant entity far off in the sky, then going outside, far from social centers, to the tops of distant mountains, can be seen as drawing closer to the divine: in other words, going inside. This turns on its head the reversal I described earlier. The opposition between inside and outside is not clearly delimited but distributed across space: one can be "inside" in very remote places and "outside" at the center of things. This complex opposition, in which inside is also outside, near is also far, is what I believe Gabra are enacting in the Jila reversal.

The final disturbance to the symmetry sketched above is the presence of women at the ritual "fora." Women are excluded from fora, which is an entirely male sphere. If I am right that the camp made at the base of Qiti is to be regarded as a special, ritualized fora, why are women there? The easy answer is that this is consistent with the reversal I have suggested: women are at fora for the same reason old men are there, because those normally associated with olla are now at fora. But that is only part of the story. The opposition Gabra make between olla and fora is linked with another between feminine and masculine. If fora is an exclusively male place, then olla, if not exclusively female, is primarily associated with the feminine, the affairs of women. The distinguishing features of main camps are tents, which all belong to women, and the performance of rituals, which belong in a sense to d'abella, the men who are women. Women go to the ceremonial "fora" at Qiti for the same reason older men go there: because fora is normally a reserve for youth and masculinity, but now, for this

Nothing is fixed

ceremony, *the places themselves are reversed*; the ceremonial fora is now a feminine location, the seat of ritual, prayers, and blessings. The reversal is not simply that women and old men go to fora camp, a masculine space; rather, it is that fora space itself becomes feminine for the ceremony. This is the reversal that d'abella embody and carry forward as they, within the moral dimensions of the institution, become women.

D'abella Encompass the Whole

By reversing oppositions in the rites described above, Gabra unite them symbolically and blur the differences between them. In the ceremonies of Jila Galana, Gabra enact the ordinary oppositions of Gabra life: they wander over the landscape in a ritual exodus to the center, the place of origin, where their relations with Waaqa are restored and revitalized, and they themselves are transformed. Thereafter, the d'abella—being both masculine and feminine, men of the outside and now of the inside—embody the very oppositions that were reversed and collapsed at their initiation.

Encompassing the whole, d'abella represent the entire community at rituals such as marriage, sorio, and Almado. I have described how at wedding ceremonies d'abella meet the groom's father at the gate of his camel corral and the bride's father at the gate of his corral. The d'abella move from outside to inside. They begin outside the corrals and proceed into each compound, entering the tents. In this way the marrying families bring the larger public into their agreement; the presence and prayers of d'abella legitimate the couple, turning a private exchange between families into a publicly sanctified marriage. The presence and approval of d'abella "certify" an event and ensure its accordance with tradition (ada).

The d'abella's shoe ceremony, with sandals facing alternately inside and outside, being blessed with oil at each turn, similarly calls attention to the moments of aggregation and dispersion, which together represent a definitive Gabra narrative, the ideal life cycle: the journey forth and the return. The d'abella, as men who have returned to the main camp, now represent both moments, the entire trip. Their authority to stand in for the whole community is expressed in their symbolic encompassment of opposition: they are at once men and women, right and left, first and last, outside and inside. The only other being to encompass opposition in this way is Waaqa, the divinity who is neither masculine nor feminine, neither right nor left, but complete, unitary, standing above opposition.

D'abella are supposed to walk behind others. In this sense they are last, but it is a peculiar kind of last—a last that suggests priority and seniority. Ramata Funani, a d'abella at Olla Sarite Alkano, whose first-born son, Jillo, was a friend, told me tongue in cheek that d'abella should really walk in front of others, not behind: "Even Waaqa will not walk in front of a d'abella," he said, a smile creasing his face. "Waaqa once walked in front of a d'abella and tripped because the d'abella was angry for being preceded." But then Ramata also said that d'abella should take the rear and let others "with stronger legs" walk in front. The account manages to express the d'abella's desire to be in front, his practice of following behind, his envy of others "with stronger legs," and his symbolic power to trip up even the divine Waaqa. Ramata suggested that following others indicates superiority: the d'abella in essence gives others permission to walk in front. It is the sort of *noblesse oblige* that prompts a superior to open the door for a subordinate, a matter of going first by going last. Recall the father's tent, pitched in the junior position south of his sons' tents.

In the story of Kedi Guura, recounted by Galgalo Shonka, an ownerless female camel with calf is enlisted to help Gabra return to their homeland across the lake. The calf travels at the front of the procession, while its mother brings up the rear. D'abella are like that female camel: they walk at the rear of a procession, they go last, but their attention is focused on the public good—the calf, representing reproduction—out front. In this way, d'abella are first and last. Like the female camel in the story, they are distinguished from others, auspicious, but also marginal. The camel was ownerless, a stranger. D'abella not only have ambiguous gender identities, but as old men they have begun to shift their attention away from the day-to-day control of their livestock to the global concerns of the larger community: rain and peace. The unintelligible language of their prayers, their bizarre encompassment of masculinity and femininity, and their seniority that is also junior, all underscore their special status as outsiders inside.

Gender and Space

Why do Gabra men denigrate women but regard d'abella, the most prestigious men, as women? What, if not sex, organizes gender assignments? What relation, if any, exists between sex and gender? How does a gender system that is apparently independent of anatomical sex remain binary? In what remains of this discussion, I want to focus these issues—gender, sex, and binary structure—toward an understanding of the d'abella institution. I begin with a structural argument.

We have seen that gender is at least partly independent of sex. Anatomical sex cannot explain gender assignments in a society with male women. Instead of sex, gender seems to be tied to spatial notions of center and periphery, or in Gabra terms, *olla* and *ala*, "inside" and "outside." The spatial argument goes like this: Gabra boys must separate themselves not only from their mothers but also from domestic centers in ways that girls do not, and it is this preponderantly male inclination to distance themselves, to go outside, away from main camps, that indexes "outside" as masculine.[20] Outside places, points of dispersion, are dangerous, vulnerable to wild animals and enemies, relatively unsocialized, and often exclusively male. Conversely, it is women who define "inside," because they make and own the tents, the sine qua non of main camps. Women and inside spaces are locations of aggregation. Women are hubs of nomadic movements; mothers, lovers, wives, sisters, and woman friends are nexus points of return and departure. The idea of "inside" is feminine. If the objects of main camps, such as tents and water and milk containers, are smooth and round, the objects of satellite camps are things like hatchets and sticks and shepherd's staffs: sharp and straight (see also Boddy 1989). The activities are different. The ways one moves through space are different: a walk across camp is full of interruptions, distractions, and interests, made in fits and starts, and as such proceeds at a pace that is relaxed and meandering; a trek outside across the distances is fast and deliberate, focused on the ground ahead and the destination. The textures are different: tents are made with soft mats, while men's corrals are made of thorny branches and stones. There are social, economic, visual, textural, and esthetic differences between the spaces. Outside and inside are gendered by the sexes that generally (though not exclusively) inhabit the respective spaces; but spaces—the elements and practices of those spaces—organize the gender identities of individuals in them. When men return as d'abella to the main camp, the moral center, the inside of Gabra space, they become women.

Spatial concepts such as inside and outside are context-specific, especially for nomads, whose places, and hence spaces, are always changing (Prussin 1995). I suggest that Gabra concepts of "masculine" and "feminine" are detached from and independent of the biological sexes in much the same way that "inside" and "outside" are detached from and independent of the material landscape. Hence,

gender : sex :: spatial concepts : material landscape

"Inside" spaces suggest not only geographic but also moral, or ethnic, centrality, while "outside" spaces suggest geographic, moral, and ethnic marginality. "Masculine" gender represents the activities and characters required and sustained by outside places, while "feminine" gender represents the activities and characters of inside places. In this sense, gender categories function as Robert Hertz (1973) observed of the right and left hands, as orientations and relations with which to think about more complex affairs. The detachment of gender and spatial categories from sexed bodies and physical places allows Gabra to use the oppositions in creative ways, to "deconstruct" the categories in practice, if not in theory.

The Space Between

We have seen that spaces can be *simultaneously* inside and outside, and that persons can be *both* masculine *and* feminine. There are echoes here of Johnson's analysis of *Billy Budd*. In the Gabra case, it is not a matter of whether one is masculine or feminine, or whether a location is outside or inside. The answer lies along a continuum and is always in some sense *both* and *neither*. The meanings resonate with one another; they reverberate, each coloring the other in subtle ways. The d'abella are women: but the fact they are men shades the meaning of their femininity, just as the fact they are women shades the meaning of their masculinity. One cannot really understand them disjunctively as either men or women, but rather as both or neither, or something else "in the space between" (Johnson 1980).

Spaces, such as main and satellite camps, olla and fora, are both inside and outside—not indifferently but complexly so. A related dynamic can be seen to apply to the masculinity and femininity of d'abella. It is not simply a matter of jumping back and forth between frames; one is not here a man and there a woman, or here inside and there outside. Rather, there is an emergent ternary character that arises from the combination, and this character is itself ineffable, represented only by the juxtaposition of opposed attributes. In this sense, we can say that gender—as well as the contrast between inside and outside—is and is not binary. This, of course, is not a deictic use of the terms "inside" and "outside." In deictic usage, "inside" and "outside" are wholly context-dependent, much like the meaning of a pointed finger. One can say of a person that she is inside a tent, and when she leaves the tent, that she is outside the tent, and if she is still in camp, she is *inside* the camp though *outside* the tent. In this absurdly limited sense, she is both inside and outside. This is deixis.

The terms point at particular contexts; to say that she is both inside and outside, one simply switches frames. But in this narrow sense the terms are not robust enough to color one another.

In Gabra usage, however, the terms are more than simply deictic. The words *olla* (main camp, or inside), *kesa* (inside, as in "in a container" or "in a family"), *ala* (outside, wild desert), and *fora* (satellite camp) evoke images, places, and moments whose meanings are at once complex and specific. Ala is the space outside the tent *and* the wilderness beyond the horizon. To be located "inside" a family is to be located safely within a tent: the idiom Gabra use to ask someone the name of her or his clan is *Balbala tamu?*, "Which door?" Thus, "inside" and "outside" work as metaphors with particular source domains.[21] The terms embrace their opposites: meanings arise in relation to the opposite or from its lack. *Olla* necessarily evokes the olla/ala relation. It is like fish and water, cars and roads, prisoners and prisons: the relation is metonymic. Outside *contains* inside. Similarly, albeit more remotely, masculinity is related to femininity, because in the Gabra view each causes, or *enables*, the other. The meanings are entangled. The absence of the other makes each incomplete; it binds the other to its lack and creates a pair, the halves of which cannot be considered discretely, without regard to the other (Derrida 1974). I say more about this below.

One connection between outside and inside, masculine and feminine, is illustrated by the persons and activities in those sorts of places. At olla, the inside of Gabra space, d'abella perform rituals that bless camels: they supervise sorio sacrifices. At sorio, camel's milk is poured into the flow of blood from the sacrificed sheep or goat, and the mixture is sopped up with clumps of grass and painted on the right sides of camels in the herd, thereby ensuring the animals' health and fertility. At the olla, camels are cared for with ritual blood and milk, itself a unity of oppositions. At fora, the outside of space, young men tend camels by taking them to ripe pastures and, when necessary, to wells. They do this to ensure the camels' health. Rituals, as I have said, cannot be performed at fora, only at olla. Thus, camels at fora are cared for by men's husbandry, with grass (and leaf browse) and water. In both places the well-being of camels is the unifying goal. We have seen that ceremonies such as sorio sacrifices imitate what people do in the rainy season: they come together, they feast, they celebrate, they give thanks to Waaqa, they pray for peace and rain. The gathering in the rainy season and the gathering for sorio rituals are separate moments, but they refer to each other: they are about the same things, rain and peace. Similarly, while olla and fora are separate places with different activities, they are nevertheless united by the health of camels. If one place is masculine and involves tasks performed by men, and the other is feminine and involves rituals supervised by men who are women, and if such concepts as masculinity and femininity are defined and given shape by these separate yet united activities, then the concepts are also defined and given shape by a common meaning—the health and care of camels (and therefore of human beings). Masculinity and femininity, inside and outside, are different qualities and sorts of places, and they mean different things, but they also mean the same thing. They encompass one another. Thus, to say only that men become women when they return as d'abella to the main camps, the structural and feminine centers, misses a more important and dynamic relation between the two places and types of men. In the Gabra world view, it is the unifying relation *between* the opposed places, persons, and moments that gives each its meaning.

Separation, Attachment, and Ambivalence

Despite their apparent complementarity, Gabra oppositions are also charged with conflict. As I have said all along, these camel-herding nomads must contend with the contradictory imperatives of separation and attachment. I have sought to show the many levels on which this dilemma occurs. The problem can be said to begin at birth with each infant's separation from its mother (Freud 1949, 1959; Mahler 1968; Pine 1971). But over an individual's life the problem expands like a fractal, a mathematical structure which replicates a geometric pattern at ever-increasing scales. The relationship between self and other is forever problematic: individuals must distinguish themselves in some way yet maintain contact with an inevitably social home base. They want "outside" freedoms but depend on "inside" entanglements.[22] It is a pan-human dilemma, but it has particular saliency and shape among pastoralists. As Michael Meeker has observed of Dinka, Nuer, Somalis, and Bedouins, they "are all very different peoples with very different pastoral ecologies. However, the pastoral way of life of each is associated in varying degrees with compromise of patriarchal authority and a problematical relationship of self and other" (1989:154).

One dimension of the problem for Gabra is generational succession, because the son is variously separated from and attached to his father, or some patron with that role, and this relation, as Meeker says, is perpetually problematic. The problem is troublesome enough that the central institution for managing social, political, and religious affairs, the luba system, is generationally organized and therefore separates the social responsibilities and practices of fathers and sons, binding them in relation to each other by keeping them apart. There are rules about the different responsibilities of fathers and sons and their obligations to each other. Men may not marry until their mothers reach menopause. What this means, given local marriage patterns, is that fathers are often in their late fifties or sixties before their first sons marry and set up households. There may be many reasons for such an arrangement, not the least of them oedipal (see Paul 1982:30; 1996b:17–33): late marriage delays the son's desire and need to supplant the father's interests with his own. Sons and fathers are ambivalent about each other. Sons need their father because he is titular owner of the family livestock until his death. He is their prototype for manhood. At the same time, the father frustrates his sons' efforts to become men by delaying their marriage and ownership of animals. Fathers need their sons because only sons can manage the day-to-day affairs of the herds. But as a man's physical powers diminish, his dependence on sons grows more acute and his control of livestock more illusory. To the extent that the luba system organizes these tensions, d'abella formally represent this ambiguous status of old men. They are valued fathers, owners, and senior men, but they are also (or their sons want them to be) increasingly feeble and out of touch with the day-to-day management of livestock.

The father's seniority over sons softens as his de facto control over the livestock erodes. But while the father's power over his herds diminishes, his authority over ritual and tradition—over culture—grows, for it is the prayers and activities of d'abella that bring rain, keep peace, and sustain life. The father's formal authority manages to increase at the same time the sons' virtual authority over the family's herds increases. It is a clever resolution to the vexing problem of succession (see Barth 1981). That it is not entirely convincing is suggested by the d'abella's complaint that they have nothing left but prayers, that they are "giraffes among sheep."

Overlying the ambivalence men feel toward fathers and sons is their ambivalence toward women, particularly women's reproductive powers. There is an extensive literature on men's envy of women, whom men imitate and belittle (Bettelheim 1962, Dundes 1976, Herdt 1981, Stoller and Herdt 1982, Paul 1982, 1996a). The combination of veneration and denigration is a classic sign of envy (see Klein 1957:6; Segal 1974:40; Paul 1996a:1–2). Gabra men are not exempt: they claim that what men do in the reproduction department is better than what women do (witness their giving "birth" to tradition and hence life itself at Jila Galana), and they denigrate women's contributions. Men call women, even older women, "children," which among other things denies them their reproductive capacity. I return to men's role in reproduction later.

Gender in the Life Cycle

D'abella represent an entire life's narrative. They are men who as boys around their mother's tent made clay camels with spit and dirt and shot birds and lizards with bows and arrows. Then, as young men, they took care of animals in distant fora camps. Later they married and reared children, and now as senior elders they have returned to main camp, the location of tents and ritual action, to pray for peace and rain and to supervise the ceremonies whose successful completion will ensure the reproduction of Gabra society. If gender is implicated in space, then it is also implicated in time, because movements through space between "inside" and "outside" occur at particular moments of the day, in the seasonal and ceremonial cycles, and throughout the life course. These movements have an ideal structure—a going forth and a return. This is what elders pray for: that when sons leave with animals to pasture, they will return. And it is for their return that elders give thanks. The journey forth is necessary, but incomplete without the return. By embodying oppositions such as masculine and feminine, outside and inside, the d'abella represent not just the return but the entire journey.[23]

Life stories have an idealized structure of going and returning, but as we saw with Galgalo Shonka and Wario Elema, they vary in myriad ways. Boys leave the immediate confines of camp to look after lambs and kids and return late in the day. Older boys leave main camp for distant satellites to look after livestock and return in the rainy season or for periodic sacrifices. Women set off with camels to distant wells and return, sometimes two days later, with water. Young men seek adventures, wage wars, steal livestock, kill wild animals, and return to tell about them. Men, who have focused much of their life's attention on livestock whose sustenance depends on what can only be found outside camps, return in old age to main camp to advise younger men, offer blessings, and say prayers that ensure peace and rain.

I want us to look carefully at the internal dynamics of the ideal life course. The course involves a departure from inside to outside and a return from outside to inside (Figure 18a). Inside, as I have said, is feminine, at least in its initial meaning: children start out life with mothers and, in fits and starts, leave them. Outside is masculine: in the Gabra view, the inclination to separate is a masculine one. A man's life thus involves a departure from a feminine location to a masculine one and a return from masculine to feminine (Figure 18b). (Locations, of course, are never fully masculine or feminine; these are ideals.)

Young boys at the center yearn for the masculine margins (Figure 18c). They claim increasing responsibility for tending animals, signaling a desire to join fathers, brothers, and other older males in the satellite camps. I remember a four-year-old boy named Adano who burst into his mother's tent shouting, *Ayo! Ayo! Ani imole bobaha indema!* "Mommy! Mommy! I am going to look after the lambs and kids!" Then he bounded off, barefoot and naked except for a tattered cloth over his shoulder and a stick in his right hand. What boys do not have—age, maturity, strength, independence—they desire, and the lack informs their longing. Boys and young men desire the dangerous distances, for it is only there that they can make good their identification with fathers and other men. The hardships of *fora* camps are romanticized by men as strengthening, toughening, hardening, and enlarging them as men. They gaze back at main camp beyond the horizon with a certain scorn for the soft femininity of the easy life there. From outside, inside looks feminine. The feminine inside is of course both repellent and desirable to young men (Figure 18d). They return to the main camps to visit their mothers, sisters, lovers, and friends, to drink milk, dance, and tell stories, to check in with their fathers. Their adventures outside are meaningless without an audience otherwise deprived of the same experiences.

Later, as the men marry in their thirties and forties, their interests and responsibilities become divided between main and satellite camps. When the father is too old to visit his animals, the sons (particularly firstborn sons) take his place as senior husbandmen, and their interests expand to include the welfare of the entire herd, not just the livestock in one *fora* camp. As sons become husbands and fathers themselves, their interests expand further to include the affairs at main camp and the wider Gabra community. They borrow and lend animals to others, and these arrangements lead to misunderstandings, disagreements, and obligations. They become entangled in disputes as contenders and as judges. The privileged center of the universe, from the point of view of these men, is less and less the particular satellite camp they happen to inhabit and

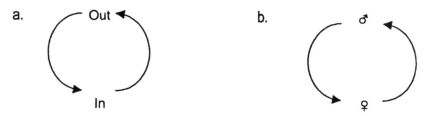

Figure 18a–b. Changing orientations over the life course of men.

Figure 18c–d. Shifting orientations of boys and young men.

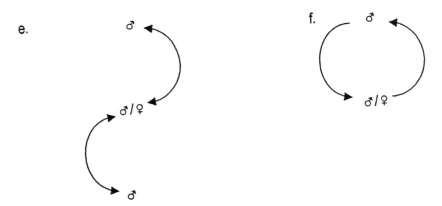

Figure 18e–f. Orientations of men late in life.

more and more the main camp around which the satellites orbit. As a man matures, so does the circumference of his concerns (Figure 18e).

Finally, as a father ages and becomes less able to follow livestock, and as his sons mature and become more responsible, the father remains increasingly at main camp, concerned with political and ritual affairs, settling conflicts, and saying prayers. His status, as I said, is at once elevated and diminished. The d'abella institution formally organizes this stage in the life cycle (though as I said, imperfectly: since the luba system is based on generation rather than age, not all d'abella have lost their vigor, and not all who have are yet d'abella). The d'abella's mixed feminine-masculine identity represents his ambiguous status. He is at once a senior man with "outside" interests in animals and a woman with "inside" interests in rituals and prayers.[24] D'abella are men who have lived outside, at the margins, and have returned to the inside, the center; they encompass the entire life journey (Figure 18f).[25]

The d'abella's return to the center is the completion of a cycle, and as such it involves something on the order of a return to infancy. This is not such a bizarre thought. Gabra are explicitly nonlinear in their understanding of time: the past repeats itself (see Robinson 1985, Tablino 1991, 1998). The generation system is cyclical, bringing men full circle through a round of roles and responsibilities. In the Borana *gada* system, after which the Gabra luba system is modeled, the d'abella grade (called *dabballe*) is the first in the sequence, rather than the last, and consists ideally of little boys—who like Gabra old men are feminine (Legesse 1973, Baxter 1978). In the cyclic sense, a Gabra boy begins at the inside, ventures out as a man, and returns to the inside as an old man to repeat his experience as a boy. This is one explanation for the jocular relationship between grandfathers and grandsons: they are structural equals.

The life-cycle explanation, however, remains incomplete, because it says nothing about why d'abella are feminine. If they are simply returning to their origin, why not make them symbolic boys instead of symbolic women? Perhaps, as I said, it is because d'abella return to a feminine space—a place of mothers as well as boys. But these structural interpretations, whether they cast the old men as "boys" or "women," fail to account for the other side of the d'abella's ambiguity. They address the d'abella's loss of status but say nothing about their elevated status as prayer-givers, ritual supervisors, and bearers of tradition. How does their being women square with their ritual *seniority*?

Women's Supplement

Men's ambivalent attitude toward both places, main camps and satellite camps, puts them always in the position of desiring what is absent but present elsewhere: at olla, they desire the freedom of fora; at fora, they desire the security and comforts of olla. Jacques Derrida's critique (1974) of Jean-Jacques Rousseau's *Confessions*, particularly the latter's use of the term "supplement," is useful here, because the ambiguity of the supplement captures the slippery dynamics of men's ambivalent desires.

Rousseau wrote about the difference between speech and writing, and following Plato, he regarded speech as more authentic, present, or real than writing. Writing, in his view, imitated speech but never quite accomplished the interpersonal communication possible with direct speech. Rousseau noticed, however, that he communicated his thoughts more clearly and accurately in writing than in speech: "If I were present" in a conversation, Rousseau wrote, "one would never know what I was worth," since shyness would inhibit his speech (quoted in Derrida 1974:142). It is Derrida who points out the paradox: writing, though a false imitation of speech, is nevertheless truer than speech. Rousseau, Derrida explains, "valorizes and disqualifies writing at the same time" (1974:141). For Rousseau, the relation between writing and speech is much the same as that between masturbation and copulation. Masturbation, like writing, is an imitation motivated by a lack—in this case the lack of a sexual partner. Masturbation is a faint imitation of copulation, but because it represents a "perfect" union between sexual partners, who are in fact one in the same person, masturbation trumps copulation as writing trumps speech.

Rousseau says that writing supplements speech. In French, the word *supplement* means both "addition" and "replacement." Derrida draws out the term's essential ambiguity: if "supplement" means "addition" then it is superfluous—it simply adds to what is already there; if it means "replacement" then it is necessary, since its presence excludes what it replaces. The singular term contains an ambiguous opposition. It is the same ambiguity as in Rousseau's observations about writing, which is at once a false imitation of speech and a truer expression.

What intrigues Derrida is the implication of this complex understanding of "supplement" for the meaning of such oppositions as writing and speech. Rather than simply opposing each other, each pole bears a critical relation to its opposite: it contains the very property the lack of which defines it as its opposite's opposite. Writing, which is supposed by Rousseau to be essentially false compared to speech, is actually capable of being truer than speech. As Barbara Johnson explains, "A and B are no longer opposed, nor are they equivalent. Indeed, they are no longer even equivalent to themselves. They are their own difference from themselves" (1981:xiii). The impulse to write is the same as the impulse to speak: to articulate across a divide of understanding. Writing and speech are both motivated by the desire to erase difference, or to alter a relation of difference. Speech already implies difference and alienation, which it sets out to overcome; speech itself is no more substantive or true than its supposed imitation.

D'abella in this sense *supplement* women, and here the term must be understood to retain the blurry and dynamic distinction between "addition" and "replacement." D'abella say they are women, but they readily acknowledge that they are not the same as women: they do not dress like women, or act like women, or fulfill any of the same functions as women. In this sense, they are supplements—that is, *additions*, augmenting the capacities that women possess otherwise. But d'abella are also *replacements* of women: they serve a necessary function which is analogous to what women do but also something women cannot do. D'abella supplement women both as additions and as replacements.

What about women do d'abella supplement?

D'abella supplement women's reproductive capacity. In the ceremony most identified with d'abella, Jila Gilana, d'abella "give birth" to tradition and therefore to life itself. D'abella enter seclusion just as women do after childbirth, and both seclusions are called *ulma*. Moreover, d'abella supplement a particular sort of reproduction: the reproduction of sons, which in this patriarchal society is the paramount goal of marriage.[26] The preeminence of sons explains the significance at marriage of the groom's mother's sandal, which the groom uses while igniting the marriage fire. The mother passes to her son the torch, so to speak, not so much of reproduction generally but of reproduction of sons specifically. Earlier I described the crown worn by married Gabra women (*malmala*), which after a woman has borne a son is completed with a metal piece across the forehead, making the whole *korma*, or "bull," like the d'abella's turban. The woman receives this metal piece, which signifies that she is the mother of a son, from her mother-in-law's own crown. A man whose wife failed to deliver a son would come under considerable pressure from his family to marry a second wife. The generic blessing from d'abella is not "bear children" or "get daughters" but *ilman d'ungat*, "kiss a son." The entire marriage ceremony can be read as a means toward getting sons.

It is men's envy of women's centrality in biological reproduction that moves them to denigrate women's contributions at the same time as they lay claim to doing something analogous to women, only better. They do this by shifting the meaning of "reproduction" away from biological reproduction, at which women have men beat hands down (Paul 1982; 1996a:2), to cultural reproduction—by which I mean prayers and rituals—at which men can be seen in Gabra society to play the central role. Gabra appear to be unique in claiming that men become women. In other societies where men are said to possess special reproductive powers, they do so as men *in extremis*—"The first order of business in being a man is: don't be a woman" (Stoller and Herdt 1982:34; see also Herdt 1981, Godelier 1986, Donham 1990, Gilmore 1990; but compare Matory 1994, Wikan 1977).

Why, then, do Gabra men become women? I think it has to do with the confluence of the two ambivalences that I have been discussing: one concerning women, whose capacities are both denigrated and envied; and the other concerning elders, who are both senior and junior, venerated and belittled. Womanhood serves Gabra as a "double-edged" metaphor, which expresses the complex position of d'abella in precisely the arena where they are said to hold special powers: reproduction.

Paul has pointed out that human growth and development require not only the biological information of genes, provided by sexual reproduction, but also the cultural information provided by interactions with caregivers and others in society (see Paul 1990, Boyd and Richerson 1985, Geertz 1973b). To paraphrase Simone de Beauvoir, one is not born but rather becomes a son, and to do that he requires a model (or models) other than his mother. This is where d'abella, as senior fathers, fulfill a reproductive function analogous to women's reproductive capacity but quite out of women's reach: d'abella, as men who are women, reproduce themselves. This is one aspect of human reproduction at which men have women beat hands down.

It is at this point that Derrida's understandings of the dynamic and ambiguous *supplement* are useful, because the meaning of the d'abella's femininity is complex and ambiguous in the same way as the supplement. D'abella, as women's supplements, are at once faint imitations and necessary replacements. Gabra understand reproduction and generativity through the trope of sexual reproduction. In the latter sense, d'abella are superfluous additions to women: imitations. They are women, but they cannot do what women can do. On the other hand, the task of reproducing Gabra sons could not be done without Gabra men—without the cultural information only they possess, over which d'abella serve as the responsible midwives. In this sense, d'abella are women's necessary replacements. Women simply cannot do what men can do in this respect. Ultimately it is not a question of whether d'abella are women or not. D'abella are women

Figure 19. A Gabra community moves camp. The family's camel herd marches in front and a line of camels loaded with tents and other possessions follows. Gabra use male camels as draft animals, but only people who cannot walk ride them.

and they are not women; they are neither women nor not-women; they are both men and women.

Conclusion

We must read the last analysis, concerning d'abella as supplements, with the previous analyses in mind; the successive interpretations do not displace one another but together form a complex explanation. D'abella are implicated not only in gender, but also in the spatial distinction between outside and inside; in the generational distinctions of seniority and succession; in the narratives of departure and return; in the reproduction of other men, who will replace them; and in the replication of tradition (*ada*) and therefore of life itself (*finna*). Each dimension—gender, space, seniority, succession, personal narrative, and reproduction—is fraught with conflict, a source of mixed feelings and ambivalent attitudes. No distinction occurs in isolation. My argument is that the d'abella and their attendant femininity can only be understood as a layering of various overlapping oppositional structures, which are perhaps best represented by the conundrum "men who are women" but are by no means limited to the opposition of gender. It is not simply that d'abella are polysemic or multivalent. They are that, but they are also the ambiguous combinations, the spaces between poles and between oppositions that make these men not just senior and junior, but also senior and feminine, junior and masculine, outside women, and inside men.

D'abella instantiate the oppositional analogies of women being to men as inside is to outside, white to red, left to right, junior to senior, and so on. They are women because they are inside, white, left, and junior. But they also subvert the analogies by embracing the oppositions. They are not simply women, inside, white, left, and junior. They are also men who retain the associations of manhood. It is in their complex bothness that d'abella represent an imagined solution to the unsolvable conflicts of nomadic life.

EPILOGUE

But first it must be noted that even the division of a species into two sexes
is not always clear-cut.

—SIMONE DE BEAUVOIR, *The Second Sex*

Dugaan d'ira inadomsitu.
Truth will not turn a man into a woman.
(Literally "Truth will not make a man dull" or "diminish the man.")

—GABRA PROVERB

I TAKE IT AS AXIOMATIC that every person is problematically related to
everyone else. Each is a social product, and therefore inextricably bound
to others; yet each is distinct and different, a maker, an agent, a producer
(Simmel 1950:58; Berger and Luckmann 1966:61). I am intrigued by the
"bothness" of such a statement. The fact that we as persons are both
products and producers seems—like Denge Doko's claims about red and
white at the start, and so many other conundrums in Gabra symbolism—to
be at once contradictory and true.

This discussion has sought to shine light on why Gabra regard d'abella
as women. The running theme has been that opposites such as "man"
and "woman" are not as discrete, distinct, or separable as they seem.
We saw how Gabra spatial distinctions between "inside" and "outside"
are reversible and collapsible, as are distinctions of seniority and even
ethnicity. We saw how individuals were simultaneously attached and
estranged from the Gabra community. We saw how weddings use symbols of
inside and outside, attachment and separation, femininity and masculinity,
to represent a unity of disparate moments and forms. And we have seen
how d'abella, the elders in charge of ceremony and prayer, encompass
oppositions such as inside and outside, senior and junior, masculinity
and femininity—and by doing so represent the ambiguous and polysemic
"space between" the poles. Indeed, taking my lead from the Gabra, this is
what I sought to say about current debates in ethnography regarding structure and post-structure, or pattern and variation. These are all complex
oppositions, the poles of which are necessarily implicated in each other.

The point is not to smooth over differences between opposites. Pattern and variation, inside and outside, man and woman, senior and junior, separation and attachment, red and white, are different. They are *also* in some sense the same. Each pole in these oppositions, as we saw in the final discussion of d'abella as supplements, is *different even from itself*, and this internal difference confounds the difference between it and its opposite. The reader will remember how red (blood) is both junior and senior to white (milk) on the basis of different criteria: precedence and strength. Blood follows milk, making white senior in precedence, but milk is easily defeated by blood, making red senior in strength. The internal difference over what constitutes seniority complicates the relation between senior and junior and challenges the meaning of seniority.

Similarly, d'abella, as women's supplements, are superfluous additions and necessary replacements of women through their different contributions to the reproduction of sons, tradition, and Gabra life. To say either that women reproduce sons or that d'abella reproduce sons is to tell only part of the story. Men are opposed to women and defined as such, in part, because they lack the ability to bear children—they cannot reproduce life. Yet they are also essential players in the reproduction of sons, tradition, rain, and therefore life, and in this sense they possess in a cultural sense the very quality they lack (and women have) biologically.

This may seem like playing with words, but it is not frivolous. The complex and internally contradictory meanings of words and concepts articulate with the complexities and internal contradictions of social processes and institutions. They allow Gabra to represent and think about the contradictory and paradoxical imperatives they face. The constraints of camel husbandry on the Chalbi Desert insist that Gabra manage an uneasy and perpetually unsatisfactory truce between social aggregation and dispersion. Their response to these constraints involves seeing themselves generally, and d'abella particularly, as both inside and outside, senior and junior, men and women. It is the internal tension of the contradiction that makes Gabra culture interesting and meaningful to its participants. T. O. Beidelman has observed that "culture coheres precisely because of its profound internal differences and even because of its inconsistencies" (1986:202). These complexities, contradictions, ambiguities, and inconsistencies are all born out of basic binary differences.

Some gender theorists have rejected binary oppositional logics as simplistic and reductionistic: binary gender looks too much like binary sex, and contemporary thinkers are rightly suspicious of isomorphic relations between these categories. The reduction of gender to sex has been shown to be mistaken on several levels. Plenty of evidence demonstrates that sex differences do not always organize gender assignments. There is as much or more variation within genders as between them. Moreover, what constitutes sex difference is no longer clear. Sex has been shown to be as constructed a category as gender. The problem, however, with the wholesale rejection of sexed bodies and binary logics is that the people who are the subjects of ethnographic study use them to think about gender, though not in any simple or reductive way. The point of this book has been to show that attention to binary patterns in thinking about gender organization need not simplify or narrow the range of possible gender expressions. The fact that adjacent binary oppositions complement and distort each other suggests some of the variation, complexity, and ambiguity that are possible within and between oppositions. Without opposition there is no ambiguous "space between."

Gabra sex and gender are binary systems, but this does not reduce gender to sex or limit the possible expressions of gender to two. The relation between sex and gender is oblique: sex organizes space; space organizes gender. Sex, like gender, may be a cultural construction, but Gabra make a sex distinction that approaches universality: human bodies either have a vagina or a penis (but see Fuasto-Sterling 1993)[1]; only bodies with a vagina can bear children, and bodies with a penis cannot; in the Gabra view, these are the two sexes, *nad'eni* (woman) and *d'ira* (man).

Males and females inhabit the Gabra landscape with different frequencies; males are more often "outside" and females are more often "inside"— not absolutely, but generally enough that Gabra make these associations. I have discussed the different practices and esthetics of these places. When men return to the inside, to the main camps, as d'abella, not simply to dwell there more or less permanently but also to take charge of its rituals and prayers, to be disposed to the collective good, they become women. Of course, the fact males predominate in one place and females in another is already a matter of gender. My argument is partly, but not completely, circular. Females do go outside and males go inside, and at least in the latter case, this change of place transforms them and reorganizes their gender in ways that cannot be sufficiently explained by their bodies alone.

Gabra thus make two sorts of distinctions, not one that is generally glossable as "gender" (cf. Butler 1990). They distinguish between sexes and they distinguish between genders. Hence d'abella, male women. Gabra do not think d'abella are female; they think they are women. It is an important distinction. The argument of some gender theorists that sex is gender collapses into a single category what is more properly and complexly left as two. Sex, like gender, may be a construction, and its construction may be shaped by others, such as gender, but this fact does not make it the same as gender. Regarding sex and gender as separate and distinct categories expands the range of gender possibilities: a male woman is different from a female woman and a male man, and distinctions of this sort could not be made without an analytic difference between gender and sex.

As organizing principles, the spatial notions of "inside" and "outside" (or center and periphery) offer distinct advantages for Gabra over others that have been proposed, such as "culture" and "nature," or "village" and "bush." The latter distinctions, though important and formative in some societies, may not occur everywhere, or everywhere the same way; and where they do, they may be too specific and concrete to resonate with the multiple tones and shadings of "inside" and "outside."

I have proposed a middle passage for thinking about Gabra gender, one that does not exclude sex or sexed bodies as relevant factors but also looks elsewhere, beyond sex, to understand gender. I find in the inside/outside polarity, charged as it is with the seminal dilemmas surrounding attachment and separation, aggregation and dispersion, a way of understanding how Gabra use gender concepts. Such distinctions are complex. What constitutes inside and outside shifts, just as what constitutes masculinity and femininity; the opposites encompass one another. But that is just the point: the triangulation of binary space (both physical and moral), sex, and gender offers exponentially more, not fewer, permutations of possible gendered meanings than does gender alone, as a single overarching category, or gender and sex together. It offers a way to describe and understand gender's complexity without reducing gender to a simple formula, simplifying gender beyond recognition, or losing its coherence in the myriad particulars.

Postscript

My wife, Carol, and I used to climb the stony escarpment above the dry Chalbi plain to see the sunrise. One morning we found the full moon about to set in the west while the sun was climbing over the horizon in the east. For a few moments, both orbs held the sky at once: the white moon, powdery as chalk, and magenta sun, dangerous as blood. Gabra, I have said, organize much of their ritual life around phases of the moon, and the full moon, *gobana*, marks the transition from the nights of lightness of the waxing moon to the nights of darkness of the waning moon, when the moon rises later and later and finally not at all. The full moon bridges the difference between light and dark; it occurs in the space between, and when it sets, shares the sky with the rising red sun.

NOTES
REFERENCES
INDEX

NOTES

Prologue

1. Denge Doko is a pseudonym. I use people's real names in this book, but occasionally I change names, and say so when I do, to protect identities.

2. There is a desert flower which blooms after the rains that Gabra call *gaale Waaqa*, "camel of god" (*Gloriosa superba*). The flower is a brilliant red; its tuberous root, which some say resembles a camel, is white. The plant is notable because it encompasses both red and white.

3. After the men got rid of Banoye, they reckoned with another woman, Qalliti, who outwitted them at every turn. Men finally conquered women through concerted action: they made them all pregnant. The psychodynamic interpretation is fairly clear: men overthrew women by leaving their mothers, asserting adult sexuality, and becoming lovers and husbands (Wood 1997a:374–392).

4. Indeed, to cast these patterns in the past tense would seem strange and disturbing to my Gabra friends and informants.

5. See Kassam and Megerssa (1994) for a discussion of the importance of these concepts in Oromo-speaking societies, such as the Gabra.

Chapter 1

1. François Dosse (1997:17) indicates that French theorists do not make the distinction that Americans do between structuralism and poststructuralism. In France, all the different forms of structuralism apparently fly a structuralist flag.

2. By contrast, Gabra conceive their divinity, Waaqa, as singular, or one, *toko*, that dwells away from Earth, *lafa*, in the sky, which is called *waqa*. Lafa/waqa is a basic opposition: the sky is far away, elsewhere, the other side, not here.

3. Robert Paul (personal communication) brought the distinction between "binary" and "dual" to my attention.

4. The word *différance* is Derrida's coinage. It combines the meanings of "difference" and "deferring," in the sense of putting something off in time. Derrida capitalizes on the term's inherent ambiguity (1982; see also Johnson 1981).

5. This in itself was not new. E. E. Evans-Pritchard (1940) had made the same observation of the Nuer in a nonstructuralist though certainly structural analysis.

6. These include clans or classes; groups or units; groups between whom marriage is prescribed or those where marriage is prohibited; exchanges where sexes are distinguished or those where sexes are merged; and groups for whom residence after marriage is significant or those for whom it is insignificant (Lévi-Strauss 1963:159–160).

7. To these ethnographic concerns must be added the literature on hermaphrodism, since biology is also ambiguous about sex identity (see Fuasto-Sterling 1993, Herdt 1994).

8. See Bradd Shore (1981) and M. Llewellyn-Davies (1981), who discuss gender reversals. Leslee Nadelson (1981) offers mixed- and same-sex arenas as an alternative contrast to the male/female distinction.

9. This definition of hegemonic fields is related to Donald Donham's definition of "ideology" (1990:49), which expresses succinctly the concept of hegemony, the intellectual and moral legitimation of political rule, developed by Gramsci.

10. The term "deconstruction" comes, through Derrida, from Martin Heidegger's *destruktion* (Dosse 1997:18).

11. There are numerous examples of culturally organized contradictions. See, for example, Turner's (1957) discussion of the conflict between matrilineality and virilocality.

Chapter 2

1. Counting nomads, who do not relish being counted, is notoriously difficult. The 1989 Government of Kenya census lists 35,726 Gabra. The census, however, was widely mistrusted: some thought the figure was too low, others that it was too high. The census does not count Gabra in Ethiopia. In addition, it seems to combine Gabra Migo and Gabra Malbe, who regard each other as related but distinct groups. Migo are largely sedentary and nominally Islamic, residing at or near urban centers such as Moyale and Isiolo (see Schlee 1990:45). Malbe are mostly rural nomads. Few Malbe consider themselves Muslim, though there are Islamic elements in their culture. This book concerns Gabra Malbe.

2. Gabra prefer to own a mix of stock, getting the bulk of their milk from camels, meat from sheep and goats, and milk and meat from cattle. Camels are seen as most reliable because they are resistant to drought and disease, and cattle as least reliable. Cattle need too much water to live for long periods in the Chalbi Desert area; they are usually kept in camps at higher, better-watered elevations and brought down to the plains in the rainy season. Gabra west of North Horr (especially Alganna) seem to favor goats and sheep, while Gabra east of North Horr (especially Galbo and Odola) privilege camels. These generalizations are

based on dead reckoning and informants' reports, not on census data (see O'Leary 1985). The dry climate and salty soils permit no agriculture. Stockless Gabra have taken up farming at better-watered Marsabit Mountain and Hurri Hills, but the future of these farms is uncertain, given the unreliable rainfall.

3. Or there may be too much rain. The "short" rains of October-November 1997 became long and longer and did not stop until after February, giving some areas more rain in five months than they would usually get cumulatively in several years (Father Tablino, personal communication). The extreme rains brought tremendous disease and death to Gabra.

4. The generalization is historically and locally variable. The Gabra range has expanded and contracted in the past 150 years. In precolonial times it seems to have been concentrated farther north of the current range (Sobania 1980, but see Schlee 1989). During the British "peace," Gabra extended their range as far south as the Ewaso Ng'iro River. Shortly after independence in 1963, the Somali, or so-called "*shifta*" (bandit), rebellion occurred in eastern Kenya, and its violence drove Gabra north and west. A similar conflict between Borana and Laikipiak Maasai probably had a similar effect in the late 1800s (Sobania 1993, and see Galgalo Shonka's story, chap. 3). Nowadays, some Gabra of Alganna and Sharbanna phratries in the western part of the region articulate with Lake Turkana and follow a slightly different axis from the Galbo, Gara, and Odola of the center and east of the region. Regardless of the location of wells, the dynamic of alternating between water and pasture remains essentially the same.

5. The environment narrows the range of options available to Gabra but by no means determines outcomes. Rendille and Somali live in similar conditions with similar economies but have different herding strategies, social organizations, and world views (Schlee 1989, O'Leary 1985, Torry 1973, I. M. Lewis 1961).

6. There are also *arjalla*, satellite camps for small stock, sheep and goats, which include women. I discuss arjalla below. The "ideal type" satellite camp, at least in the eyes of men, is fora; it is the social opposite of main camp, or olla.

7. Gabra women's dress is much the same as Borana women's dress, except that Gabra women wear distinctive beaded anklets.

8. Following Bourdieu (1977) and Ortner (1989), I believe that gender is organized through ordinary practices. Practices, of course, are not perfectly divided between males and females. Girls as well as boys identify with camels; boys as well as girls identify with life in and around the tents.

9. I have wondered whether "women" is the right equivalent for *nad'eni*. It may after all refer to some quality shared by males and females, rather than to what I gloss as "women." But "women" preserves the sense I have that women, wives, mothers, are the primary "source domain" (Lakoff 1987) for a term that they extend to males metaphorically. This itself is a complex issue, analogous to the famous Bororo statement "We are parrots" or the Nuer "Twins are birds." In these cases, as well as the Gabra "D'abella are women," people know the difference

between categories at the same time as they assert identity across them (T. Turner 1991).

10. Gabra draw a sharp distinction between girls (*intala*) and women (*nad'eni*), defined by marriage. A girl may have no sexual contact with a man.

11. *Abbera* is also a general term of respect between a younger man and an elder.

12. Gabra women weave the mats, called *dasse*, like sturdy rugs, leaving fibers long on one side to form a thick, protective thatch.

13. Gabra seem to prefer two types of trees for fencing, though there are others: *d'ad'acha*, or *Acacia tortilis*, and *sigirso*, or *Acacia reficiens*. D'ad'acha has a long, straight thorn, like a toothpick; sigirso has a curved thorn like a cat's claw.

14. Except the olla yaa, where tents form a circle. Here sheep and goat corrals lie within the circle of tents and the camel corrals without, forming an extensive interlocking barrier around the entire camp. I also saw several ordinary camps that were much harassed by hyenas and circled up, with the vulnerable sheep and goats inside.

15. Hence the Gabra proverb *Iyesi bad'a argat dinqa oli hiqa*, "When a beggar gets into the front of the tent, he soon moves to the back."

16. See Torry (1973) and O'Leary (1985) for more detailed discussions of herd management, which I shall not attempt here.

17. To say "close of day" is only half right. The Gabra "day," *ayana*, a span of twenty-four hours and a named unit of a week, *torban*, begins after noon (see Tablino 1991). Tuesday, Talassa, ends at noon Tuesday when Wednesday, or Arba, begins. American and European calendars count daytimes; Gabra count nights.

18. Sorio Nagaya is a sacrifice, usually of a sheep or goat, performed in front of a family's tent on specified days during three auspicious lunar months: Somdera, Somdera Ege, and Yaaka. The months are known as "camel months," or *jia galla*. The sacrifices are thought to be especially beneficial to camels, and blood from the victim is painted on the sides of camels. If a father, mother, or eldest son is not present, a family does not perform sorio. Marriages are also held in these months (Tablino 1991; see chapter 4).

19. Women who are *chabana* (usually for sexual activity before they are married) are not only ritually outcast, like men, but socially outcast as well; they must leave the community, often being married off to Rendille.

20. Gabra eat only those wild animals that they perceive as having a domestic parallel. Thus they will eat giraffes because they are like camels, buffalo because they are like cattle, and several species of gazelle and antelope because they remind them of sheep and goats. Gabra will not normally eat birds, eggs, or fish (but see chapter 3). They kill lion, elephant, or rhinoceros for prestige, but they do not eat the meat.

21. Gabra say that killing enemies and taking trophies is done less frequently now than before the colonial era. I did not accompany men on raids during my

fieldwork. But I knew men who wore ivory *arbora* bracelets signifying they had killed, and I heard, from victims as well as raiders, many stories about raids, several of which occurred during my stay.

22. The Galayoli clan of Galbo is believed to have descended directly from Somali ancestors. An Odola friend told me that Odola descended from Garre Somali. He said that long ago a Somali leader visited them from Wajir, but they refused to return to Somalia with him because their camels preferred the Golbo plains of the present Gabra area. He left them the distinctive white d'abella's turban, so that although they could not read the Koran, they would thus remember their Islamic roots. See Schlee (1989).

23. Gabra are not alone in connecting inside with sociality. Susan Rasmussen (1996:14), in an analysis of Tuareg tents, argues that seminomadic Tuareg also see inside as public and social, outside as wild, dangerous, and solitary. Tuareg cosmology and mythology, she writes, "oppose the classic nomadic tent (*ehan*) and civilization on the one hand to the wild and solitude (*essuf*), on the other" (1996:17). See also Riesman (1977).

24. Yaa are permanently constituted camps some of whose officers and members change at transition ceremonies for d'abella. Each yaa is defined by three sacred objects—a drum, a horn, and a pair of firesticks—whose custodians and other elected leaders constitute the core community of the yaa.

25. The olla/ala distinction may function as a "key symbol" or "root metaphor." In this case, Gabra extend a logic from a familiar set of experiences to make sense of other, less familiar domains (Ortner 1973:1340–41; see also Lakoff and Johnson 1980 and Lakoff 1987).

26. Another story has a Borana son domesticating "wild" camels, an act that resulted in his father's banishing him and his generations to the arid Golbo plains below the Mega Escarpment.

27. One of Schlee's informants suggested that the name "Gabra" may be derived from *gabar*, a Borana word meaning "slave" or "vassal" (Schlee 1989:98; see also Maud 1904). Lambert Bartels (1983) notes that Matcha Oromo, far to the north in Ethiopia, use the word *gabaro*, or *gabare*, to refer to Oromo clans that do not descend directly from Borana (see also Haberland 1963:141–144; Hultin 1982; Kassam 1987:55; Hassen 1990:63ff.; Blackhurst 1996:246). Borana use the word *gabara* to mean "become a Gabra" (Leus 1995:318). Gabra who know Amharic said the cognate Amhara word *gabar*, "one who gives tribute," may have some relation to the name "Gabra." It could be that "Gabra" is derived from one or the other of these terms, but this is speculative. Even if true, it would not be clear what it meant historically.

28. Gabra, of course, would assert that the father is always the owner. Baxter (personal communication) has pointed out that livestock are a "bundle of rights . . . but, above all, a bundle of responsibilities." In this sense, fathers tend to have the primary rights, while sons more often have primary responsibilities.

Still, sons exercise considerable control over livestock and certainly entertain the fantasy that they are owners.

29. The story goes that Alganna used to be senior, but in a dispute, Alganna and Sharbanna agreed to yield seniority to the one whose tethered sheep survived a night in the wild. Sharbanna tricked Alganna by removing the Sharbanna sheep in the middle of the night and returning it before dawn, so Sharbanna's sheep was safe when Alganna's was being eaten by hyenas. They gained seniority through deception.

30. See also Donald Donham's discussion (1990:110–111) of the Maale idiom of ownership, which is much the same as Gabra. Ownership, like seniority, is fraught with complexity, since "owning" animals is contingent on claims by others on the animals (see Storas 1991 for a somewhat analogous case of Turkana livestock relations). Gabra inheritance is based on primogeniture; the firstborn inherits all stock that the father has not already promised to others, including junior sons. Thus, at a father's death, some animals will go to junior sons.

31. Gara are seniormost among the five phratries by virtue of performing their transition ceremonies for d'abella one year ahead of the rest.

32. Red and white are important symbolic colors, linked with blood and milk. At sorio sacrifices (Sorio Nagaya) during the three camel months, when the animal's throat is slit open, the owner pours milk into the flowing blood, and in this way makes a unity out of duality.

33. The terms *gada* and *luba* are metonyms. *Gada* is the name, signifying "rule," of a specific grade within the Borana system; *luba* is the general word for a generationally organized set, or group, of men, whatever its grade. The word *luba* may derive from the passive verb *lubboma*, "to be forced or ordered."

34. This is true for Galbo and Odola. In Alganna, there are two sets between fathers and sons (Torry 1973, 1978).

35. In other phratries, qomicha and yuba grades are collapsed, so sons enter the system as political elders when their fathers retire—a considerably different solution to the problem of succession between fathers and sons, but one that nevertheless supports the argument that tension between the generations is an important dynamic in the system.

36. See also chapter 5. Among the Borana, too, a man has only to touch a *gadamoji*, a leader, or his *kalacha* headpiece to find inviolable sanctuary (Baxter, personal communication).

37. The descriptions of the grades are ideal types. I knew rude and aggressive d'abella, and qomicha who were old and wise and ritually oriented. But the generalizations do conform to what Gabra told me about the grades and what I observed as general traits aspired to by men in them.

38. In the past two centuries, transitions seem to have occurred every fourteen, twenty-one, or twenty-eight years—always multiples of the seven-year "week"

cycles mentioned above. Gara hold transition ceremonies, called Jila Galana, in Qamisa, or Thursday, years; the other phratries follow in Gumata, or Friday, years. According to Robinson (1985), Gabra inducted new generations of d'abella in 1867 and again in 1888. Tablino (1988) and Robinson (1985) have reported that subsequent transitions were held in 1909, 1923, 1951, 1972, and 1986. Tablino (personal communication) said he has heard that the Gara phratry will hold its jila in 1999, which means Galbo will likely hold theirs in 2000.

Chapter 3

1. I tape-recorded interviews with Galgalo Shonka and other elders, which Yara and I later transcribed and translated. Galgalo liked being recorded and remarked how the tape captured his words exactly as he said them.

2. The conflation of past and present is also a theme in Crapanzano's (1980:35) life history of Tuhami, a man who weaves past and present toward an emergent truth.

3. The story that follows illustrates Gabra-typical oscillations of dispersion and aggregation.

4. Galgalo spoke no English. What follows is a translation by my assistant Yara and me.

5. Hodson (1970) refers to lowland Borana as "Hofta." The word may refer to Borana who have been "left behind" or excluded from the gada generation-set system (Torry 1978).

6. The fact that the women remarried indicates that Gabra did not regard their marriage to the white man as legitimate, since Gabra women may not remarry after divorce, abandonment, or widowhood.

7. Tablino (1989) and Robinson (1985), who have studied Gabra concepts of time and history, report that this year corresponds to 1899. Galgalo's narrative seems to collapse events that others (see Robinson 1984, Tablino 1989, Sobania 1980) say occurred, in reverse sequence, in 1899 and 1900. I am less interested in the actual order of events than in their significance to Galgalo.

8. In other accounts the raiders were Turkana. In fact, Galgalo seems to collapse different attacks associated with a Laikipia Maasai-Samburu-Rendille alliance in the eighteenth and nineteenth centuries (Oba 1996).

9. Galgalo Shonka did not know his full name. He was probably Alfred W. Haylett, a missionary in Marsabit in the early 1930s (Tablino 1999).

10. Also known as David Dabasso (Maciel 1985; Baxter, personal communication).

11. Evelyn Mary Haylett. She lived only several months in Marsabit before she died (Tablino 1999).

12. Presumably a Mr. and Mrs. R. Hacking (Tablino 1999).

13. This is myrrh, resin from a tree (*Commiphora abyssinica*) that grows in the region, which Gabra chew and affix to their eyebrows at new moons and on days of sacrifices.

14. Galgalo and his wife, Ele, had eight children, six sons and two daughters. The third, fourth, and sixth-born sons had all gone to school. The third, Denge, continued on to seminary and became an Anglican priest at Bubissa. The first two sons and the fifth remained, unschooled, with their father. When I knew the family, the youngest was attending high school at Marsabit. Neither of the daughters, now married, attended school.

15. Galgalo Shonka died in January 1996, after I left the field (Tablino, personal communication). His eldest son, Elema, died of a puff adder's bite in 1998 (B. J. Lindquist, personal communication.)

16. There are many examples of close relationships between ethnographers and marginal, albeit articulate, informants, such as Victor Turner's (1967) friendship with Muchona and Crapanzano's (1980) with Tuhami.

17. Maikona's adult male population numbered more than three hundred during my fieldwork, yet there were fewer than fifty regular wage-earning jobs.

18. Corinne Kratz discusses the similar case of an Okiek man, abandoned as a child by his father, creating a life's narrative around this problematic relationship (1997).

19. Wario and I spoke with each other mainly in English.

20. Gabra women are not supposed to remarry. This, her second marriage, would not have been regarded as legitimate. It is one among many reasons that Wario's father was considered odd.

21. She left at night so her husband or other elders would not try to stop her. It is also customary to make long treks at night to avoid the heat of day.

22. Ayana was said to have originated far to the north in Ethiopia, founded by a man named Sheikh Hussein. For more on Ayana in and around Ethiopia, see Trimingham (1965), H. S. Lewis (1984), Hassen (1990), and Aguilar (1994). Baxter reports that Ayana was practiced by Burji and Konso in the early 1950s but by the 1980s had spread to most settlements and other ethnic groups (personal communication).

23. *Mora* is a prized strip of stomach fat that is taken from a slaughtered animal. The animal sacrificed after a child's birth is named after the fat. *Elemo* is a young male sheep; *korbes* is a young male goat.

24. The North Horr mission sits surrounded by a fence within the permanent settlement near the North Horr wells.

25. If they used the word "Oromo" they were probably using the broader class term to emphasize a connection between themselves and the Borana-Gabra students. On the other hand, they may have said "Orma," but "Oromo" would have been a more familiar word to Wario; Gabra call the Orma "Wardaa."

26. *Changaa* is KiSwahili for distilled alcohol, or "moonshine."

Chapter 4

1. I was struck at weddings by the symbolic elaboration of ordinary things—the daily work of pitching tents, building corrals, tending animals. In fact, the idealized performance of the ordinary seemed to be characteristic of ceremonies generally. This is instructive. At the very least, the ritual elaboration of the ordinary suggests what aspects of life Gabra believe need rehearsal, formalization, and divine attention. The ordinary is also metaphoric. Like most of us, Gabra used familiar objects and practices to think about less familiar things, to express complex and transcendent meanings, and to resolve what cannot be resolved (Turner 1967, Lakoff and Johnson 1980).

2. There are other ceremonies that I might have described in as much detail, such as men's initiation rites. The last transition ceremonies for d'abella, for instance, occurred in 1986, but before my fieldwork (Kassam 1987, Tablino 1989, Schlee 1990, and Stiles 1991 offer perceptive eyewitness accounts). I collected many Gabra memories of that series of events, some of which I recount later. The aim of this chapter is not to talk about d'abella, whom we turn to with full attention in the next chapter, but to illustrate a symbolic logic, a logic of reversal and juxtaposition.

3. The Roman Catholic church has baptized more than two thousand Gabra; the Church of the Province of Kenya (Anglican) estimates it has more than one thousand Gabra adherents. Two smaller missionary churches, the African Inland Church at Marsabit and Kalacha and the Evangelical Lutheran Church in Kenya at Marsabit, each have fewer than one hundred Gabra followers. I was unable to get estimates from Muslim missionaries, but Islamic friends believed that the number of Muslim Gabra equaled the overall number of Christian Gabra. Both were concentrated in urban centers (see also Tablino 1999, Daystar 1982).

4. The two Somd'era months are adjacent; Yaaka follows five months later. Since the lunar year of twelve months is shorter than the solar year, there is no enduring correspondence between Western and Gabra months. The months also cycle independently of the seasons.

5. Gabra elders complained that "modern" children who had grown up in towns or attended boarding schools were refusing arranged marriages in favor of love matches. Even then, however, many performed the traditional ceremonies in order to maintain membership in the community. One young man from Maikona, a university student in Nairobi, told me, "Unless I feel I should no longer be part of the community, I must marry the way these people are marrying. There is no shortcut."

6. Gabra kin terms regard cousins within the patriline as siblings, even those several times removed, as in the example here, and refer to them by the same name; hence, they are "classificatory" equivalents.

7. Torry's data show that, among the five phratries, Galbo married Galbo 83 percent of the time; Alganna married endogamously 76 percent; Gara, 63 percent; Sharbana, 56 percent; and Odola, 50 percent (1973:303). For marriages outside the phratry, each also showed striking preferences to marry from one or two other phratries.

8. Gabra seemed to prefer to marry within their phratry from the opposite moiety. I spent most time with Galbo, the most endogamous of the five phratries, whose senior Jiblo moiety was exogamous, preferring brides from clans of the junior Lossa moiety. Lossa men married either Jiblo brides, or Lossa brides from other clans. Outside Galbo, however, Torry (1973:301) found no particular moiety bias. My own data suggested considerable variation, and outside Galbo, little phratry endogamy. But like Torry, I noticed interphratry biases: Alganna and Sharbanna tended to intermarry, as did Galbo and Odola. These phratries also overlapped geographically and shared ritual and political affairs.

9. Gabra enjoy playing like this with words that sound like other words and have multiple connotations. In this way they share a certain affinity with Derrida. See also Turner's discussion of etymological play among Ndembu (1957).

10. Coffee was available in markets and shops at Marsabit and trading centers near water points. It came mainly, though not exclusively, from Ethiopia, and the coffee ceremony was surely an influence, via Borana, of highland Ethiopia on Gabra.

11. The pattern of groom's family going to bride's family was reversed if the groom's family lived in the yaa. The yaa camped in a circle rather than a line, and it sought to preserve the circle. Rather than have important members of the yaa leave for a marriage, creating a gap, the bride's family came to them.

12. Or two d'abella and two women—always an even number.

13. The word may be a compound of *sarma*, "respect" or "veneration," also the term for a camel given by a mother's brother to a man who has killed an enemy, and *muche*, "something small."

14. This is an important distinction indicating something about the different characters of d'abella and other elders. I take it up in the next chapter.

15. Waata called themselves Gabra if they lived among Gabra. They were said to be the remnants of supposedly autochthonous hunters and gatherers. Gabra denigrated Waata as people with poor pastoral skills, greedy to eat their animals rather than allow them to multiply; but Gabra also gave Waata ritual respect, in that their blessings were desired and their curses feared (Kassam 1986a; see also Kratz 1994 for a parallel relationship between Maasai and Okiek).

16. In town marriages, wedding guests increasingly were expected to bring money as a gift for the couple.

17. The bride did not help to build the tent at her own wedding. The wedding tent was pitched without her, while she spent the day outside camp tending her father's camels.

18. A brother or friend would often help him shave his scalp.

19. Only married men had stools. An unmarried man sat on the ground, a rock, his heels, or somebody else's stool. The barchuma or man's stool was carved from a single piece of wood, with a broad, round, concave seat and two rectilinear legs. The seat was around two feet in diameter, and the stool stood about a foot and a half off the ground. Strips of skin from animals the owner had sacrificed were tied around the stool's legs. The stool stood for its owner: if a man was away from home, his stool could occupy his place at ceremonies. Others might sit on someone else's barchuma, except his father and men of his father's generation, who would not. I often saw visiting men, gathered for prayers in front of someone's tent, ask earnestly about the owner of a stool they were about to sit on so as not to sit on a "son's" seat.

20. Collecting firewood was normally women's work. Except at fora, men fetched firewood only when a wife was secluded after childbirth and at weddings.

21. There are two sticks, each forty to fifty centimeters long, used for making a fire. One serves as base, with a small concavity the size of a pea carved in its side. It lies atop the sandal, swaddled in a tatter of old cloth and dry dung. The other serves as drill, one end whittled to a dull point. The drill rests in the groove and stands perpendicular to the base. The groom and his three companions—and any other men who want to join in—take turns rotating the drill vigorously between their palms, as if warming their hands or coiling clay, making the drill spin in the groove. Taking turns, the men soon have a whiff of smoke and an ember. Lifted to the wind in the piece of cloth, the dung blazes, and the blaze is set into a pile of kindling wood already prepared nearby. Only men made fire; women rekindled fires with existing coals in their own hearth or borrowed embers from a neighbor's. (Many men and women, of course, now use wooden matches.)

22. The translations are interpretations, meant to convey coherent meanings for expressions that are cryptic and idiomatic in the original.

23. The marriage ceremony echoed male circumcision, with its emphasis on turning away from boyish pranks and privileges toward the responsibilities of manhood. The boy's severed foreskin was burned by his mother in a fire she kindled with, among other things, broken arrows, the implements of boyhood. Like a groom, the boy preparing for circumcision bathed and removed his old clothes and, once circumcised, put on a new cloth. The circumciser received the boy's left sandal, and the mother his right sandal, gifts that emphasized the boy's new start in life, for he now required new sandals. The gifts also linked mother and circumciser as fellow agents of the boy's birth and development and foreshadowed the boy's marriage, when his mother would offer her right sandal as a platform for making the wedding fire.

24. The state when a man merely trembles is *irroqab*, or *irrokom*. It was not until I returned from the field that I realized this might be *irro qaba*, literally "he has a bracelet," and that *irro*, a special bracelet, may signify he has killed an

enemy in battle. Thus, it could be that heroes, who wear the irro bracelet, are more likely to control iwachis: hence, their restrained trembling is irroqab.

25. Selecting songs to include in this discussion was difficult. This song and the men's song above emphasize issues of solidarity and separation in ways that helped me to recognize the themes in others.

26. Gabra call both evening and morning stars *bakalcha*. What we consider different planets they regard as one, the center of the universe. The fire in the nabo of the yaa, from which all yaa households kindled their hearth fires, was also called *bakalcha*. I never heard Gabra call the marriage fire, the one built by groom and companions, *bakalcha*, but they did compare it to the nabo fire; and they stressed the importance of using this "outside" fire to start the first fire inside the couple's new tent. The marriage and nabo fires were thus connected and linked explicitly to a cosmological center. The goal at weddings seemed to be to hand over the bride about an hour before first light, which because the Chalbi is close to the equator occurs shortly after five a.m. the year around.

27. Compare the groom's request for gift animals with similar exchanges at Maasai (Spencer 1988) and Okiek (Kratz 1989) weddings.

28. The husband saved the foreleg bones of both *chibra* and *moila* (the sheep slaughtered before the wedding) sacrifices and hung them in a bundle from his leather kit inside the tent. When the wife delivered her first child, the husband hung the bones from a high branch in a thorny d'ad'acha tree, if the child was a boy, or a fruity, thornless mad'era tree, if a girl. Again we see a textural difference between the straight and thorny masculine character and the smooth and round feminine. I never found a Gabra who could explain the practice of hanging the chibra bones. High places are associated with Waaqa. The gesture could be a sort of thanksgiving offering to divinity for having provided a child prayed for at the wedding. More likely, according to Paul Baxter (personal communication), it distracted the evil eye (*buda*) away from the infant.

29. Or earlier, depending on the propitiousness or unpropitiousness of the day, Mondays and Thursdays being ideal, and Tuesdays, Wednesdays, and Saturdays particularly avoided.

30. Probably a reference to dawn, *bari*; hence, gifts for the beginning, or dawning, marriage.

31. See Torry (1973:324–327) for additional detail on these exchanges.

Chapter 5

1. The *malmala* crown worn by women is modified after a woman has borne a son, and then it is also called *korma*.

2. The qallu is a sort of hereditary high priest who serves in ritual contexts as an intermediary to the divine. All men of his clan, and certain other senior clans

in both moieties, are said to be minor qallu; they dispense the white clay used in making ceremonial paint and plastering d'abellas' turbans.

3. So laden with meaning is the hitu that when a d'abella retires he must undo its powers in a private ceremony by dipping it four times in a bowl of milk. The powers of the turban are unclear: d'abella collectively curse a person by placing its seam on the right side, rather than the left, of their head; this position makes the turban exert a dangerous force on the cursed. Non-d'abella are enjoined not to touch the turban, not only in respect for the institution but also, they said, because touching it would harm the uninitiated. Certainly the turban is a powerful symbol, representing the d'abella.

4. The reader will remember that the groom on his wedding night, fresh and clean and newly shaven, as if reborn, wears only plain white cloth; and rather than wear the customary *gombora* shorts, he wraps the white cloth around him like a sarong.

5. The term *d'iro* is a vocative meaning "men!" or "friends!" It is used by the groom at weddings to call men to sing. It also refers metonymically to animals stolen from enemies in a raid.

6. Alternatively, they had killed a lion, elephant, or rhinoceros.

7. As I have said, Waaqa is thought to enjoy nothing better than the sizzle and smell of frying coffee.

8. Goats are loud and aggressive, always bleating, while sheep are thought to be peaceful because they are comparatively quiet.

9. Words are powerful, and their use is controlled in other arenas as well. The reader will recall that in sodda (kin avoidance) relations established by marriage the names of certain affines may never be uttered, and if they are, a small gift must be given to restore respect.

10. D'abella are an elite group, but not a select group, since virtually all men become d'abella if they live long enough.

11. One might wonder whether the term *nad'eni* is appropriately translated as "woman" or "women." Perhaps it refers to some third quality in which women and some men participate (such as Bororo and parrots; see T. Turner 1991). There was, however, little question that Gabra saw women, married females, mothers of children with husbands and lovers, as prototypical nad'eni. Those women were a "source domain" (Lakoff and Johnson 1980, Lakoff 1987) for the meaning behind d'abella as women. Gabra recognized that calling d'abella *nad'eni* warranted explanation, while calling women *nad'eni*, in the ordinary use of the term, required no explanation.

12. Gabra are aware of women's red menstrual blood. It is a subject they did not willingly discuss with me, one that they seemed uncomfortable talking about. Women breastfeed babies for three years, during which period they are sexually abstinent. It occurs to me that menstruation is probably relatively rare: women are ideally amenorrheic, either pregnant or lactating. Menstruation may suggest

infertility, which would make it an unsavory topic and its blood an ominous sign. The color white's association with femininity may emphasize the link between femininity and reproduction.

13. This is analogous to the American notion that children do not fear Santa Claus, though of course they sometimes do.

14. I was once on a long journey with a d'abella, and when night fell I asked if it was all right for him to keep walking. He said d'abella may *continue* walking at night, so long as they walk to their own camp where they will be recognized.

15. They venture away from the tent "protected" with eyes blackened by charcoal, head covered, and carrying a staff. Women in *ulman* may be visited. The seclusion exempts women from work, giving them a long rest, during which time others, including their husbands, do their work for them, as in the time of Banoye.

16. See also Bettelheim (1962) and Shapiro (1989). "Predominant in the ethnographic record is evidence of how men have defined the reproduction of cultural instructions as an exclusively male prerogative" (Paul 1996a:19).

17. I did not witness the Jila Galana ceremonies; the last transition occurred in 1986, seven years before I went to the field, and the ritual would not be repeated again until 2000 at the earliest, five years after I left. However, I talked at length with Gabra about the rites. Kassam (1987), Tablino (1989, 1998), Schlee (1990), and Stiles (1991) offer perceptive eyewitness accounts of the 1986 ceremonies.

18. Father Tablino, who has written about Jila Galana, visited the site after the 1986 jila. He and other outsiders were excluded from this particular ceremony. He describes (Tablino 1989) four small stone enclosures, which may represent the north and south doorways of the nabo. His description does not completely square with what elders told me. The accounts I heard were no doubt cooked or truncated. My aim, however, is to describe not the event but what it meant to people afterwards.

19. Shivering suggests passion and strong feelings to Gabra, and the shivering man here may be linked to iwachis, the convulsions of men who lose their minds when singing songs about brave deeds. It occurs to me that it may also be linked with the initial convulsions of a slaughtered animal, since the man from Boru Umuro is positioned and treated as a sacrificial victim.

20. Girls must also separate themselves from their mothers, but their separation occurs within main camp, at the social center, reinforcing the association between the encampment and women.

21. Here I am following Lakoff and Johnson (1980), who explore how metaphor imports elements of the familiar and concrete to the less familiar and abstract.

22. This sort of tension is played out in the Gabra board game sadeka (Wood 1997a).

23. Across the gender divide, the literature is full of examples of women, especially late in life, changing gender identities, even becoming men or manlike

(see Evans-Pritchard 1940, Turner 1957, Skultans 1970, Oboler 1980, Poole 1981, Rasmussen 1987, 1997). The fact that we have a better understanding of the mutability of women's gender than men's reflects a bias toward women in gender studies generally (Gilmore 1990)—a bias this book may help to correct.

24. The split masculine/feminine identity of d'abella mirrors the mixed-sex demographics of the place where d'abella are most identified, the main camp. This is a key social division in Gabra society, the exclusively male arena of the fora camps and the mixed male-and-female arenas of the main camps. Leslee Nadelson (1981) called attention to this important social division in a study of an Amazonian society. In that case, rituals occurred in the exclusively male sphere. In the Gabra case, it is just the reverse: rituals are performed by men but always in the mixed arena.

25. See Bradd Shore's discussion (1996:207–231) of the Murngin master narrative, or "foundational schema," which involves an inside-outside walkabout, and therefore represents a similar case.

26. It always interested me that, while Gabra reckon human ancestries through males (and prefer males), they reckon camel ancestries through females (and prefer females). The lender of a female camel has ongoing rights in its female offspring; the lender of a bull has no such claims, even though herdsmen usually know the identity of a calf's sire. This fact of camel matrilines gives added meaning to the female *sarma* camel's wearing the bull camel's *jilba* collar. None of this is to suggest that Gabra do not know or care about the pedigree of a camel's male line, just that for ownership purposes it does not matter.

Epilogue

1. Gabra have no concept of human hermaphroditism, as far as I am aware. Assuming that hermaphrodites are born, as they must be, and their ambiguous status is apparent, they must be reared with a specific sexual assignment, expelled from society, or killed. My evidence for the last possibility is obviously thin, considering that I never heard of such a case. But there is precedent for infanticide in Gabra society. Gabra once killed twins, if firstborn, presumably because they were anxious about the duality of a status that is supposed to be unitary. Moreover, Gabra are greatly troubled, as I have mentioned, by the hyena, the females of which have an organ like a penis: the hyena personifies evil and wildness; it is the antithesis of humanity. A baby with ambiguous genitalia would probably frighten Gabra enough that they would want to kill it or to abandon it, which would probably mean giving it to a Waata family to foster.

REFERENCES

Aguilar, Mario. 1994. "The Eagle Talks to a *Kallu*: Waso Borana Ritual Perception of Ethiopia." In *New Trends in Ethiopian Studies*, vol. 2, *Social Sciences*, edited by H. G. Marcus, pp. 756–762. Lawrenceville, N.J.: Red Sea Press.

Aguilar, Mario. 1995. "African Conversion from a World Religion: Religious Diversification by the Waso Boorana in Kenya." *Africa* 65(4):525–544.

Almagor, Uri. 1989. "Dual Organization Reconsidered." In Maybury-Lewis and Almagor, eds., pp. 19–32.

Anderson, Perry. 1984. *In the Tracks of Historical Materialism*. Chicago: University of Chicago Press.

Andrzejewski, B. W. 1957. "Some Preliminary Observations on the Borana Dialect of Galla." *Bulletin of the School of African and Oriental Studies* 19:354–374.

Asad, Talal. 1973. "Two European Images of Non-European Rule." In *Anthropology and the Colonial Encounter*, edited by Talal Asad, pp. 103–118. London: Ithaca Press.

Bake, Gernot. 1991. "Water Sources." In *Range Management Handbook of Kenya*, vol. 2, edited by H. J. Schwartz et al., pp. 53–73. Republic of Kenya, Ministry of Livestock Development.

Bartels, Lambert. 1983. *Oromo Religion*. Berlin: Dietrich Reimer.

Barth, Fredrik, ed. 1969. *Ethnic Groups and Boundaries: The Social Organization of Cultural Difference*. London: Allen and Unwin.

Barth, Fredrik. 1981. "Role Dilemmas and Father-Son Dominance in Middle Eastern Kinship Systems." In *Features of Person and Society in Swat: Collected Essays on Pathans*. London: Routledge and Kegan Paul.

Barth, Fredrik. 1987. *Cosmologies in the Making: A Generative Approach to Cultural Variation in Inner New Guinea*. Cambridge: Cambridge University Press.

Bassi, Marco. 1994. "Gada as an Integrative Factor of Political Organization." In *A River of Blessings: Essays in Honor of Paul Baxter*, edited by D. Brokensha, pp. 15–30. Syracuse, N.Y.: Maxwell School of Citizenship and Public Affairs.

223

Bateson, Gregory. 1958. *Naven: A Survey of the Problems Suggested by a Composite Picture of the Culture of a New Guinea Tribe Drawn from Three Points of View*. Stanford: Stanford University Press.

Bateson, Gregory. 1972. "Form, Substance, and Difference." In his *Steps to an Ecology of Mind*, pp. 448–464. New York: Ballantine.

Baxter, P. T. W. 1954. *The Social Organization of the Galla of Northern Kenya*. Ph.D. dissertation, University of Oxford.

Baxter, P. T. W. 1972. "Absence Makes the Heart Grow Fonder: Some Suggestions Why Witchcraft Accusations Are Rare among East African Pastoralists." In *The Allocation of Responsibility*, edited by M. Gluckman, pp. 163–191. Manchester U.K.: Manchester University Press.

Baxter, P. T. W. 1978. "Boran Age-sets and Generation-sets: *Gada* a Puzzle or a Maze?" In Baxter and Almagor, eds., pp. 151–182.

Baxter, P. T. W., and Uri Almagor, eds. 1978. *Age, Generation and Time: Some Features of East African Age Organizations*. New York: St. Martin's.

Baxter, P. T. W., Jan Hultin, and Alessandro Triulzi, eds. 1996. *Being and Becoming Oromo: Historical and Anthropological Enquiries*. Uppsala: Nordiska Afrikainstitutet/Red Sea Press.

Beaman, A. W. 1981. *The Rendille Age-set System in Ethnographic Context*. Ph.D. dissertation, Boston University.

Beauvoir, Simone de. 1952. *The Second Sex*. New York: Knopf.

Beidelman, T. O. 1973. "Kaguru Symbolic Classification." In Needham, ed., pp. 128–166.

Beidelman, T. O. 1986. *Moral Imagination in Kaguru Modes of Thought*. Bloomington: Indiana University Press.

Berger, Peter, and Thomas Luckmann. 1966. *The Social Construction of Reality: A Treatise in the Sociology of Knowledge*. New York: Anchor.

Bergmann, Martin. 1971. "Psychoanalytic Observations on the Capacity to Love." In *Separation-Individuation*, edited by J. McDevitt and C. Settlage, pp. 15–40. New York: International University Press.

Bettelheim, Bruno. 1962. *Symbolic Wounds*. New York: Collier.

Blackhurst, Hector. 1996. "Adopting an Ambiguous Position: Oromo Relationships with Strangers." In Baxter, Hultin, and Triulzi, eds., pp. 239–250.

Blacking, John. 1990. "Growing Old Gracefully: Physical, Social, and Spiritual Transformations in Venda Society, 1956–1966." In *Anthropology and the Riddle of the Sphinx*, edited by Paul Spencer, pp. 48–66. London: Routledge.

Boddy, Janice. 1989. *Wombs and Alien Spirits: Women, Men, and the Zar Cult in Northern Sudan*. Madison: University of Wisconsin Press.

Bourdieu, Pierre. 1977. *Outline of a Theory of Practice*. Cambridge: Cambridge University Press.

Boyd, Robert, and Peter Richerson. 1985. *Culture and the Evolutionary Process.* Chicago: University of Chicago Press.

Braidotti, Rosi. 1991. *Patterns of Dissonance.* New York: Routledge.

Brown, Judith, and Virginia Kerns. 1985. *In Her Prime: A New View of Middle-aged Women.* South Hadley, Mass.: Bergin and Garvey.

Butler, Judith. 1990. *Gender Trouble, Feminism and the Subversion of Identity.* New York: Routledge.

Butler, Judith. 1994. "Contingent Foundations: Feminism and the Question of 'Postmodernism.'" In *The Postmodern Turn: New Perspectives on Social Theory*, edited by S. Seidman, pp. 153–170. Cambridge: Cambridge University Press.

Caillois, Roger. 1984. "Mimicry and Legendary Psychasthenia." *October* 31:17–32.

Cerulli, Enrico. 1922. "The Folk-literature of the Galla of Southern Abyssinia." In *Harvard African Studies*, vol. 3, edited by E. A. Hooton, pp. 9–228. Cambridge, Mass.: Harvard University Press.

Chodorow, Nancy. 1978. *The Reproduction of Mothering: Psychoanalysis and the Sociology of Gender.* Berkeley: University of California Press.

Clifford, James. 1988. *The Predicament of Culture: Twentieth-century Ethnography, Literature, and Art.* Cambridge, Mass.: Harvard University Press.

Conway, J., S. Bourque, and J. Scott. 1989. "Introduction." In their *Learning about Women: Gender, Politics, and Power.* Ann Arbor: University of Michigan Press.

Crapanzano, Vincent. 1980. *Tuhami: Portrait of a Moroccan.* Chicago: University of Chicago Press.

Dahl, G., and A. Hjort. 1976. *Having Herds: Pastoral Herd Growth and Household Economy.* Stockholm: University of Stockholm.

D'Andrade, Roy, and Claudia Strauss, eds. 1992. *Human Motives and Cultural Models.* New York: Cambridge University Press.

Daystar Communications. 1982. *Unreached Peoples of Kenya Project: Gabbra Report.* Ken Shingledecker, project coordinator. Nairobi: Daystar.

Derrida, Jacques. 1972. "Interview/Jacques Derrida by J.-L. Houdebine and Guy Scorpetta." *Diacritics* 2(4):35–43.

Derrida, Jacques. 1974. *Of grammatology.* Baltimore: Johns Hopkins University Press.

Derrida, Jacques. 1982. "Différance." In his *Margins of Philosophy*, pp. 3–27. Chicago: University of Chicago Press.

Dews, Peter. 1987. *Logics of Disintegration: Poststructuralist Thought and the Claims of Critical Theory.* New York: Verso.

Diemberger, Hildegard. 1993. "Blood, Sperm, Soul and the Mountain: Gender Relations, Kinship and Cosmovision among the Khumbo (NE Nepal)." In *Gendered Anthropology*, edited by Teresa del Valle, pp. 88–127. London: Routledge.

Donham, Donald. 1990. *History, Power, Ideology: Central Issues in Marxism and Anthropology*. Cambridge: Cambridge University Press.

Donham, Donald, and Wendy James, eds. 1986. *The Southern Marches of Imperial Ethiopia: Essays in History and Social Anthropology*. Cambridge: Cambridge University Press.

Dosse, François. 1997. *History of Structuralism*. Vols. 1, 2. Translated by Deborah Glassman. Minneapolis: University of Minnesota Press.

Douglas, Mary. 1957. "Animals in Lele Religious Symbolism." *Africa* 27:46–58.

Dumont, Louis. 1970. *Homo hierarchicus: The Caste System and Its Implications*. Chicago: University of Chicago Press.

Dundes, Alan. 1976. "A Psychoanalytic Study of the Bullroarer." *Man* n.s. 11:220–238.

Durrell, Lawrence. 1958. *Balthazar*. New York: E. P. Dutton.

Evans-Pritchard, E. E. 1940. *The Nuer: A Description of the Modes of Livelihood and Political Institutions of a Nilotic People*. New York: Oxford University Press.

Evans-Pritchard, E. E. 1956. *Nuer Religion*. New York: Oxford University Press.

Field, Chris. 1970. *Preliminary Report on the Ecology and Management of Camels, Sheep, and Goats in Northern Kenya*. Nairobi: UNESCO/UNEP.

Foucault, Michel. 1978. *The History of Sexuality*. Vol. 1. New York: Vintage.

Fox, James. 1989. "Category and Complement: Binary Ideologies and the Organization of Dualism in Eastern Indonesia." In Maybury-Lewis and Almagor, eds., pp. 33–56.

Fratkin, Elliot. 1987. "Age-sets, Households, and the Organization of Pastoral Production: The Ariaal, Samburu, and Rendille of Northern Kenya." *Research in Economic Anthropology* 8:295–314.

Fratkin, Elliot. 1991. *Surviving Drought and Development: Ariaal Pastoralists of Northern Kenya*. Boulder, Colo.: Westview.

Fratkin, Elliot. 1992a. "Traveler's Journal." *Africa News*, May 11–24, p. 4.

Fratkin, Elliot. 1992b. "Maa-speakers of the Northern Desert: Recent Developments in Ariaal and Rendille Identity." In Spear and Waller, eds., pp. 273–289.

Fratkin, Elliot. 1998. *Ariaal Pastoralists of Kenya: Surviving Drought and Development in Africa's Arid Lands*. Boston: Allyn and Bacon.

Fratkin, Elliot, Kathleen Galvin, and Eric Roth, eds. 1994. *African Pastoralist Systems: An Integrated Approach*. Boulder, Colo.: Lynne Rienner.

Freud, Sigmund. 1918. *Totem and Taboo: Resemblances between the Psychic Lives of Savages and Neurotics*. New York: Vintage.

Freud, Sigmund. 1949. *An Outline of Psycho-analysis*. New York: W. W. Norton.

Freud, Sigmund. 1958 [1915]. "Observation on Transference-love." In *Standard Edition of the works of Freud*, edited by J. Strachey, vol. 12, pp. 157–171. London: Hogarth.

Freud, Sigmund. 1959. *Inhibitions, Symptoms and Anxiety*. New York: Norton.

Fuasto-Sterling, Anne. 1993. "The Five Sexes: Why Male and Female Are Not Enough." *Sciences* 33:20–25.

Geertz, Clifford. 1973a. "Thick Description: Toward an Interpretive Theory of Culture." In his *The Interpretation of Cultures*, pp. 3–30. New York: Basic Books.

Geertz, Clifford. 1973b. "The Growth of Culture and the Evolution of Mind." In his *The Interpretation of Cultures*, pp. 55–83.

Geertz, Clifford. 1988. *Works and Lives: The Anthropologist as Author*. Stanford: Stanford University Press.

Gilmore, David. 1990. *Manhood in the Making: Cultural Concepts of Masculinity*. New Haven: Yale University Press.

Girard, Rene. 1979. "Myth and Ritual in Shakespeare: *A Midsummer Night's Dream*." In *Textual Strategies: Perspectives in Post-structuralist Criticism*, edited by J. Harari, pp. 189–212. Ithaca, N.Y.: Cornell University Press.

Gleick, James. 1987. *Chaos: Making a New Science*. New York: Viking.

Gluckman, Max. 1955. *Custom and Conflict in Africa*. Oxford: Blackwell.

Godelier, Maurice. 1986. *The Making of Great Men*. Cambridge: Cambridge University Press.

Goody, Jack, ed. 1958. *The Developmental Cycle of Domestic Groups*. Cambridge: Cambridge University Press.

Gutmann, David. 1987. *Reclaimed Powers: Men and Women in Later Life*. Evanston, Ill.: Northwestern University Press.

Haberland, Eike. 1963. *Galla Süd-Äthiopiens*. Stuttgart: W. Kohlhammer.

Harari, Josue. 1979. "Critical Factions/Critical Fictions." In *Textual Strategies: Perspectives in Post-structuralist Criticism*, edited by J. Harari, pp. 17–72. Ithaca, N.Y.: Cornell University Press.

Hassen, Mohammed. 1990. *The Oromo of Ethiopia*. Cambridge: Cambridge University Press.

Heine, B., and A. Kassam. 1985. *Borana Wild Plants*. Ms., Cologne/Nairobi. [Published as B. Heine and M. Brenzinger, 1988, *Plant Concepts and Plant Use: An Ethnobotanical Survey of the Semi-arid and Arid Lands of East Africa, Part IV: Plants of the Borana*. Saarbrücken and Fort Lauderdale: Breitenbach.]

Herdt, Gilbert. 1981. *Guardians of the Flutes*. New York: McGraw-Hill.

Herdt, Gilbert. 1994. "Third Sexes and Third Genders." In *Third Sex, Third Gender: Beyond Sexual Dimorphism in Culture and History*, edited by G. Herdt, pp. 21–81. New York: Zone.

Herlocker, D. 1979. *Vegetation of Southwestern Marsabit District, Kenya*. D-1. Nairobi: Integrated Project in Arid Lands (UNESCO).

Hertz, Robert. 1973 [1909]. "The Pre-eminence of the Right Hand: A Study in Religious Polarity." In Needham, ed., pp. 3–31.

Herzfeld, Michael. 1985. *The Poetics of Manhood: Contest and Identity in a Cretan Mountain Village*. Princeton: Princeton University Press.

Hinnant, John. 1978. "The Guji: *Gada* as a Ritual System." In Baxter and
    Almagor, eds., pp. 207–243.
Hinnant, John. 1989. "Ritual and Inequality in Guji Dual Organization." In
    Maybury-Lewis and Almagor, eds., pp. 57–76.
Hodson, Arnold W. 1970 [1927]. *Seven Years in Southern Abyssinia.* Westport,
    Conn.: Negro Universities Press.
Holland, Dorothy, and Naomi Quinn. 1987. *Cultural Models in Language and
    Thought.* Cambridge: Cambridge University Press.
Hultin, Jan. 1982. "The Oromo Expansion Reconsidered." *N.E.A. Journal of
    Research on Northeast Africa* 1:188–203.
Jakobson, Roman. 1971. *Selected Writings.* The Hague: Mouton.
Johnson, Barbara. 1980. "Melville's Fist: The Execution of *Billy Budd.*" In
    The Critical Difference: Essays on the Contemporary Rhetoric of Reading,
    edited by B. Johnson, pp. 79–109. Baltimore: Johns Hopkins University
    Press.
Johnson, Barbara. 1981. "Translator's Introduction." In Jacques Derrida, *Dissem-
    ination,* pp. vii–xxxiii. Chicago: University of Chicago Press.
Johnson, Barbara. 1987. "Nothing Fails like Success." In *A World of Difference,*
    edited by B. Johnson, pp. 11–24. Baltimore: Johns Hopkins University
    Press.
Kant, Immanuel. 1965. *Critique of Pure Reason.* New York: St. Martin's.
Kassam, Aneesa. 1982. "The Fox in Gabbra Oral Folktales." *Kenya Past and
    Present* 14:34–43.
Kassam, Aneesa. 1984. *La geste de Renard: Variations sur un conte Gabbra.* Ph.D.
    thesis, Sorbonne.
Kassam, Aneesa. 1986a. "The Gabbra Pastoralist/Waata Hunter-Gatherer Sym-
    biosis: A Symbolic Interpretation." *Sprache und Geschichte in Afrika* 7:189–
    204.
Kassam, Aneesa. 1986b. "The Fertile Past: The Gabra Concept of Oral Tradition."
    Africa 56:193–209.
Kassam, Aneesa. 1987. "The Process of Becoming: Gabra Oromo Transition Rites
    (Jilla)." *Azania* 22:55–75.
Kassam, Aneesa, and Gemetchu Megerssa. 1994. "*Aloof alolla*: The Inside and
    the Outside: Boran Oromo Environmental Law and Methods of Conserva-
    tion." In *A River of Blessings, Essays in Honor of Paul Baxter,* edited by
    D. Brokensha, pp. 85–98. Syracuse: Maxwell School of Citizenship and
    Public Affairs.
Kassam, Aneesa, and Gemetchu Megerssa. 1996. "Sticks, Self, and Society in
    Booran Oromo: A Symbolic Interpretation. In *African Material Culture,*
    edited by M. J. Arnoldi et al., pp. 145–166. Bloomington: Indiana University
    Press.
Katz, Cindi, and Janice Monk, eds. 1993. *Full Circles: Geographies of Women over
    the Life Course.* London: Routledge.

Katz, Richard. 1982. *Boiling Energy: Community Healing among the Kalahari Kung.* Cambridge, Mass.: Harvard University Press.

Keith, Jennie. 1980. "The Best Is Yet to Be: Toward an Anthropology of Age." *Annual Review of Anthropology* 9: 339–364.

Klein, Melanie. 1957. *Envy and Gratitude.* New York: Basic Books.

Klein, Melanie. 1986. *The Selected Melanie Klein.* New York: Free Press.

Knauft, Bruce. 1996. *Genealogies for the Present in Cultural Anthropology.* New York: Routledge.

Kopytoff, Igor. 1987. "The Internal African Frontier: The Making of African Political Culture." In *The African Frontier*, edited by I. Kopytoff, pp. 3–84. Bloomington: Indiana University Press.

Kratz, Corinne. 1989. "Genres of Power: A Comparative Analysis of Okiek Blessings, Curses, and Oaths." *Man* n.s. 24:636–656.

Kratz, Corinne. 1994. *Affecting Performance: Meaning, Movement, and Experience in Okiek Women's Initiation.* Washington, D.C.: Smithsonian Institution Press.

Kratz, Corinne. 1995. "Personhood and Complex Agency in Okiek Marriage Arrangement." Paper presented at the annual meeting of the American Anthropological Association.

Kratz, Corinne. 1997. "Conversations and Lives." In *Words and Lives*, edited by D. W. Cohen et al. Chicago: University of Chicago Press.

Krige, Eileen J., and J. D. A. Krige. 1943. *The Realm of a Rain-Queen: A Study of the Pattern of Lovedu Society.* London: Oxford University Press.

Kruuk, H. 1972. *The Spotted Hyena: A Study of Predation and Social Behavior.* Chicago: University of Chicago Press.

Lacan, Jacques. 1977. *The Four Fundamental Concepts of Psycho-analysis.* New York: W. W. Norton.

Lakoff, George. 1987. *Women, Fire, and Dangerous Things.* Chicago: University of Chicago Press.

Lakoff, George, and Mark Johnson. 1980. *Metaphors We Live By.* Chicago: University of Chicago Press.

Lauretis, Teresa de. 1984. *Alice Doesn't: Feminism, Semiotics, Cinema.* London: Macmillan.

Lauretis, Teresa de, ed. 1986. *Feminist Studies/Critical Studies.* London: Macmillan.

Legesse, Asmarom. 1973. *Gada: Three Approaches to the Study of African Society.* New York: Free Press.

Legesse, Asmarom. 1989. "Adaptation, Drought, and Development: Boran and Gabra Pastoralists of Northern Kenya." In *African Food Systems in Crisis*, edited by R. Hoss-Ashmore and S. Katz, pp. 261–279. New York: Gordon and Breach.

Leonardo, Micaela di. 1991. "Gender, Culture, and Political Economy: Feminist Anthropology in Historical Perspective." In *Gender at the Crossroads*

of Knowledge: Feminist Anthropology in the Postmodern Era, edited by
M. di Leonardo, pp. 1–48. Berkeley: University of California Press.

Leus, Ton. 1995. *Borana Dictionary: A Borana Book for the Study of Language
and Culture.* Yaaballo, Ethiopia: Catholic Church Dadim.

Levine, Donald. 1985. *The Flight from Ambiguity: Essays in Social and Cultural
Theory.* Chicago: University of Chicago Press.

Lévi-Strauss, Claude. 1944. "Reciprocity and Hierarchy." *American Anthropologist* 46:266–268.

Lévi-Strauss, Claude. 1960. "On Manipulated Sociological Models." *Bijdragen
tot de Taal-, Land- en Volkenkunde* 116:45–54.

Lévi-Strauss, Claude. 1963. *Structural Anthropology.* New York: Basic Books.

Lévi-Strauss, Claude. 1969 [1949]. *The Elementary Structures of Kinship.* Boston:
Beacon.

Lewis, H. S. 1966. "The Origins of the Galla and Somali." *Journal of African
History* 6:27–46.

Lewis, H. S. 1984. "Spirit Possession in Ethiopia: An Essay in Interpretation." In
*Proceedings of the Seventh International Conference of Ethiopian Studies,
University of Lund, 1982*, pp. 466–480. Addis Ababa: Institute of Ethiopian
Studies.

Lewis, I. M. 1961. *A Pastoral Democracy: A Study of Pastoralism and Politics
among Northern Somali of the Horn of Africa.* New York: Oxford University
Press.

Lienhardt, R. Godfrey. 1961. *Divinity and Experience: The Religion of the Dinka.*
London: Oxford University Press.

Lindholm, Charles. 1982. *Generosity and Jealousy: The Swat Pukhtun of Northern
Pakistan.* New York: Columbia University Press.

Llewellyn-Davies, Melissa. 1978. "Two Contexts of Solidarity among Pastoral
Maasai Women." In *Women United, Women Divided*, edited by P. Caplan
and J. M. Bujra, pp. 206–237. London: Tavistock.

Llewellyn-Davies, Melissa. 1981. "Women Warriors and Patriarchs." In *Sexual
Meanings*, edited by S. Ortner and H. Whitehead, pp. 330–358. Cambridge:
Cambridge University Press.

Lyons, John. 1977. *Semantics.* Cambridge: Cambridge University Press.

Maciel, Mervyn. 1985. *Bwana Karani.* Braunton, U.K.: Merlin Books.

Mahler, Margaret. 1968. *On Human Symbiosis and the Vicissitudes of Individua-
tion.* With M. Furer. New York: International Universities Press.

Matory, J. Lorand. 1994. *Sex and the Empire That Is No More: Gender and the
Politics of Metaphor in Oyo Yoruba Religion.* Minneapolis: University of
Minnesota Press.

Maud, Philip. 1904. "Exploration in the Southern Borderland of Abyssinia."
Geographical Journal 23:552–579.

Maybury-Lewis, David. 1960. "The Analysis of Dual Organizations: A Methodological Critique." *Bijdragen tot de Taal-, Land- en Volkenkunde* 116:2–44.

Maybury-Lewis, David, and Uri Almagor, eds. 1989. *The Attraction of Opposites: Thought and Society in the Dualistic Mode*. Ann Arbor: University of Michigan Press.

Mead, Margaret. 1949. *Male and Female: A Study of the Sexes in a Changing World*. New York: William Morrow.

Meeker, M. 1989. *The Pastoral Son and the Spirit of Patriarchy: Religion, Society, and Person among East African Stock Keepers*. Madison: University of Wisconsin Press.

Merton, Robert. 1976. *Sociological Ambivalence and Other Essays*. New York: Free Press.

Moore, Henrietta. 1986. *Space, Text, and Gender: An Anthropological Study of the Marakwet of Kenya*. Cambridge: Cambridge University Press.

Moore, Henrietta. 1988. *Feminism and Anthropology*. Minneapolis: University of Minnesota Press.

Moore, Henrietta. 1994. *A Passion for Difference*. Bloomington: Indiana University Press.

Murphy, Robert. 1971. *The Dialectics of Social Life: Alarms and Excursions in Anthropological Theory*. New York: Basic Books.

Nadelson, Leslee. 1981. "Pigs, Women, and the Men's House in Amazonia: An Analysis of Six Mundurucu Myths." In *Sexual Meanings*, edited by S. Ortner and H. Whitehead, pp. 240–272. Cambridge: Cambridge University Press.

Needham, Rodney, ed. 1973. *Right and Left: Essays on Dual Symbolic Classification*. Chicago: University of Chicago Press.

Needham, Rodney. 1987. *Counterpoints*. Berkeley: University of California Press.

Nuckolls, Charles. 1991. "Culture and Causal Thinking: Prediction and Diagnosis in a South Indian Fishing Village." *Ethos* 17:5–51.

Nuckolls, Charles. 1996. *The Cultural Dialectics of Knowledge and Desire*. Madison: University of Wisconsin Press.

Oba, Gufu. 1996. "Shifting Identities along Resource Borders: Becoming and Continuing to be Boorana Oromo." In Baxter, Hultin, and Triulzi, eds., pp. 117–131.

Obeyesekere, Gananath. 1981. *Medusa's Hair: An Essay on Personal Symbols and Religious Experience*. Chicago: University of Chicago Press.

Obeyesekere, Gananath. 1990. *The Work of Culture*. Chicago: University of Chicago Press.

Oboler, Regina S. 1980. "Is the Female Husband a Man? Women/Women Marriage among the Nandi of Kenya." *Ethnology* 19:69–88.

O'Leary, Michael. 1985. *The Economics of Pastoralism in Northern Kenya: The Rendille and the Gabra*. F-3. Nairobi: Integrated Project in Arid Lands (UNESCO).

Ortner, Sherry. 1973. "On Key Symbols." *American Anthropologist* 75:1338–1346.

Ortner, Sherry. 1974. "Is Female to Male as Nature Is to Culture?" In *Women, Culture, and Society*, edited by M. Rosaldo and L. Lamphere, pp. 67–87. Stanford: Stanford University Press.

Ortner, Sherry. 1984. "Theory in Anthropology since the Sixties." *Comparative Studies in Society and History* 26:126–166.

Ortner, Sherry. 1989. *High Religion: A Cultural and Political History of Sherpa Buddhism*. Princeton: Princeton University Press.

Ortner, Sherry. 1996. *Making Gender: The Politics and Erotics of Culture*. Boston: Beacon.

Ortner, Sherry, and Harriet Whitehead, eds. 1981. *Sexual Meanings: The Cultural Construction of Gender and Sexuality*. Cambridge: Cambridge University Press.

Oyama, Susan. 1985. *The Ontogeny of Information: Developmental Systems and Evolution*. Cambridge: Cambridge University Press.

Paul, Robert. 1982. *The Tibetan Symbolic World: Psychoanalytic Explorations*. Chicago: University of Chicago Press.

Paul, Robert. 1987. "The Question of Applied Psychoanalysis and the Interpretation of Cultural Symbolism." *Ethos* 15:82–102.

Paul, Robert. 1989. "Psychoanalytic Anthropology." *Annual Review of Anthropology* 19:177–202.

Paul, Robert. 1990. "What Does Anybody Want? Desire, Purpose, and the Acting Subject in the Study of Culture." *Cultural Anthropology* 5:431–451.

Paul, Robert. 1996a. "Symbolic Reproduction and Sherpa Monasticism." In *Denying Biology*, edited by U. Linke and W. Shapiro, pp. 51–73. New York: University Press of America.

Paul, Robert. 1996b. *Moses and Civilization: The Meaning behind Freud's Myth*. New Haven: Yale University Press.

Peletz, Michael. 1996. *Reason and Passion: Representations of Gender in a Malay Society*. Berkeley: University of California Press.

Pine, Fred. 1971. "On the Separation Process: Universal Trends and Individual Differences." In *Separation-Individuation*, edited by J. McDevitt and C. Settlage, pp. 113–130. New York: International University Press.

Poole, Fitz John Porter. 1981. "Transforming 'Natural' Women: Female Ritual Leaders and Gender Ideology among Bimin-Kuskusmin." In Ortner and Whitehead, eds., pp. 116–165.

Prussin, Labelle. 1995. *African Nomadic Architecture: Space, Place, and Gender*. Washington, D.C.: Smithsonian Institution Press.

Prussin, Labelle. 1996. "When Nomads Settle: Changing Technologies of Building and Transport and the Production of Architectural Form among the

Gabra, Rendille, and the Somalis." In *African Material Culture*, edited by M. Arnoldi et al. pp. 73–102. Bloomington: Indiana University Press.

Quinn, Naomi. 1987. "Convergent Evidence for a Cultural Model of American Marriage." In *Cultural Models in Language and Thought*, edited by D. Holland and N. Quinn, pp. 173–192. Cambridge: Cambridge University Press.

Quinn, Naomi. 1991. "The Cultural Basis of Metaphor." In *Beyond Metaphor: A Theory of Tropes in Anthropology*, edited by James Fernandez, pp. 56–93. Stanford: Stanford University Press.

Quinn, Naomi, and Dorothy Holland. 1987. "Culture and Cognition." In their *Cultural Models in Language and Thought*, pp. 3–40. Cambridge: Cambridge University Press.

Rasmussen, Susan. 1987. "Interpreting Androgynous Women: Female Aging and Personhood among the Kel Ewey Tuareg." *Ethnology* 26:17–30.

Rasmussen, Susan. 1996. "The Tent as Cultural Symbol and Field Site: Social and Symbolic Space, 'Topos,' and Authority in a Tuareg Community." *Anthropological Quarterly* 69:14–26.

Rasmussen, Susan. 1997. *The Poetics and Politics of Tuareg Aging: Life Course and Personal Destiny in Niger*. Dekalb: Northern Illinois University Press.

Rich, Adrienne. 1980. "Compulsory Heterosexuality and Lesbian Existence." *Signs: Journal of Women in Culture and Society* 5:631–660.

Riesman, Paul. 1977. *Freedom in Fulani Social Life: An Introspective Ethnography*. Chicago: University of Chicago Press.

Robinson, Paul. 1985. *Gabra Nomadic Pastoralism in Nineteenth and Twentieth Century Northern Kenya: Strategies for Survival in a Marginal Environment*. Ph.D. dissertation, Northwestern University.

Rosaldo, Michelle. 1974. "Women, Culture and Society: A Theoretical Overview." In *Women, Culture, and Society*, edited by M. Rosaldo and L. Lamphere, pp. 17–42. Stanford: Stanford University Press.

Roth, Eric A. 1993. "A Reexamination of Rendille Population Regulation." *American Anthropologist* 95:597–611.

Schlee, Günther. 1989. *Identities on the Move: Clanship and Pastoralism in Northern Kenya*. Manchester, U.K.: Manchester University Press.

Schlee, Günther. 1990. "Holy Grounds." In *Property, Poverty and People: Changing Rights in Property and Problems of Pastoral Development*, edited by P. T. W. Baxter and R. Hogg, pp. 45–54. Manchester, U.K.: Department of Social Anthropology, University of Manchester.

Schlee, Günther. 1994. "Ethnicity Emblems, Diacritical Features, Identity Markers: Some East African Examples." In *A River of Blessings, Essays in Honor of Paul Baxter*, edited by D. Brokensha, pp. 129–143. Syracuse: Maxwell School of Citizenship and Public Affairs, Syracuse University.

Scott, Joan. 1986. "Gender: A Useful Category of Historical Analysis." *American Historical Review* 91:1053–1075.

Scott, Joan. 1988. *Gender and the Politics of History.* New York: Columbia University Press.

Scott, Joan. 1994. "Deconstructing Equality-versus-Difference: Or, the Uses of Poststructuralist Theory for Feminism." In *The Postmodern Turn: New Perspectives on Social Theory*, edited by S. Seidman, pp. 282–298. Cambridge: Cambridge University Press.

Segal, Hanna. 1974. *Introduction to the Work of Melanie Klein.* New York: Basic Books.

Shapiro, Warren. 1989. "The Theoretical Importance of Pseudo-procreation Symbolism." *Psychoanalytic Study of Society* 14:72–88.

Shongolo, Abdullahi. 1994a. "The Gumi Gaayo Assembly of the Boran: A Traditional Legislative Organ and Its relationship to the Ethiopian state and a modernizing World." *Zeitschrift für Ethnologie* 119:27–58.

Shongolo, Abdullahi. 1994b. "Adaptive Responses of Pastoralists to the Drought of 1991/92 in Northern Kenya: A Comparative Study of Boran and Gabra Pastoralists of Moyale." Consultancy report to Marsabit Development Programme (GTZ), Moyale.

Shore, Bradd. 1981. "Sexuality and Gender in Samoa: Conception and Missed Conception." In Ortner and Whitehead, eds., pp. 192–215.

Shore, Bradd. 1996. *Culture in Mind: Cognition, Culture, and the Problem of Meaning.* New York: Oxford University Press.

Simmel, Georg. 1950. *The Sociology of Georg Simmel.* Edited and translated by K. Wolff. Glencoe, Ill.: Free Press.

Simmel, Georg. 1968. *The Conflict in Modern Culture and Other Essays.* New York: Teacher's College Press.

Skultans, V. 1970. "The Symbolic Significance of Menstruation and Menopause." *Man* n.s. 5:639–651.

Sobania, Neal. 1979. *A Background History to the Mount Kulal Region of Northern Kenya.* Nairobi: UNESCO.

Sobania, Neal. 1980. *The Historical Tradition of the Peoples of the Eastern Lake Turkana Basin, c. 1840–1925.* Ph.D. dissertation, University of London (SOAS).

Sobania, Neal. 1988. "Fishermen Herders: Subsistence, Survival and Cultural Change in Northern Kenya." *Journal of African History* 29:41–26.

Sobania, Neal. 1990. "Social Relationships as an Aspect of Property Rights: Northern Kenya in the Pre-colonial and Colonial Periods." In *Property, Poverty and People: Changing Rights in Property and Problems of Pastoral Development*, edited by P. T. W. Baxter and R. Hogg, pp. 1–19. Manchester, U.K.: Department of Social Anthropology, University of Manchester.

Sobania, Neal. 1991. "Feasts, Famines and Friends: Nineteenth-century Exchange and Ethnicity in the Eastern Lake Turkana Regional System." In *Herders, Warriors, and Traders*, edited by P. Bonte and J. Galaty, pp. 118–141. Boulder, Colo.: Westview.

Sobania, Neal. 1993. "Defeat and Dispersal: The Laikipiak and Their Neighbours at the End of the Nineteenth Century." In Spear and Waller, eds., pp. 105–119.

Soga, Toru. 1997. "The Camel Exchange System among the Gabra: Patterns and Consequences of Inheritance." In *Ethiopia in Broader Perspective: Papers of the XIIIth International Conference of Ethiopian Studies*, vol. 2, edited by K. Fukui et al., pp. 597–615. Kyoto: Shokado.

Spear, Thomas. 1981. *Kenya's Past*. London: Longman.

Spear, Thomas. 1993. "Introduction." In Spear and Waller, eds., pp. 1–18.

Spear, Thomas, and Richard Waller, eds. 1993. *Being Maasai: Ethnicity and Identity in East Africa*. London: James Currey.

Spencer, Paul. 1973. *Nomads in Alliance: Symbiosis and Growth among the Rendille and Samburu of Kenya*. London: Oxford University Press.

Spencer, Paul. 1988. *The Maasai of Matapato: A Study of Rituals of Rebellion*. Bloomington: Indiana University Press.

Stiles, Daniel. 1991. "The Gabbra Jilla." *Kenya Past and Present* 23:23–34.

Stoller, Robert, and Gilbert Herdt. 1982. "The Development of Masculinity: A Cross-cultural Contribution." *Journal of the American Psychoanalytic Association* 30:29–59.

Storås, Frode. 1991. "Cattle Complex or Begging Complex: Livestock Transactions and the Construction of Turkana Society." In *The Ecology of Choice and Symbol: Essays in Honor of Fredrik Barth*, edited by R. Grønhorg et al., pp. 50–65. Bergen, Norway: Alma Mater Forlag.

Strathern, Marilyn. 1981a. "Self Interest and the Social Good: Some Implications of Hagen Gender Imagery." In Ortner and Whitehead, eds., pp. 166–191.

Strathern, Marilyn. 1981b. "Culture in a Netbag: The Manufacture of a Subdiscipline in Anthropology." *Man* n.s. 16:665–688.

Tablino, Paolo. 1980. *I Gabbra del Kenya*. Bologna: E.M.I.

Tablino, Paolo. 1989. *African Traditional Religion: Time and Religion among the Gabra Pastoralists of Northern Kenya*. Marsabit, Kenya: Catholic Diocese of Marsabit.

Tablino, Paolo. 1991 [1988]. "The Calculation of Time among the Gabra of Kenya." *Bulletin des études africaines* 8(16):97–107.

Tablino, Paolo. 1996. "Being Gabra Today." In Baxter, Hultin, and Triulzi, eds., pp. 114–116.

Tablino, Paolo. 1999. *The Gabra: Camel Nomads of Northern Kenya*. Translated by C. Salvadori. Nairobi: Pauline Publications Africa.

Taussig, Michael. 1993. *Mimesis and Alterity: A Particular History of the Senses*. New York: Routledge.

Thompson, Paul. 1985. "Women in the Fishing: The Roots of Power between the Sexes." *Comparative Studies in Society and History* 27:3–32.

Torry, William. 1973. *Subsistence Ecology among the Gabra: Nomads of the Kenya/Ethiopia Frontier.* Ph.D. dissertation, Columbia University.

Torry, William. 1978. "Gabra Age Organization." In Baxter and Almagor, eds., pp. 183–206.

Trawick, Margaret. 1988. "Ambiguity in the Oral Exegesis of a Sacred Text: *Tirukkovaiyar* (or the Guru in the Garden), Being an Account of a Tamil Informant's Responses to Homesteading in Central New York State." *Cultural Anthropology* 3:316–351.

Trawick, Margaret. 1990. *Notes on Love in a Tamil Family.* Berkeley: University of California Press.

Trimingham, S. J. 1965. *Islam in Ethiopia.* London: Frank Cass.

Trubetzkoy, N. S. 1969. *Principles of Phonology.* Berkeley: University of California Press.

Turner, Terrence. 1991. " 'We are parrots,' 'Twins are birds,' the Play of Tropes as Operational Structures." In *Beyond Metaphor: The Theory of Tropes in Anthropology,* edited by James Fernandez, pp. 121–158. Stanford: Stanford University Press.

Turner, Victor. 1957. *Schism and Continuity in an African Society: A Study of Ndembu Village Life.* Manchester, U.K.: Manchester University Press.

Turner, Victor. 1967. *The Forest of Symbols: Aspects of Ndembu Ritual.* Ithaca: Cornell University Press.

Waller, Richard. 1985. "Ecology, Migration, and Expansion in East Africa." *African Affairs* 84:347–370.

Waller, Richard. 1993. "Conclusions." In Spear and Waller, eds., pp. 290–302.

Waller, Richard, and Neal Sobania. 1994. "Pastoralism in Historical Perspective." In Fratkin et al., eds., pp. 45–68.

West, Cornel. 1994. "The New Cultural Politics of Difference." In *The Postmodern Turn: New Perspectives on Social Theory,* edited by S. Seidman, pp. 65–81. Cambridge: Cambridge University Press.

Wikan, Unni. 1977. "Man Becomes Woman: Transsexualism in Oman as a Key to Gender Roles." *Man* n.s. 12:304–319.

Wood, John. 1997a. *When Men Are Women: Opposition and Ambivalence among Gabra Nomads of East Africa.* Ph.D. dissertation, Emory University.

Wood, John. 1997b. "Inside the Outside: The Construction of Pastoral Identities at the Margins of Kenya and Ethiopia." In *Ethiopia in Broader Perspective: Papers of the XIIIth International Conference of Ethiopian Studies,* vol. 2, edited by K. Fukui et al., pp. 688–705. Kyoto: Shokado.

Yanagisako, Sylvia J., and Jane F. Collier. 1987. "Toward a Unified Analysis of Gender and Kinship." In their *Gender and Kinship: Essays toward a Unified Analysis,* pp. 14–50. Stanford: Stanford University Press.

INDEX

abba, 43, 68; *abba dibe*, 78, 97; *abba magalata*, 90; *olla*, 45; *abba uchuma*, 90, 177; *abba wara*, 48, 153
abbera, 43
Abudo Halake, 60, 130–31
abuya, 174
ada, 39, 110, 122, 177
ala, and *olla*, 59–60
alcohol abuse, 119–21
Almado, 38, 110, 150; and women, 4, 43
amasso, 151
ambiguity: and ambivalence, 29; of *d'abella*, 166–67; of genders, 14; precision of, 26
ambivalence, 28–31; in Gabra society, 31–32; origins of term, 30; social origins of, 30–31
angafa, 68–69, 129, 147
arjalla, 44
attachment. *See* separation and attachment
avoidance rules, for in-laws, 130–31
ayana, 108

bakalcha, 80, 160, 218n26
Banoye, story of, 6–7, 207n3
barchuma, 99, 147, 174
barito (wedding gifts), 164
Barth, Fredrik, 190
Beauvoir, Simone de, 20
Beidelman, T. O., 14, 201
Billy Budd, 26–28, 187
binary opposition, 201–2; and difference,

23; and dualism, 16; and gender, 202; and male domination, 22
bita, 45
boji, 168
Borana, 63; raids with, 64; relations with, 63–65
Boru Umuro, 180, 220n19
boys: circumcision of, 217n23; days of, 51
bride: tent of, 148; wedding procession of, 160–61
bridewealth, 132; procession of, 142–43
Butler, Judith, 20

camels, at wells, 58
Catholic Church, 104, 215n3
ceremonial objects of *d'abella*, 171
chabana, 126, 210n19
Chalbi Desert, 34, 201
cheko, 62
Christian Children's Fund, 119
Christian conversions, 215n3
circumcision of boys, 217n23
clothing: of *d'abella*, 41, 170–71; of men and women, 40
coffee, 163, 216n10; offering at weddings, 148; for prayers, 132
conflict: and compromise, 30; between individual and society, 31; psychodynamic origins of, 29
cultural models, 7

d'abella, 166–99; clothing of, 41, 170–71; as male women, 5, 175–78; with